Comfortable
in the
Kitchen

Meredith Laurence

Photography by Jessica Walker

Walah!, LLC Publishers
Philadelphia

First Edition

Published in the United States by Walah!, LLC Publishers

walah@me.com

Library of Congress Cataloging-in-Publication Data
Laurence, Meredith.
        Blue jean chef : comfortable in the kitchen /
    Meredith Laurence ; photography by Jessica Walker.
        p. cm.
        Includes index.
        ISBN-13: 978-0-9827540-3-0
        ISBN-10: 0-9827540-3-5

        1. Cooking, American. 2. Cookbooks.   I. Title.

    TX715.L38 2010   641.5973
                                QBI10-600120

Printed in China

Book design by Janis Boehm
www.bound-determined.com

Photography by Jessica Walker
www.jessicawalkerphotography.com

Table of Contents

Table of Contents

Meat and Poultry

Fish and Seafood

Vegetables

Table of Contents

Breakfast

Desserts and Treats

Index

Acknowledgements

In addition to my parents who have always believed in me and given me so much, including my love of food, my sincere thanks go to...

Eric Theiss for supporting me through this project from the start.

Grace Lee at Sonshine Trade for making the printing process smooth and seamless.

Janis Boehm for her beautiful book design and attention to detail.

Jessica Walker for gorgeous photography.

Lisa Ventura, Bonne Di Tomo and Lynn Willis for their delicious food preparations and for styling more than just the food.

Joseph McAllister for testing so many recipes and feeding so many friends with the results!

Norma Laurence, Elaine McDougall and Hamish Taylor for making such a thorough proofreading and editing team with very different perspectives. Any typos remaining in the book should be addressed directly to one of them!

… and especially to Anne Symes for testing recipes, tasting recipes, reading every word, encouraging me, and mostly for being my pillar.

Introduction

Everybody knows a good cook – someone who seems so comfortable in the kitchen, at ease with preparing meals for no matter how many people. Some of those people may have a natural gift for cooking, but being a good cook is a skill that can be learned and mastered by anyone. I think I've always been comfortable in the kitchen, whether it was my mother's kitchen growing up, a restaurant kitchen, a cooking school kitchen, a test kitchen or a television studio kitchen set. Perhaps my comfort level stems from a genuine love of food, but I think it's more likely that my knowledge of basic cooking technique and a lot of practice has made the kitchen my favorite place to be.

Of all the kitchens I've worked in and cooking jobs I've had, the most gratifying experience for me has been teaching others to cook. I love seeing someone else's joy in learning how to cut an onion the right way, or his or her pleasure in creating a successful meal for the first time. Watching someone's confidence and enjoyment in the kitchen grow makes me happy. That is what I hope will happen with this book.

This book is structured to build a level of comfort in any cook. Each section of the book contains "Basic" recipes. These are recognizable dishes, which range from classic comfort meals to dishes worthy of a dinner party, but they include detailed explanations of why the recipe is written the way it is. These Basic recipes will give you a solid understanding of the cooking techniques used to create that dish successfully.

Once you have the basic cooking technique, the next step is to practice. Repeating the same recipe over and over again in order to master a technique is not much fun, and certainly no family wants the cook of the house to do that either! So, each Basic recipe is followed by four other recipes using the same technique, but with different ingredients so that you are creating very different meals. And there you have it – knowledge of basic cooking techniques and practice. My hope is that readers of this book will then feel confident enough to improvise, incorporating their own ingredient ideas and creating meals that are truly their own. Feeling comfortable.

I have also included a few additional recipes in each section, called Blue Jean Chef Favorites. You'll see them marked with a star at the top of the page. These recipes don't necessarily fit into one of the Basic groups, but are some of my favorite dishes and I wanted to include them in this book. I hope you enjoy them too.

As I did with every cooking class I ever taught, I do have to set a few ground rules that will contribute not only to your success, but also to your happiness in the kitchen.

First rule – read the recipe from start to finish before you begin cooking. This is critical in order to know if you have all the ingredients, as well as if you have enough time to complete the recipe. If you want to go one step further, reading the "Recipe Explained!" section will give you a better understanding of the recipe.

Second rule – buy the very best ingredients you can. A finished dish can only taste as good as its ingredients. Local, seasonal produce always tastes better than produce that is out of season, or shipped in from another country.

Third rule – do your mise en place. This means do all your prep work first. Chop what needs to be chopped. Measure what needs to be measured. This makes cooking much less stressful and more relaxing. Of course, you can start a step of the recipe in the middle of doing your mise en place if that first step in the recipe requires some time. You'll know this because you will have read the recipe all the way through first!

Fourth rule – taste your food before you take it to the table. You'd be surprised how many people forget this step, but it's really important. You should always take a few seconds to taste the food and re-season it if necessary before you decide a dish is done.

So, with explanations of basic cooking techniques, delicious practice recipes, a few favorite recipes of my own and some ground rules, I hope you'll feel comfortable – as comfortable in the kitchen as you are in your blue jeans!

Soups
and
Salads

Soups and salads can act as starters to a meal, or they can step up and play the role of main course. This is especially true if you pair a soup and salad together for a delicious lunch or dinner. The soups that follow fall into one of two groups – chunky soups and thick puréed soups – and the salads include lots of interesting ingredients, not just lettuce and vinaigrette.

Basic Chicken Noodle Soup

Chicken noodle soup is considered by many to be the best remedy for a cold or the flu. I've given a lot of thought to this matter, and I've decided that in order for the soup to be at all restorative, it must be homemade. It's the love that goes into making this soup for someone who is sick that holds the healing power. Try this version – it is so much better than anything from a can.

SERVES

8 - 10

1 tablespoon olive oil

1 onion, finely chopped (about 1 cup)

2 carrots, finely chopped (about 1 cup)

2 ribs celery, finely chopped (about 1 cup)

2 cloves garlic, finely chopped

½ teaspoon dried thyme

1 bay leaf

2 quarts good quality or homemade chicken or vegetable stock

3 cups shredded cooked chicken

1½ cups wide egg noodles

salt, to taste

freshly ground black pepper

¼ cup chopped fresh parsley

1. Heat a stockpot or Dutch oven over medium heat. Add the olive oil and lightly sauté the onion, carrot and celery until tender – about 6 to 8 minutes. Add the garlic, thyme and bay leaf and cook for another minute. Add the chicken stock and bring to a simmer. Simmer for 20 minutes.

2. Add the cooked chicken and noodles to the pot and cook until noodles are al dente – about 6 to 8 minutes. Remove the bay leaf from the soup, season with salt and pepper, add parsley and serve immediately.

Recipe Explained!

● A good chunky soup must have a flavorful broth, tasty vegetables and tender, flavorful components, like chicken, beef, pork, or noodles and other grains.

● It is critical that you use a good stock. If you don't make your own stock, buy the very best stock that you can, or buy twice as much stock as you need and reduce it to a half of its original volume to concentrate the flavor.

● In this recipe, as with all the recipes for chunky soups, the vegetables are cooked in oil first. This helps establish their flavor. Then they are simmered in the broth just until tender.

● Some recipes for chicken noodle soup cook the chicken in the broth. This is great to enhance the flavor of the broth, but it takes flavor away from the chicken. Use leftover chicken if you have it on hand or cook it especially for the soup. Grilled chicken will add a smoky, grilled flavor to the soup, which is very nice. Sautéed chicken is tasty as well.

● This recipe cooks the noodles in the soup to save a step. Cooking the noodles (or any starchy ingredient) in the soup, rather than adding cooked noodles to the soup, will make the soup a little cloudy, but will give the noodles more flavor. The noodles will, of course, continue to absorb liquid as they sit in the soup. Keep in mind that if you save leftovers of this soup and re-heat it another day, you may need to thin the soup with more stock or water. Each time you reheat the soup, the noodles will get softer and softer, but the soup will still be delicious.

Beef and Barley Soup

This soup is very thick and stew-like. It makes a good meal on a winter's night with just a side salad or a slice of crusty bread.

1 tablespoon olive oil

1 pound beef stew meat

1 onion, chopped
(½-inch pieces; about 1 cup)

2 carrots, chopped
(½-inch pieces; about 1 cup)

2 stalks celery, chopped
(½-inch pieces; about 1 cup)

3 cloves garlic, finely chopped

1 teaspoon dried thyme

1 bay leaf

2 to 3 quarts beef stock

½ cup pearl barley
(regular or quick-cooking)

salt, to taste

freshly ground black pepper

¼ cup chopped fresh parsley

1. Heat a stockpot or Dutch oven over medium to medium-high heat. Add the olive oil and, in batches so you don't overcrowd the pan, brown the stew meat on all sides, seasoning with salt and pepper as you go. Remove the browned meat from the pot and set aside.

2. In the same pot, sauté the onion, carrot and celery until tender and starting to brown – about 10 to 12 minutes. Add the garlic, thyme and bay leaf and cook for another minute.

3. Return the beef to the pot and add two quarts of the beef stock. Bring to a simmer and simmer gently for 60 minutes, or until the beef is tender.

4. Add the barley to the pot and continue to simmer for 45 minutes. Thin the soup to your desired consistency with more beef stock and heat through. Season the soup with salt and pepper and add the parsley. Remember to remove the bay leaf from the soup before serving.

If you prefer a thinner soup, cook the barley separately in 1½ cups of water for 30 to 45 minutes, and then add it to the soup. This will also make the soup less cloudy and less like a stew. (If you are using quick-cooking barley, it will cook in about 10 to 12 minutes.)

Pork and White Bean Soup

This is another soup that can be a whole meal unto itself. I like to finish it with cilantro, but if you don't like cilantro, parsley is a good substitute.

3 slices of bacon, chopped
(1-inch pieces)

1 pound pork tenderloin, cubed
(1-inch pieces)

1 onion, chopped
(½-inch pieces; about 1 cup)

2 carrots, chopped
(½-inch pieces; about 1 cup)

2 ribs celery, chopped
(½-inch pieces; about 1 cup)

4 cloves garlic, minced

1 teaspoon dried oregano

½ teaspoon hot red pepper flakes

1 bay leaf

1 (28 ounce) can diced tomatoes

2 quarts chicken stock

3 (15 ounce) cans white beans,
drained and rinsed

salt, to taste

freshly ground black pepper

¼ cup chopped fresh cilantro

1. Heat a stockpot or Dutch oven over medium heat. Add the bacon and cook until crispy. Remove the bacon pieces with a slotted spoon and set aside. Drain off the bacon fat, leaving 1 tablespoon in the pot.

2. In batches, so that you don't overcrowd the pot, brown the pork tenderloin pieces on all sides, seasoning with salt and pepper as you go. Remove the browned pork and set aside with the bacon.

3. Using the same pot, lightly sauté the onion, carrot and celery until tender – about 6 to 8 minutes. Add the garlic, oregano, hot red pepper flakes and bay leaf, and cook for another minute. Return the cooked pork and bacon to the pot, add the tomatoes and chicken stock, and bring to a simmer. Simmer for 60 minutes, or until the pork is tender.

4. Add the beans to the pot and heat through – about 5 minutes. Remove the bay leaf from the soup, season with salt and pepper, add cilantro and serve immediately.

Asian Shrimp Noodle Soup

This noodle soup has an entirely different flavor from the chicken noodle soup, but the concept is the same. It is light and refreshing, and suitable for any season. Don't forget to squeeze the lime wedges into the soup before enjoying it.

24 large raw shrimp, unpeeled

1 quart vegetable stock

1 tablespoon vegetable oil

1 red onion, sliced (about 1 cup)

2 carrots, cut into julienne strips
(about 1 cup)

2 ribs celery, sliced on the bias
(¼-inch slices; about 1 cup)

2 cloves garlic, minced

2 tablespoons grated fresh ginger

1 red chili pepper, halved

2 (15 ounce) cans coconut milk

½ pound rice vermicelli noodles

1 tablespoon soy sauce

3 green onions, sliced

¼ cup fresh cilantro leaves

1 lime, cut into wedges

1. Peel and devein the shrimp, reserving the shells. Set the peeled shrimp aside and reserve. Combine the vegetable stock and reserved shrimp shells in a saucepan. Simmer together for 30 minutes. Then strain out and discard the shrimp shells, reserving the stock.

2. Heat a stockpot or Dutch oven over medium heat. Add the vegetable oil and lightly sauté the onion, carrot and celery until tender – about 6 to 8 minutes. Add the garlic, ginger, chili pepper halves and cook for 1 to 2 minutes. Add the reserved vegetable stock and coconut milk, and bring to a simmer. Simmer for 20 minutes.

3. Meanwhile, in a separate bowl or saucepan, pour boiling water over the rice noodles and let them sit while the soup simmers.

4. Drain and add the noodles to the soup, along with the shrimp, soy sauce and green onions. Simmer just until the shrimp is pink and opaque – about 2 to 4 minutes. Add the cilantro and serve with the lime wedges.

 To easily peel shrimp, start peeling from underneath at the legs and peel the shell away from the body. To devein the shrimp, make a shallow slit along the back of the shrimp to reveal the black "vein" or intestine. Simply remove this with the tip of your paring knife and wipe it on a paper towel.

Sausage and Lentil Soup

*I love lentils and they make a delicious combination with the sausage in this hearty soup.
Lentils are very high in protein and dietary fiber, low in fat, and are also a very good source of iron.
Who knew something so tasty could be good for you!*

SERVES

8 - 10

1 tablespoon olive oil

1 pound spicy Italian sausage,
removed from casing and coarsely crumbled

1 onion, chopped
(½-inch pieces; about 1 cup)

2 carrots, chopped
(½-inch pieces; about 1 cup)

2 ribs celery, chopped
(½-inch pieces; about 1 cup)

2 cloves garlic, minced

½ teaspoon dried thyme

½ teaspoon dried rosemary

1 bay leaf

2 to 3 quarts chicken stock

2 cups dried French green (Puy) lentils

salt, to taste

freshly ground black pepper

¼ cup chopped fresh parsley

1. Heat a stockpot or Dutch oven over medium heat. Add the olive oil and brown the sausage for 6 to 8 minutes.

2. Add and lightly sauté the onion, carrot and celery until tender – about 6 to 8 minutes. Add the garlic, thyme, rosemary and bay leaf and cook for another minute. Add 2 quarts of the chicken stock and lentils, and bring to a simmer. Simmer for 45 minutes. Check the consistency of the soup and thin with more chicken stock if desired. Heat through.

3. Remove the bay leaf from the soup, season with salt and pepper, add parsley and serve immediately.

Choose French green lentils (also known as Puy lentils) for this soup. They hold their shape better than other lentils, which can get a little mushy when overcooked. Sometimes little pebbles can get mixed in with lentils, so be sure to pick through them and rinse them to remove any stone dust before cooking.

Basic Cream of Vegetable Soup

This soup is so easy to make and yet so satisfying to eat. Because you are puréeing the soup at the end, there is no need for precision when chopping the vegetables – just try to keep them roughly the same size so that they cook evenly. Adding cream at the end is completely optional, although it does give the soup a luxurious texture. As for what vegetables to use, try any combination of vegetables that you like!

SERVES

6 - 8

2 tablespoons butter

1 tablespoon olive oil

1 onion, chopped (about 1 cup)

1 to 2 cloves of garlic, minced

1 potato, peeled and chopped (about 1 cup)

3 cups vegetables, chopped

4 sprigs fresh thyme sprigs

1 bay leaf

water, as needed

½ to 1 cup heavy cream

1 teaspoon salt, or more to taste

freshly ground black pepper

1. Melt the butter along with the olive oil in a stockpot or Dutch oven over medium heat. Add the onion and cook for 5 to 7 minutes. The onion should be translucent, not brown. Add the garlic and cook for an additional minute.

2. Add the potato, vegetables, thyme sprigs and bay leaf and continue to cook for another 5 to 10 minutes. Add enough water to just cover the vegetables. Simmer for 20 minutes. Remove the thyme sprigs and the bay leaf.

3. Using a blender, food processor, food mill or immersion blender, purée the soup until no lumps remain and the soup is smooth. Return the soup to the stovetop and add the cream, salt and freshly ground black pepper. If the soup needs to be thinned, just add water until you've reached the desired consistency. Heat through and serve.

Recipe Explained!

● You can always make a hearty and non-fat vegetable soup by just boiling vegetables in water and then puréeing them. However, in this version, I start by cooking the vegetables in a combination of butter and olive oil. Butter adds great flavor, but it burns at a relatively low temperature. Olive oil can reach a higher temperature before burning. Using the two together gives you the best of both worlds – flavor and higher heat potential. By cooking the vegetables in fat before adding liquid, the vegetables can release more of their natural flavor.

● The potato is included in the ingredients to help thicken the soup, regardless of what vegetables you choose to use. For instance, if you make a zucchini soup, you might need a little thickening help from the potato. On the other hand, if you are making a sweet potato soup, the potato is really not necessary.

● I use only as much water as I need to simmer the vegetables – just enough to cover them by an inch. This is because it is a quicker process to purée the vegetables in less liquid (fewer batches). If you need more liquid in order to purée the vegetables, just add a little water. Once everything is puréed, you can add more liquid until you've reached the desired consistency. It is much easier to add liquid than take it out!

Cream of Tomato Soup

Cream of tomato soup is one of the most popular soup flavors. The key to this soup is to use the best tomatoes you can find. Only use fresh tomatoes if you're making this at peak tomato season (late summer). Otherwise, you're better off using good quality canned tomatoes.

SERVES

6 - 8

2 tablespoons butter

1 tablespoon olive oil

1 onion, chopped (about 1 cup)

1 to 2 cloves of garlic, minced

1 teaspoon dried basil leaves

4 pounds fresh tomatoes, peeled, seeded and chopped OR 2 (28 ounce) cans tomatoes

¾ cup heavy cream

1 teaspoon salt, or more to taste

freshly ground black pepper

¼ cup chopped fresh basil (optional)

1. Melt the butter along with the olive oil in a stockpot or Dutch oven over medium heat. Add the onion and cook for 5 to 7 minutes. The onion should be translucent, not brown. Add the garlic and dried basil, and cook for an additional minute.

2. Add the tomatoes and bring the soup to a boil. Reduce the heat and simmer the soup with the lid askew for 30 minutes.

3. Using a blender, food processor, food mill or immersion blender, purée the soup until no lumps remain and the soup is smooth. Return the soup to the stovetop and add the cream, salt and freshly ground black pepper. If the soup needs to be thinned, just add some water until you've reached the desired consistency. Heat through and serve with fresh basil sprinkled on top if desired.

TIP

If you're using canned tomatoes for this soup, look for San Marzano tomatoes. These are a variety of plum tomatoes originally from a small town near Naples, Italy. They have a thicker flesh and fewer seeds than Roma tomatoes, with a stronger, sweeter and less acidic flavor.

Cream of Mushroom Soup

This soup uses a little flour, rather than a potato to help thicken it. It can be very rich, so a little will go a long way.

¾ ounce dried wild mushrooms

3 cups chicken or mushroom stock, divided

2 tablespoons butter

1 tablespoon olive oil

1 onion, chopped
(about 1 cup)

1 clove garlic, minced

1 teaspoon fresh thyme leaves, chopped

1 pound brown mushrooms, sliced
(about 6 cups)

3 tablespoons flour

½ - 1 cup heavy cream

½ teaspoon salt, or more to taste

freshly ground black pepper

¼ cup chopped fresh chives

1. Bring 1 cup of the chicken or mushroom stock to a boil. Remove from the heat and pour the stock into a heat-proof bowl. Add the dried mushrooms and let them soak for 30 minutes. After 30 minutes, gently lift the mushrooms out of the stock, pat dry with a paper towel and set aside. Pass the soaking liquid through a very fine strainer or paper coffee filter to remove any dirt and reserve.

2. Melt the butter along with the olive oil in a stockpot or Dutch oven over medium heat. Add the onion and cook for 5 to 7 minutes. The onion should be translucent, not brown. Add the garlic and fresh thyme and cook for an additional minute.

3. Add the fresh mushrooms along with the drained, reconstituted dried mushrooms. Increase the heat to medium-high and cook the mushrooms for 5 to 6 minutes, stirring occasionally. Sprinkle in the flour, and stir to coat all the mushrooms. Cook for 1 to 2 minutes. Add the remaining stock and strained mushroom soaking liquid. Bring the mixture to a boil. Reduce the heat and simmer for 10 to 15 minutes.

4. Using a blender, food processor, food mill or immersion blender, purée the soup until no lumps remain and the soup is smooth. Return the soup to the stovetop and add the heavy cream, salt and freshly ground black pepper. If the soup needs to be thinned, just add some water until you've reached the desired consistency. Heat through and serve with fresh chives sprinkled on top.

TIP

Dried mushrooms add a lot of flavor to the soup, but can be very gritty. As you soak them in hot liquid, the grit will fall to the bottom of the bowl. Be sure to lift the mushrooms out of this liquid by hand (rather than draining them into a colander) so that you are sure to separate the mushrooms from the dirt. Don't forget to keep that delicious soaking liquid, but strain it through a fine strainer first.

Curried Sweet Potato Soup

The secret ingredient in this recipe is orange juice! It brightens the flavor considerably and makes this hearty soup feel a little lighter. This is a good soup to make in a huge batch and freeze for a rainy day.

SERVES
6 - 8

2 tablespoons butter

1 tablespoon olive oil

½ onion, chopped (about ½ cup)

5 to 6 sweet potatoes, peeled and diced (about 6 cups)

1 tablespoon curry powder

4 cups chicken stock, vegetable stock or water

¾ cup orange juice

½ teaspoon salt, or more to taste

freshly ground black pepper

½ cup sour cream (optional)

3 tablespoons chopped fresh parsley

1. Melt the butter along with the olive oil in a stockpot or Dutch oven over medium heat. Add the onion and cook for 5 to 7 minutes, just until the onion is translucent, not brown.

2. Add the sweet potatoes and curry powder, and continue to cook for another 6 to 8 minutes. Add the chicken stock, vegetable stock or water and continue to simmer for another 20 minutes. Stir in the orange juice.

3. Using a blender, food processor, food mill or immersion blender, purée the soup until no lumps remain and the soup is smooth. Return the soup to the stovetop and thin the soup with water until you've reached the desired consistency. Add salt and freshly ground black pepper. Serve with a dollop of sour cream and chopped parsley to garnish.

Potato Leek Soup
Vichysoisse

Potato leek soup has been around for the ages. However, Vichysoisse, the cold version of the soup, only really appeared in the early 20th century. Most food historians agree that Vichysoisse was first served to the public at the Ritz Carlton in New York City by Chef Louis Diat, who fondly remembered cooling his mother's potato leek soup with milk before eating it. He named it after Vichy, a town near his home in France.

SERVES

6 - 8

2 tablespoons butter

1 tablespoon olive oil

4 leeks, cleaned and sliced
(½-inch pieces)

3 sprigs fresh thyme

8 baking potatoes, peeled and chopped
(½-inch cubes; about 8 to 9 cups)

water, as needed

1 cup heavy cream

1 teaspoon salt, or more to taste

freshly ground black pepper

¼ cup chopped fresh chives

1. Melt the butter along with the olive oil in a stockpot or Dutch oven over medium heat. Add the leeks and cook over medium heat until tender – about 8 minutes.

2. Add the fresh thyme sprigs and potatoes and continue to cook with the leeks for another 5 minutes. Add enough water to cover the potatoes, and bring everything to a boil. Reduce the heat to a simmer and simmer for 30 minutes, or until the potatoes are soft. Remove the thyme sprigs.

3. Using a blender, food processor, food mill or immersion blender, purée the soup until no lumps remain and the soup is smooth. Return the soup to the stovetop and add the heavy cream, salt and freshly ground black pepper. If the soup needs to be thinned, just add some water until you've reached the desired consistency. Heat through and serve with chives sprinkled on top.

4. If you choose to serve this soup cold, chill the soup before you add the chives and then thin it with a little water or a little milk or heavy cream. Before serving, taste again and re-season if necessary with salt and freshly ground black pepper. Sprinkle with chopped fresh chives.

TIP

To clean leeks, cut off the dark green top of the leek where it naturally wants to break if you bend the leek from end to end. Then, slice the leek in half lengthwise and soak in cold water for 10 minutes or so, separating the leaves with your hands to remove any embedded dirt there. Dry the leeks on a clean kitchen towel and proceed with the recipe.

Cream of Lobster Soup

This is a decadent soup, usually made for a special occasion. With this in mind, this recipe is designed for two people as a significant course, or four people as a small starter to a meal.

SERVES

2 – 4

2 tablespoons butter

½ onion, chopped (about ½ cup)

1 carrot, chopped (about ½ cup)

1 clove garlic, peeled and smashed

2 sprigs of fresh thyme

1 bay leaf

2 lobster tails in the shell
(about 5 to 6 ounces each)

½ cup white wine

½ cup canned tomatoes in juice

2 cups chicken stock

½ cup cream

1 tablespoon chopped fresh tarragon

¼ teaspoon salt, or more to taste

freshly ground black pepper

¼ cup crème fraiche or sour cream (optional)

1. Melt the butter in a stockpot or Dutch oven over medium heat. Cook the onion and carrot for 5 to 10 minutes. The onion should be translucent, but not brown. Add the garlic, thyme sprigs and bay leaf and cook for an additional minute.

2. Add the lobster tails (in their shells) to the pot and let them cook for about 4 minutes, turning them occasionally. The shells will turn pink. Add the white wine and the tomatoes with their juice and simmer with the lobster tails for 10 minutes. Add the chicken stock and continue to simmer for another 20 minutes.

3. Remove the lobster tails from the pot and once they are cool enough to handle, crack the shells and remove the meat, keeping the meat in one piece as much as possible. Discard the shells and reserve the meat.

4. Remove the thyme sprigs and bay leaf from the pot and then, using a blender, food processor, food mill or immersion blender, purée the soup until no lumps remain and the soup is smooth. Return the soup to the stovetop and add the cream and fresh tarragon. Bring to a simmer and season to taste with salt and freshly ground black pepper.

5. Slice the lobster meat into medallions and place them in the bottom of the serving bowls. Pour the hot soup on top. Garnish with a dollop of crème fraiche or sour cream.

Crème fraiche is a soured cream. It is thicker than heavy cream and less sour than sour cream. It's absolutely worth making the effort to find it in your grocery store. If not, substitute sour cream, or make your own crème fraiche by heating 1 tablespoon of buttermilk and 1 cup of heavy cream together until just warm (about 85° F). Then let this mixture sit at room temperature for 8 to 24 hours until it thickens. Cover and refrigerate and use as needed.

Basic **Balsamic Vinaigrette**

Having a decent vinaigrette recipe is essential for all cooks. Here's one that is easy to put together and versatile for all sorts of salads and meals.

MAKES ABOUT

1 cup

¼ cup balsamic vinegar

½ shallot, finely chopped
(about 2 tablespoons)

1 tablespoon Dijon mustard

1 teaspoon brown sugar

½ teaspoon salt

freshly ground black pepper

¾ cup olive oil

1. Mix the vinegar, shallot, mustard, sugar, salt and pepper in a small bowl, measuring glass or vinaigrette bottle. Whisk until the sugar has dissolved and no lumps of mustard remain.

2. Add the olive oil and whisk together. Serve over greens, vegetables, cooked fish or chicken, roasted potatoes…the list goes on and on.

Recipe Explained!

The basic ratio for vinaigrette is three-parts oil to one-part vinegar (3:1). With this ratio you can make any vinaigrette you like. There are just a few simple rules and helpful hints that will make things easier:

● Always start with the vinegar and always end with the oil. Other ingredients, like mustard, sugar, salt or honey, will dissolve in vinegar but will remain clumpy or grainy in oil. Make the oil the last thing you add.

● Try to add something sweet. Sugar is an emulsifier, which is an ingredient that will help keep the oil and vinegar in suspension. While it is not foolproof, a vinaigrette with a little sugar in it (or honey, or anything sweet) will stay together longer, like a good marriage! Don't fret if the oil and vinegar separate – a little whisking will bring it back together.

● Use the best olive oil you have. Extra virgin olive oil is made from the first cold pressing of the olives and has a superior taste to pure olive oil.

● Not all vinegars are created equal. A measure of good vinegar is one that is at least 6% acidity. If it doesn't say that it is 6% acidity on the bottle, it probably isn't!

Mixed Greens
with Oranges, Endive and Pecans

This salad uses a combination of citrus juice and vinegar as the acidic ingredients in the dressing. Because citrus juice is also sweet, you can use less oil than what the regular 3:1 ratio normally calls for. I love the addition of blue cheese to this salad, but it is completely optional.

SERVES

4

3 oranges, divided

2 tablespoons balsamic vinegar

1 tablespoon whole-grain mustard

2 teaspoons honey

¼ teaspoon salt

freshly ground black pepper

2 tablespoons extra virgin olive oil

½ cup pecan halves

5 ounces mixed baby greens or mesclun mix

2 heads Belgian endive, sliced on the bias (½-inch slices)

¼ cup fresh parsley leaves

¼ to ½ cup crumbled blue cheese (optional)

1. To make the vinaigrette, squeeze the juice from one orange into a mixing bowl. Add the balsamic vinegar, mustard, honey, salt and pepper and whisk together. Add the olive oil and whisk to combine.

2. Lightly toast the pecans, either in a 350° F oven on a cookie sheet for 10 minutes or so, or in a dry skillet on the stovetop.

3. Place the mixed greens into a salad bowl. Slice the endive and add that to the bowl along with the fresh parsley leaves. Peel and segment the remaining two oranges and add the segments to the salad, along with the toasted pecans. Dress the salad with the vinaigrette (you many not use the entire quantity of dressing), toss gently and serve.

4. For a tasty indulgence, crumble some blue cheese over the salad.

To segment an orange, slice off the top and the bottom of the orange. Then run your knife down the sides of the orange, curving with the shape of the orange, to cut away all the peel and pith. Carefully, make slices on either side of the membranes separating the orange segments, loosening the segments from the orange. Be sure to do this over a bowl to catch all the juices!

Endive, Radicchio and Apple Salad
with Walnuts

Belgian endive and radicchio are both bitter greens that make for a very refreshing salad. It's sometimes nice to have a salad that is different from the traditional mixed green salad. Combined with the sweet apple and salty cheese, this makes a tasty salad starter that is elegant enough for any dinner party.

SERVES

6 - 8

6 heads of Belgian endive, thinly sliced on a bias

½ head of radicchio, thinly sliced

3 apples, thinly sliced

½ cup walnut halves

¼ cup chopped fresh parsley

1 tablespoon white wine vinegar

½ teaspoon Dijon mustard

¼ teaspoon salt

freshly ground black pepper

3 tablespoons olive oil

1 ounce Parmesan cheese, peeled into shards with a vegetable peeler

1. Slice the endive and the radicchio into thin shreds. A mandolin or manual slicer are good tools to use. If not, use a chef's knife and practice your knife skills! Place the shredded endive and radicchio into a bowl.

2. Leave the peel on the apple and slice off the four sides of the apple around the core. Discard the core and slice the apple into thin slices. Add the apple slices to the bowl with the endive and radicchio.

3. Toast the walnuts in a 350° F oven for 10 to 12 minutes. Coarsely chop the walnuts and add them to the bowl, along with the fresh parsley.

4. In a separate small bowl, whisk the vinegar and mustard together and add the salt and pepper. Whisk in the olive oil. Pour the dressing over the salad and toss. Finish the salad by topping it with peelings of Parmesan cheese and another grind or two of black pepper.

Beet Salad with Goat Cheese Crostini

I've encountered several people who have told me they don't like beets, only to discover that they've only tried the canned variety. If that's you, please try beets again. They are earthy and delicious and very easy to prepare. Give them a second chance!

4 medium beets, scrubbed

olive oil

salt

freshly ground black pepper

¼ cup water

8 slices of baguette

2 teaspoons red wine vinegar
(raspberry flavored red wine vinegar
is very nice on beets)

2 tablespoons olive oil

½ teaspoon salt

freshly ground black pepper

4 handfuls of mixed baby greens

2 tablespoons chopped fresh chives

3 to 4 ounces goat cheese

1. Pre-heat the oven to 400° F. Scrub any dirt off the beets, but leave the skins on. Place the beets in a shallow pan and drizzle with olive oil. Season with salt and pepper and add ¼ cup of water to the pan (the water will help the skins come off more easily after roasting). Cover with a lid or aluminum foil, and transfer the pan to the oven for 45 to 50 minutes, or until the beets are tender when pierced with a knife. When cool enough to handle, peel the beets with a paring knife and slice them into wedges.

2. While the beets are cooking, slice the baguette and drizzle each slice with a little olive oil. Toast the baguette slices in the oven for 10 minutes or until lightly browned. Set aside.

3. Toss all the beet wedges in a bowl with the vinegar, olive oil, salt and pepper. Place a handful of the mixed greens on each plate and divide the beet mixture between the plates, drizzling any remaining dressing over the top. Sprinkle with the chives.

4. Just before serving, spread the goat cheese on the toasted baguette slices and broil for 2 to 3 minutes to warm through. Place two crostini on each plate and serve.

Classic White Coleslaw

I love the monochromatic quality of this coleslaw, elevating it from a deli counter to an elegant garden party setting. Of course, you can add color and make it more traditional by substituting red cabbage for some of the green cabbage and tossing in some shredded carrots if you like.

1 green cabbage, halved, cored and thinly sliced (about 4 to 5 cups)

1 white onion, thinly sliced (about 1 cup)

3 tablespoons sugar

½ cup white wine vinegar

1 teaspoon mustard powder

1 tablespoon celery seed

½ cup vegetable oil

½ teaspoon salt

freshly ground black pepper

1. Slice the cabbage and the onion in very thin slices, preferably using a slicer or mandolin. Mix the two together in a large bowl, and toss with 2 tablespoons of the sugar and a dash of salt. Set aside.

2. In a small saucepan, bring the vinegar, mustard powder, 1 tablespoon of sugar and celery seed to a boil. Stir to dissolve the sugar. Remove the saucepan from the heat and whisk in the vegetable oil. Pour the hot vinaigrette over the cabbage and onions and toss well. Season to taste with salt and pepper, cover and refrigerate for a few hours.

TIP You can buy pre-packaged shredded cabbage in a bag at most grocery stores to make this salad super easy to throw together.

Lemony White Bean Salad
with Feta Cheese

This salad is so easy to make, but so tasty. With beans being a great source of protein and fiber, this salad can easily be turned into a nice light meal for two all on its own.

SERVES

2 - 4

2 (15 ounce) cans of white beans, drained and rinsed

¼ medium red onion, finely chopped (about ½ cup)

½ cup fresh parsley leaves

½ cup thinly sliced radishes

½ cup pitted black olives (oil-cured or Kalamata olives)

½ cup crumbled feta cheese

2 tablespoons lemon juice

½ teaspoon salt

freshly ground black pepper

2 tablespoons olive oil

1. Combine the white beans, red onion, parsley leaves, radishes, black olives and feta cheese in a salad bowl.

2. In a separate bowl, whisk together the lemon juice, salt, pepper and finally the olive oil. Drizzle the dressing over the salad and toss well.

Beet and Orange Salad

With its alternating slices of orange and red, this salad is spectacular. The tarragon gives the dish a unique and complementary licorice flavor, but you can use chives if you prefer.

SERVES

4

4 medium beets

olive oil

salt

freshly ground black pepper

¼ cup water

4 oranges, divided

2 teaspoons white wine vinegar

½ shallot, finely chopped
(about 2 tablespoons)

½ teaspoon salt

2 tablespoons roughly chopped fresh tarragon
(or fresh chives)

¼ cup extra virgin olive oil

coarse sea salt (optional)

1. Pre-heat the oven to 400° F. Scrub any dirt off the beets, but leave the skins on. Place the beets in a shallow pan and drizzle with olive oil. Season with salt and pepper and add ¼ cup of water to the pan (the water will help the skins come off more easily after roasting). Cover with a lid or aluminum foil, and transfer the pan to the oven for 45 to 50 minutes, or until the beets are tender when pierced with a knife. When the beets are tender, remove them from the oven. When cool enough to handle, peel the beets and slice them into ¼-inch slices.

2. Prepare three of the oranges by removing all the peel and pith. Start by cutting off both ends of the orange. Then cut the peel away from the flesh with a paring knife, making a curved slice down from one end to the other. Slice these oranges into ¼-inch slices.

3. Squeeze the juice from the remaining orange into a small bowl. Add the vinegar and mix well. Add the shallots, salt and tarragon to the orange juice and vinegar, and whisk in the olive oil.

4. Arrange the beet and orange slices on a platter, shingling them on top of each other alternately either in circles or in rows. Drizzle the vinaigrette over everything and season again with a little coarse sea salt if desired.

Potato Salad
with Bacon, Corn and Green Onions

Who doesn't love potato salad? Add bacon and corn to the mix and you've got a winner.
This version is sure to please at any picnic. Just make sure you make enough!

1 pound small fingerling potatoes, scrubbed and cut into bite-sized pieces

4 slices of bacon, cooked and crumbled

4 radishes, thinly sliced (about ½ cup)

1 carrot, thinly sliced (about ½ cup)

1 stalk celery, sliced (about ½ cup)

2 green onions, thinly sliced

½ cup corn kernels (fresh or frozen)

1 tablespoon chopped fresh parsley

2 teaspoons chopped fresh dill

1/3 cup mayonnaise

1 tablespoon Dijon mustard

2 teaspoons fresh lemon juice

salt

freshly ground black pepper

1. Bring a medium saucepot of salted water to a boil. Boil the potatoes until they are tender to a knifepoint. Drain. Toss the potatoes with the cooked bacon, radish, carrot, celery, green onion, corn, parsley and dill.

2. In a separate bowl, combine the mayonnaise with the Dijon mustard, lemon juice, salt and pepper.

3. Add the mayonnaise mixture to the potatoes and toss well. Serve immediately by itself, or over a bed of greens.

Snacks
and
Sandwiches

If you're looking for a light meal, a snack or sandwich might fit the bill. Here you'll also find substantial nibbles like pizzas and nachos. Serve these to a crowd and you'll have happy guests. Crostini are traditional cocktail snacks, but even grilled cheese sandwiches can be cut into little squares for hors d'oeuvres that please everyone.

Basic **Grilled Cheese Sandwich**

Whether you're making it plain and simple, or dressing it up with more adult ingredients, a grilled cheese sandwich is worth making properly. It may have just three ingredients, but made the right way it can go from simple to sublime.

SERVES

4

butter, softened

8 slices sandwich bread

6 ounces grated Cheddar cheese
(about 1½ cups)

1. Spread the butter on one side of all eight slices of bread. Assemble the sandwiches by placing four of the slices butter side down on a work surface. Divide the cheese between these four slices and top with the remaining four slices of bread, butter side up.

2. Pre-heat a skillet or griddle (ideally square in shape) over medium heat. Add the assembled sandwiches and fry on both sides until nicely browned – about 2 to 3 minutes per side. Serve immediately.

Recipe Explained!

● Spreading the butter on the bread, rather than adding butter to the skillet to fry these sandwiches, will ensure that you will have evenly browned sandwiches.

● Grated cheese melts faster and more evenly than sliced cheese. Grate your cheese whenever possible.

● Choose your bread carefully. With so few ingredients, the bread can really make a difference to the quality of the sandwich. Try English muffin bread, Texas toast bread, or egg bread – all of these brown beautifully. You can also add flavor to the sandwich just by choosing tomato bread, fruit and nut bread, or olive rosemary bread.

● Don't make the bread slices too thick – if the bread is too thick, it will be more difficult for the cheese to melt and for the bread to get crispy.

● A square skillet or griddle will allow you to cook four sandwiches at once. With a round skillet, you'll have to work in batches.

● Try using a sandwich or bacon press. A bacon press works well to compress the sandwiches, giving them even contact with the hot pan so they brown very evenly. It also helps to keep the heat in the pan and melt the cheese.

Grilled Apple and Cheddar Cheese Sandwich

If you like a slice of cheese with your apple pie, then this sandwich is for you. It's a classic combination of salty and sweet flavors. Add a little heat to melt the cheese and it's perfect.

butter, softened

8 slices sourdough bread, sliced ½-inch thick

1 Granny Smith or other green apple, thinly sliced

6 ounces grated Cheddar cheese (about 1½ cups)

1. Spread the butter on one side of all eight slices of bread. Assemble the sandwiches by placing four of the slices butter side down on a work surface. Place the apple slices on the four pieces of bread and then divide the grated Cheddar cheese between the sandwiches. Top with the remaining four slices of bread, butter side up.

2. Pre-heat a skillet or griddle (ideally square in shape) over medium heat. Add the assembled sandwiches and fry on both sides until nicely browned – about 2 to 3 minutes per side. Serve immediately.

Croque Monsieur and Madame

The Croque Monsieur sandwich is essentially a grilled ham and cheese sandwich but with cheese sauce poured on top and broiled to perfection. Top it with a fried egg and it becomes a Croque Madame. The sandwich is such a standard item on French café menus, that even McDonald's restaurants in France offer their version of the classic - a "Croque Mc'Do"!

SERVES

4

2 teaspoons butter

1 tablespoon flour

1½ cups milk, room temperature

¼ cup grated Parmesan cheese

¼ cup grated Gruyère or other Swiss cheese

pinch freshly grated nutmeg

⅛ teaspoon salt

Freshly ground black pepper

butter, softened

8 slices French bread (not baguette, but large crusty loaf), sliced ½-inch thick

Dijon mustard

8 slices ham (about 8 ounces)

6 ounces grated Gruyère or other Swiss cheese (about 1½ cups)

4 eggs (only for Croque Madame)

1. Melt the butter in a small saucepan over medium heat. Add the flour and cook the two together for about 2 minutes, stirring constantly. Whisk in the milk, breaking up any lumps that form. Bring the mixture to a boil, stirring constantly. Once the sauce has come to the boil and thickened, remove the pan from the heat and stir in the two cheeses. Season with nutmeg, salt and pepper, and set aside.

2. Pre-heat the broiler and position the oven rack about four inches from the top of the oven. Butter one side of all eight slices of bread, and spread the Dijon mustard on the other sides. Assemble the sandwiches as follows: bread (butter side down, mustard side up) – ham – cheese – ham – bread (mustard side down, butter side up).

3. Pre-heat an oven-safe skillet or griddle (ideally square in shape) over medium heat. Add the assembled sandwiches and fry on both sides until nicely browned – about 2 to 3 minutes per side.

4. Leaving the sandwiches in the pan, spread some of the cheese sauce (made above) on the top of each sandwich. Pop the skillet under the broiler until the cheese sauce has melted and browned lightly. Serve immediately.

5. To make a Croque Madame: fry the eggs in a separate skillet while the sandwiches are under the broiler. Cook the eggs sunny-side up or over-easy and place one on the top of each finished sandwich.

Sweet Chocolate and Berry Sandwich

I can't decide if this sandwich should be eaten in the morning, for lunch, or late at night. Either way, it's sure to be a sandwich you won't soon forget! It's delicious and decadent, and makes an excellent dessert, cut into quarters.

SERVES

4

butter, softened

8 slices cinnamon raisin bread

½ cup chocolate hazelnut spread

½ cup raspberry jam

24 raspberries

1. Spread the butter on one side of all eight slices of bread. Assemble the sandwiches by placing the bread slices butter side down on a work surface. Divide and spread the chocolate hazelnut spread on four of the slices of bread. Divide and spread the raspberry jam on the other four slices of bread. Press the raspberries into the four slices of chocolate covered bread, and top with the jam covered slices.

2. Pre-heat a skillet or griddle (ideally square in shape) over medium heat. Add the assembled sandwiches and fry on both sides until nicely browned – about about 2 to 3 minutes per side. Enjoy with a tall glass of milk!

Western Grilled Cheese Sandwich

This is a take-off on a Western omelette, incorporating all the traditional ingredients of the omelette – ham, peppers and cheese. If you want to make a really hearty sandwich, you can even add the egg. Simply scramble an egg separately and tuck it inside with the other ingredients before frying the sandwich. Sounds like breakfast to me!

SERVES

4

butter, softened

8 slices whole wheat bread, sliced ½-inch thick

6 ounces grated Swiss cheese (about 1½ cups), divided

1 to 2 roasted red bell peppers, peeled and sliced (store-bought are fine)

4 slices ham (about 4 ounces), halved

1. Spread the butter on one side of all eight slices of bread. Assemble the sandwiches by placing four of the slices butter side down on a work surface. Divide half of the cheese between these four slices and add the roasted red pepper and ham. Top with the remaining cheese and then with the remaining four slices of bread, butter side up.

2. Pre-heat a skillet or griddle (ideally square in shape) over medium heat. Add the assembled sandwiches and fry on both sides until nicely browned – about 2 to 3 minutes per side.

TIP There are three ways to roast red bell peppers if you want to make them at home. You can grill them on an outdoor grill, roast and char them directly over the flame of a gas burner, or cut them in half and broil them in your oven. Whatever method you use, make sure you roast the peppers until the skin is completely black. Place the roasted peppers in a paper bag. This will allow the peppers to cool but trap the steam, which will make them easier to peel. Once cool, peel away the skins and the peppers are ready to use.

Basic Nachos

For all those people who write to me asking for a recipe for nachos, this one's for you! The key to good nachos is to have crispy chips, oozing cheese, but no sogginess. If the chips around the edge of the dish brown a little more than the rest, that's a good sign.

SERVES

6 – 8

8 ounces Cheddar cheese, grated
(about 2 cups)

8 ounces Pepper Jack cheese, grated
(about 2 cups)

1 large bag of corn tortilla chips

1 jar tomato salsa, or your own homemade salsa

1 cup sour cream

guacamole (optional)

1. Pre-heat the oven to 350˚ F.

2. Combine the cheeses in a small bowl. Layer the ingredients evenly as follows on a baking sheet or oven-safe ceramic platter: corn tortilla chips, a good handful of cheese, modest dollops of the salsa, more chips, more cheese, more salsa, more chips, more cheese, and so on until you've run out of ingredients, making sure you end with a layer of cheese.

3. Bake in the oven for 10 to 15 minutes, or until all the cheese has melted and is bubbling. Remove and serve with sour cream, guacamole and any remaining salsa.

Recipe Explained!

● Use thick corn tortilla chips. These are less likely to get soggy from wet ingredients. White corn tortilla chips are the most common chips for nachos, but a mixture of white and blue corn chips adds interest and color to the dish.

● Use good cheese. Cheese that you grate yourself is generally better quality than pre-grated cheese. Nachos are really all about the cheese, so use the best.

● You can put almost any ingredient on nachos, although there is something to be said for keeping it simple. The only rule is that if you use an ingredient that requires cooking (like chicken or beef), it must be pre-cooked before going on the chips.

● Spread the ingredients as evenly as you can. No-one likes to get the chip with nothing on it. Each chip should have at least a little of some topping. Building the nachos in layers

helps distribute the toppings more evenly.

● If possible, try to use a platter or baking pan that you can cook and serve on. This will make serving the nachos much easier, as you won't have to transfer them. If you don't have an oven-to-table pan, use a baking sheet lined with parchment paper or a silicone liner that will allow you to slide the nachos off onto a serving platter.

Chicken Nachos
with Avocado, Monterey and Pepper Jack Cheeses

This is one of my favorite nacho dishes. It's simple, but satisfying. The critical factor is that the avocados MUST be ripe. If your avocados are not ripe, wait a day or two before making this. You won't regret it.

SERVES

6 – 8

4 ounces Monterey Jack cheese, grated (about 1 cup)

8 ounces Pepper Jack cheese, grated (about 2 cups)

1 large bag of corn tortilla chips

1 jar tomato salsa or your homemade salsa

2 cups shredded cooked chicken

2 avocados, diced and peeled

2 green onions, sliced on the bias

1 cup sour cream (optional)

1. Pre-heat the oven to 350° F.

2. Combine the cheeses in a small bowl. Layer the ingredients evenly as follows on a baking sheet or oven-safe ceramic platter: corn tortilla chips, a good handful of cheese, modest dollops of salsa, chicken, avocado, green onions, more chips, more cheese, more salsa, more chicken, more avocado, more green onions, and so on until you've run out of ingredients, making sure you end with a layer of cheese.

3. Bake in the oven for 10 to 15 minutes, or until all the cheese has melted and is bubbling. Remove and serve with sour cream and any remaining salsa.

TIP

To speed up the ripening process of an avocado, place it in a paper bag with an apple or a banana. The apple or banana will emit ethylene gas, which accelerates ripening. Conversely, if your avocados are really ripe and you're not making the nachos for a couple of days, store the avocados in the refrigerator which will help them last a little longer.

Chili and Cheddar Cheese Nachos

These nachos are so hearty they really are a meal unto themselves.

1 tablespoon vegetable oil

½ onion, chopped (about ½ cup)

2 tablespoons chili powder

1 pound lean ground beef

¼ cup tomato paste

¼ cup water

1 large bag of corn tortilla chips

12 ounces Cheddar cheese, grated
(about 3 cups)

3 Jalapeño peppers, sliced

1 cup sour cream

guacamole (optional)

1. Pre-heat the oven to 350° F.

2. Heat a skillet or sauté pan over medium-high heat. Add the vegetable oil and cook the onions until tender and just starting to brown – about 5 to 7 minutes. Add the chili powder and cook for 1 more minute. Add and brown the ground beef. Stir in the tomato paste and water, and simmer the mixture until cooked through – about 10 minutes.

3. Layer the ingredients evenly as follows on a baking sheet or oven-safe ceramic platter: corn tortilla chips, a good handful of cheese, a couple spoonfuls of beef chili, some Jalapeño slices, more chips, more cheese, more beef chili, more Jalapeño, and so on until you've run out of ingredients, making sure you end with a layer of cheese.

4. Bake in the oven for 10 to 15 minutes, or until all the cheese has melted and is bubbling. Remove and serve with sour cream and guacamole.

TIP Much of the spicy heat of a pepper lies in the veins and seeds of the pepper. If you like spicy foods, leave the edible seeds in the pepper when you slice it. If, on the other hand, you have a lower tolerance to spice, seed the peppers first and then slice them and add them to the recipe.

Black Bean and Corn Nachos

To really do these nachos justice, you have to use fresh corn rather than frozen corn kernels. Save this recipe for the summer months and try it on the barbecue for a little smoky nuance.

8 ounces Pepper Jack cheese, grated (about 2 cups)

8 ounces Cheddar cheese, grated (about 2 cups)

1 large bag of corn tortilla chips

2 (15 ounce) cans black beans, drained and rinsed

1½ cups fresh corn kernels

1 jar tomato salsa, or your own homemade salsa

1 cup sour cream

guacamole

1. Pre-heat the oven to 350° F.

2. Combine the cheeses in a small bowl. Layer the ingredients evenly as follows on a baking sheet or oven-safe ceramic platter: corn tortilla chips, a good handful of cheese, some black beans, some corn kernels, modest dollops of salsa, more chips, more cheese, more black beans, more corn kernels, more salsa, and so on until you've run out of ingredients, making sure you end with a layer of cheese.

3. Bake in the oven for 10 to 15 minutes, or until all the cheese has melted and is bubbling. Remove and serve with sour cream, guacamole and any remaining salsa.

Mango and Jalapeño Nachos

Nachos take a tropical twist in this version.

8 ounces Cheddar cheese, grated
(about 2 cups)

8 ounces Monterey Jack cheese, grated
(about 2 cups)

1 large bag of corn tortilla chips

2 mangoes, peeled and diced

3 Jalapeño peppers, sliced

½ cup packed fresh cilantro leaves

1 cup sour cream

guacamole (optional)

1. Pre-heat the oven to 350° F.

2. Combine the cheeses in a small bowl. Layer the ingredients evenly as follows on a baking sheet or oven-safe ceramic platter: corn tortilla chips, a good handful of cheese, some mango, some Jalapeño slices, some cilantro, more chips, more cheese, more mango, more Jalapeño, more cilantro, and so on until you've run out of ingredients, making sure you end with a layer of cheese.

3. Bake in the oven for 10 to 15 minutes, or until all the cheese has melted and is bubbling. Remove and serve with sour cream and, if you like, guacamole.

TIP Mangoes are extremely slippery without their peel. To dice them easily, slice off the sides of the mango, as closely as possible to the long flat seed inside. Then score each half of the mango flesh into dice, cutting right down to the skin, but not through it. Invert the piece of mango as though you were trying to turn it inside out, and simply cut the dice off the peel.

Basic Tomato and Cheese Pizza

This is a pretty foolproof pizza dough recipe, and there's a lot to be said about a basic tomato and cheese pizza. Once you've mastered the basics, there's a world of pizza opportunity out there. Try making one on the grill – it adds a great smoky flavor.

Serves 3 as a main course or 6 to 8 as an appetizer

MAKES

3 pizzas

Dough:

1 teaspoon active dry yeast

1 cup warm water, about 90° – 100°F

2 tablespoons olive oil

3 cups bread flour

1 teaspoon salt

Topping for three pizzas:

1½ cups tomato sauce (homemade, store bought, or the Basic Marinara Sauce on page 72)

1½ cups grated cheese (Mozzarella, Asiago, ricotta salata, or any cheese you like)

1 tablespoon chopped fresh basil or oregano

1. Sprinkle the yeast into the warm water. Within about 5 minutes, you should see foam or froth on top of the water. If nothing happens, the yeast may be dead and unusable, in which case discard and start again with new yeast. Once the yeast has foamed, add the olive oil to the water and yeast.

2. Combine the flour and salt in the bowl of a stand mixer or a large mixing bowl. Add the yeast mixture and mix until the dough comes together. Then knead the dough for about 10 minutes in a stand mixer, or 20 minutes by hand, until it becomes smooth and elastic.

3. Place the dough in an oiled bowl, covered with plastic wrap, and let it rise in a warm place until doubled in bulk – about 2 hours. Punch the dough down, and divide it into three equal pieces. Roll these pieces into balls and let them rest, covered, for at least 15 minutes. (If you plan on making this dough well in advance, freeze the dough balls in oiled baggies.)

4a. To cook in the oven: Pre-heat the oven to 500° F. Shape a pizza dough ball into whatever shape you like, stretching the dough as thinly as desired. Spread the tomato sauce on the dough and scatter the cheese over the top. For a thin crust pizza, bake on a pre-heated pizza stone for 8 to 10 minutes. For a deep-dish pizza, bake in a deep-dish pizza pan for 10 to 12 minutes.

4b. To cook on an outdoor grill: Pre-heat the grill until very hot. Shape a pizza dough ball into whatever shape you like, stretching the dough as thinly as desired. Brush the dough lightly with oil and grill one side of the dough for 2 to 3 minutes on a medium hot part of your grill. When the dough has set enough to turn, flip it over, spread the tomato sauce on the grilled side of the dough and scatter the cheese over the top. Close the lid and grill the pizza for 5 to 7 minutes.

5. Once the dough has cooked, and the cheese is brown and bubbling, remove the pizza from the oven or outdoor grill, and immediately sprinkle the fresh basil or oregano on top. Slice and enjoy.

TIP

Defrost frozen pizza dough balls at room temperature for a several hours, or overnight in the refrigerator. If defrosted in the refrigerator, be sure to leave the dough out on the counter for a couple of hours to bring it to room temperature before trying to stretch it.

Mushroom Pizza
with Lemon, Garlic and Mint

This has always been one of my favorite pizzas. The combination of lemon, garlic and mint added at the end of cooking adds a fresh burst of flavor. Use whatever combination of mushrooms you enjoy, but I find Portobello mushrooms work really well.

MAKES

2 pizzas

Dough:

2 Pizza dough balls (from Basic Tomato and Cheese Pizza Recipe on page 55)

Topping for two pizzas:

6 ounces Fontina cheese, grated (about 1½ cups)

8 ounces wild mushrooms, thinly sliced (about 3 cups)

2 teaspoons olive oil

salt

freshly ground black pepper

1½ tablespoons chopped lemon zest

2 small cloves garlic, minced

3 tablespoons chopped fresh mint

1. Follow the instructions for making pizza dough in the Basic Tomato and Cheese Pizza recipe.

2a. To cook in the oven: Pre-heat the oven to 500° F. Shape a pizza dough ball into whatever shape you like, stretching the dough as thinly as desired. Scatter the Fontina cheese on the dough. Toss the mushrooms with the olive oil, salt and pepper and distribute them on top of the cheese. For a thin crust pizza, bake on a pre-heated pizza stone for 8 to 10 minutes. For a deep-dish pizza, bake in a deep-dish pizza pan for 10 to 12 minutes.

2b. To cook on an outdoor grill: Pre-heat the grill until very hot. Shape a pizza dough ball into whatever shape you like, stretching the dough as thinly as desired. Brush the dough lightly with oil and grill one side of the dough for 2 to 3 minutes on a medium hot part of your grill. Meanwhile, toss the mushrooms with olive oil, salt and pepper. When the dough has set enough to turn, flip it over and scatter the Fontina cheese on the grilled side of the dough. Distribute the mushrooms on top of the cheese. Close the lid and grill the pizza for 5 to 7 minutes.

3. While the pizza is cooking, combine the lemon zest, garlic and mint in a small bowl. Once the dough has cooked and the cheese is brown and bubbling, remove the pizza from the oven or outdoor grill and immediately sprinkle the mint, lemon zest and garlic mixture on top. Cut into wedges and serve.

TIP

Fontina is a cow's milk cheese that melts well and has a very smooth texture. If you can't find Fontina, try substituting Gouda, Emmental, Gruyère, Taleggio or Edam.

Potato, Bacon, Rosemary and Blue Cheese Pizza

The key to this pizza is making sure the potato slices are super thin. A mandolin or slicer works well for this task.

MAKES

2 pizzas

Dough:

2 Pizza dough balls (from Basic Tomato and Cheese Pizza Recipe on page 55)

Topping for two pizzas:

2 Yukon Gold potatoes, very thinly sliced on a mandolin or slicer

2 teaspoons olive oil

salt

freshly ground black pepper

6 slices of bacon, cooked and chopped

1 tablespoon chopped fresh rosemary

4 ounces blue cheese, crumbled (about 1 cup)

1. Follow the instructions for making pizza dough in the Basic Tomato and Cheese Pizza recipe.

2a. To cook in the oven: Pre-heat the oven to 500° F. Shape a pizza dough ball into whatever shape you like, stretching the dough as thinly as desired. Toss the sliced potatoes with the olive oil, salt and pepper, and spread onto the pizza dough in an even layer, overlapping slightly. Scatter the bacon pieces and rosemary on the potatoes and crumble the blue cheese on top. For a thin crust pizza, bake on a pre-heated pizza stone for 8 to 10 minutes. For a deep-dish pizza, bake in a deep-dish pizza pan for 10 to 12 minutes.

2b. To cook on an outdoor grill: Pre-heat the grill until very hot. Shape a pizza dough ball into whatever shape you like, stretching the dough as thinly as desired. Brush the dough lightly with oil and grill one side of the dough for 2 to 3 minutes on a medium hot part of your grill. Meanwhile, toss the sliced potatoes with the olive oil, salt and pepper. When the dough has set enough to turn, flip it over and spread the potato slices onto the grilled side of the dough in an even layer, overlapping slightly. Scatter the bacon pieces and rosemary on the potatoes and crumble the blue cheese on top. Close the lid and grill the pizza for 5 to 7 minutes.

3. Once the dough has cooked and the cheese is melted and bubbling, remove from the oven or outdoor grill, cut into wedges and serve immediately.

 TIP If you are not a big fan of blue cheese, substitute a cheese that you do like – try Asiago or Monterey Jack cheese.

Chicken and Broccoli White Pizza

A pizza dough really is like a blank canvas – you can add anything you like to fill in the picture. This version is a simple pizza with clean flavors. Miss the tomato sauce? Add a few slices of fresh tomatoes.

MAKES

2 pizzas

Dough:

2 Pizza dough balls (from Basic Tomato and Cheese Pizza Recipe on page 55)

Topping for two pizzas:

6 ounces Swiss cheese, grated (about 1½ cups)

2 skinless, boneless chicken breasts, cooked and shredded

2 crowns of broccoli, cut into bite-sized pieces and blanched

1 clove garlic, minced

salt

freshly ground black pepper

1. Follow the instructions for making pizza dough in the Basic Tomato and Cheese Pizza recipe.

2a. To cook in the oven: Pre-heat the oven to 500° F. Shape a pizza dough ball into whatever shape you like, stretching the dough as thinly as desired. Distribute half of the Swiss cheese on the dough. Arrange the cooked chicken and broccoli pieces on top. Sprinkle the minced garlic over the pizza, season with salt and pepper, and finish with the remaining cheese. For a thin crust pizza, bake on a pre-heated pizza stone for 8 to 10 minutes. For a deep-dish pizza, bake in a deep-dish pizza pan for 10 to 12 minutes.

2b. To cook on an outdoor grill: Pre-heat the grill until very hot. Shape a pizza dough ball into whatever shape you like, stretching the dough as thinly as desired. Brush the dough lightly with oil and grill one side of the dough for 2 to 3 minutes on a medium hot part of your grill. When the dough has set enough to turn, flip it over and distribute half of the Swiss cheese on the grilled side of the dough. Arrange the cooked chicken and broccoli pieces on top. Sprinkle the minced garlic over the pizza, season with salt and pepper, and finish with the remaining cheese. Close the lid and grill the pizza for 5 to 7 minutes.

3. Once the dough has cooked and the cheese is brown and bubbling, remove from the oven or outdoor grill, cut into wedges and serve immediately.

TIP
To cook the broccoli, blanch it in boiling water for 3 to 4 minutes, or steam the broccoli for a more nutritious result. Broccoli steams very quickly in the microwave. Place ¼ cup of water in a bowl with the broccoli florets and microwave for 2 to 3 minutes.

BET Breakfast Pizza
Bacon, Egg and Tomato

This is a great pizza for a fun weekend brunch. I first made this pizza when I was working in Vermont at a restaurant called The Commons. During our Sunday brunches we made pizza after pizza after pizza...

Dough:

2 Pizza dough balls (from Basic Tomato and Cheese Pizza Recipe on page 55)

Topping for two pizzas:

8 slices of bacon, cooked

2 – 3 plum tomatoes, sliced

6 ounces Cheddar cheese, grated (about 1½ cups)

2 eggs

salt and freshly ground black pepper

1 tablespoon chopped fresh parsley

1. Follow the instructions for making pizza dough in the Basic Tomato and Cheese Pizza recipe.

2. Pre-heat the oven to 500˚ F. Shape a pizza dough ball into whatever shape you like, stretching the dough for a thin crust pizza. Place the bacon slices on the pizza dough (4 slices per pizza). Arrange the tomato slices on top and then scatter the cheese over everything. Season with salt and pepper. For eggs over hard, crack the egg on top of the pizza just before it goes into the oven for 8 to 10 minutes. For eggs over easy, cook the pizza for 4 to 5 minutes and then crack the egg on top and return it to the oven to finish cooking for another 4 to 5 minutes.

3. Once the dough has cooked, the egg white has cooked through and the cheese is melted and bubbling, remove the pizza from the oven and sprinkle the parsley on top. Cut into wedges and serve immediately.

TIP

If you choose to split one pizza between two people, use two eggs on the pizza so both people get an egg.

Basic Tomato and Basil Crostini

"Crostini" and "Bruschetta" are often used interchangeably to refer to toasted bread topped with a savory mixture. What's the difference? Generally the bread for bruschetta is more substantial and grilled, while the bread for crostini is cut in small pieces and baked. Which will you make?

MAKES ABOUT

30 crostini

1 baguette

olive oil

4 vine-ripened tomatoes

½ small shallot, finely chopped (about 2 tablespoons)

1 tablespoon balsamic or red wine vinegar

2 tablespoons extra virgin olive oil

½ teaspoon salt

freshly ground black pepper

1 clove garlic, peeled and left whole

20 leaves fresh basil, thinly sliced

1. Pre-heat the oven to 350° F.

2. Slice the baguette on the bias into ½-inch slices and place on a baking sheet. Brush the baguette slices with the olive oil and toast in the oven until lightly browned – about 20 minutes. Remove from the oven and let cool slightly.

3. While the baguette is toasting, prepare the tomato mixture. Cut the tomatoes in half horizontally and remove the seeds with your fingers. Chop the tomatoes and place in a bowl. Add the shallot, vinegar, olive oil, salt and pepper. Mix well.

4. Once out of the oven and just cool enough to handle, rub each baguette slice very lightly with the clove of garlic. A little goes a long way here, so don't rub too hard.

5. Top each baguette slice with some of the tomato mixture. Place on a platter, and sprinkle the shredded fresh basil over the top.

Recipe Explained!

● If you are using baguette for the crostini, the baguette should be sliced on the bias so that there is more surface area to top.

● Don't make the bread slices too thick. That will make the crostini difficult to eat.

● Finish preparing crostini as close to serving time as possible so that they don't lose their crunch.

● You can toast the bread for crostini ahead of time and store the toasted bread in an air-tight container. Then top them just before serving.

● Grilling the bread adds great flavor to these recipes. If you decide to grill, use larger pieces of bread, which are easier to manage. Then, call it bruschetta!

White Bean, Rosemary and Pecorino Crostini

Another great combination of simple flavors, these crostini make a great snack and are pretty too.

1 baguette

olive oil

1 (14 ounce) can white beans, drained

¼ cup chopped roasted red bell pepper (store-bought are fine)

1 tablespoon red wine vinegar

2 tablespoons olive oil

½ shallot, finely chopped (about 2 tablespoons)

½ teaspoon fresh rosemary, chopped very finely

¼ teaspoon salt

freshly ground black pepper

4 ounces Pecorino cheese

1. Pre-heat the oven to 350° F.

2. Slice the baguette on the bias into twenty ½-inch slices and place on a baking sheet. Brush the baguette slices with the olive oil and toast in the oven until lightly browned – about 20 minutes. Remove from the oven and let cool.

3. While the baguette is toasting, combine the white beans, red pepper, vinegar, oil, shallot, rosemary, salt and pepper. Toss well and let sit.

4. Heap the bean mixture on the cooled baguette slices and place on a platter. Using a peeler, peel shards of the Pecorino cheese and scatter on top. Serve immediately.

Tuna and Black Olive Crostini

There are very few ingredients in this snack, so make sure those ingredients are of excellent quality. Delicious Italian tuna and oil-cured black olives will make this crostini one of your favorites.

1 baguette

olive oil

2 cans tuna, packed in water, drained

½ lemon, juiced (about 1 tablespoon)

2 tablespoons chopped fresh parsley

½ cup black olives, pitted and chopped

2 tablespoons extra virgin olive oil

salt

freshly ground black pepper

1. Pre-heat the oven to 350° F.

2. Slice the baguette on the bias into twenty ½-inch slices and place on a baking sheet. Brush the baguette slices with the olive oil and toast in the oven until lightly browned – about 20 minutes. Remove from the oven and let cool.

3. While the baguette is toasting, combine the tuna, lemon juice, parsley, olives, olive oil, salt and pepper.

4. Heap spoonfuls of the tuna mixture onto the cooled baguette slices and serve immediately.

Pear and Blue Cheese Crostini

Bosc pears are my preference for this crostini, but Anjou or Bartlett pears work well too.

1 baguette

olive oil

2 tablespoons butter

3 pears, peeled and diced

1 tablespoon brown sugar

½ cup crumbled blue cheese

2 – 3 tablespoons finely chopped fresh chives

1. Pre-heat the oven to 350° F.

2. Slice the baguette on the bias into twenty ½-inch slices and place on a baking sheet. Brush the baguette slices with the olive oil and toast in the oven until lightly browned – about 20 minutes. Remove from the oven and let cool.

3. Heat a skillet over medium heat. Add the butter, pears and brown sugar to the skillet and cook for 4 to 5 minutes, or until the pears are tender and lightly browned.

4. Let the pears cool and then spoon them onto the toasted cooled baguette slices. Top with crumbles of blue cheese and garnish with a little chopped fresh chive.

TIP

Unlike most fruit, pears actually ripen faster once they have been picked off the tree. Don't worry if the pears you bring home are firm to the touch. They will ripen quickly on your kitchen counter, especially if stored in a paper bag. To check the ripeness of a pear, press just below the stem. If it yields to the pressure of your thumb, it is ripe.

Caramelized Onion, Goat Cheese and Bacon Crostini

The components used in this crostini are great to have on hand in your pantry, so save any leftovers. Caramelized onions are delicious in a sandwich or on a pizza, and the brown sugared bacon works very nicely in a salad or a pasta sauce.

MAKES ABOUT

30 crostini

8 slices of bacon, preferably thick-cut

2 tablespoons brown sugar

3 tablespoons olive oil

4 sweet onions, peeled and sliced (about 6 to 7 cups)

½ teaspoon salt

freshly ground black pepper

½ cup water

1 baguette

olive oil

4 ounces goat cheese, crumbled

3 tablespoons chopped fresh chives

1. Pre-heat the oven to 350° F.

2. Lay the bacon slices out flat on a baking sheet and sprinkle the brown sugar on top of each slice. Bake in the oven until the bacon is browned and crispy – about 35 minutes. Break the cooked bacon into 1- to 2-inch pieces and set aside.

3. In a large Dutch oven or sauté pan, heat three tablespoons of olive oil and add all the sliced onion. Cook on medium heat until the onions start to brown. Stir regularly to encourage the onions to brown evenly, scraping up any brown bits that accumulate on the bottom of the pan. Reduce the heat if the onions start to brown too quickly or too much. Once the onions are brown, season with salt and pepper and stir in the water. Once the water has been incorporated, the onions should have an almost creamy appearance.

4. Slice the baguette on the bias into ½-inch slices and place on a baking sheet. Brush the baguette slices with the olive oil and toast in the oven until lightly browned – about 20 minutes. Remove from the oven and let cool.

5. Assemble the crostini by spooning some of the onions on each cooled baguette slice. Crumble some of the goat cheese on top of the onions and then finish it off with a good piece of bacon and a sprinkling of chives on each.

Tuna Salad Sandwich with Capers and Pickles

When I worked in the test kitchen at the Center for Culinary Development in San Francisco, we all used to make tuna salad sandwiches with different "secret" ingredients. Of them all, my favorite combination was briny capers and sweet pickles.

SERVES

4

2 cans of tuna, packed in water, drained

2 tablespoons mayonnaise

1 rib celery, finely chopped

1 tablespoon capers, rinsed and chopped

2 tablespoons sweet pickles, chopped

6 radishes, sliced or chopped

salt

freshly ground black pepper

8 slices sourdough or ciabatta bread

1 head butter lettuce

1. In a bowl, mix together the tuna, mayonnaise, celery, capers, pickles, radishes, salt and pepper. Combine well with a fork.

2. Toast the bread slices under the broiler until lightly brown. (You could also use a toaster for this, but if you're toasting eight slices, the broiler will get them all done at the same time.)

3. Divide the tuna salad between four of the slices of toasted bread. Cover each with a couple of leaves of the butter lettuce and top with the second piece of toasted bread. Slice in half and enjoy.

Egg Salad Sandwich with Anchovies

Growing up in Calgary, Canada, my family occasionally went for day trips into the Rocky Mountains. Sometimes on these trips, my father would bring his special egg and anchovy sandwiches. They were not a big hit with my friends, but I loved them.

SERVES

4

6 eggs

1 rib of celery, finely chopped

1 tablespoon mayonnaise

2 teaspoons chopped fresh chives

salt

freshly ground black pepper

8 slices whole wheat or multi-grain bread

1 (2 ounce) tin anchovies

1 head butter lettuce

1. Hard boil the eggs, allow them to cool and peel them. Chop the eggs and place them in a bowl.

2. To this bowl, add the celery, mayonnaise, chives, salt and pepper. (Go easy with the salt, since the anchovies are very salty.) Mash the mixture together with a fork and set aside.

3. Toast the bread slices under the broiler until lightly brown. (You could also use a toaster for this, but if you're toasting eight slices, the oven will get them all done at the same time.)

4. Divide the egg salad between four of the slices of toasted bread. Place 2 to 3 fillets of anchovy on each sandwich. Cover each with a couple of leaves of the butter lettuce and top with the second piece of toasted bread. Slice in half and enjoy.

TIP

Anchovies can be stored in a sealed container in the refrigerator, covered in oil, for up to two months.

Pasta

There are so many possibilities with pasta. The recipes in this section are grouped into marinara-based pastas and cheese-based pastas. It's important to know the basics. Knowing how to make a good marinara sauce and a good cheese sauce are two essential components of any cook's repertoire. With those two building blocks, you can construct any number of pasta dishes.

Basic Marinara Sauce

This is an important sauce to have in any cook's repertoire. It's easy to put together and nice to have on hand, since it can be used for so much more than just pasta.

SERVES

8 - 10

3 tablespoons olive oil

3 cloves garlic, finely chopped
(about 1 tablespoon)

pinch hot red pepper flakes

2 (28 ounce) cans of crushed tomatoes OR 6 cups chopped fresh tomatoes

½ to 1 teaspoon salt

½ teaspoon sugar (optional)

¼ cup chopped fresh parsley or basil

1. Add the olive oil, garlic and hot red pepper flakes to a deep sauté pan or Dutch oven, and then heat the pan over medium heat. Cook gently until the garlic is fragrant, but do not brown.

2. Add the tomatoes and bring to a simmer. Simmer for about 20 to 30 minutes, stirring occasionally. Season with salt and sugar if desired (you may find it needs no sweetening.) Stir in the fresh parsley or basil.

3. Serve over pasta or in any number of dishes.

Recipe Explained!

● The first thing you'll notice about this recipe is that it does not call for the pan to be pre-heated. Heating the oil and garlic with the pan (instead of pre-heating the pan) allows a more gentle garlic taste to flavor the oil.

● You may find three tablespoons of olive oil a lot to use. You can cut down on this quantity, but it adds flavor as well as a smooth texture to the finished sauce. If flavor is at the forefront of my mind, I use the full 3 tablespoons. If I'm thinking of my waistline, however, I tend to cut back.

● Whether to use crushed or diced canned tomatoes is often just a matter of personal preference. I use crushed tomatoes in a basic marinara sauce. When I want actual chunks of tomato in my sauce, I go for the diced variety, as you'll see in the subsequent recipes. Using fresh tomatoes is certainly an option, but be sure the tomatoes you're using are ripe. Making a marinara is a great way to use up tomatoes at the end of the season if you have a surplus on hand and, if you properly can or freeze the sauce, you will be able to enjoy them well into winter.

● Pay attention to the heat under the pan while it simmers. If the heat is too high, the sauce will boil too rapidly. A boiled sauce will lose too much liquid and be thick and bitter. If this happens by accident, add a little water to loosen the sauce.

Pasta à la Norma

This is one of my favorite tomato-based pasta dishes. It was named in honor of Bellini's popular opera of the same name. Both were considered fantastic!

SERVES

4 - 6

1 eggplant, sliced (1-inch slices)

kosher salt, to salt the eggplant

1 tablespoon olive oil

2 cloves garlic, sliced

¼ teaspoon hot red pepper flakes

1 (28 ounce) can of diced tomatoes OR 3 cups chopped fresh tomatoes

½ teaspoon salt

olive oil

1 pound dried pasta

½ cup crumbled ricotta salata cheese or grated Parmesan cheese

¼ cup chopped fresh parsley or basil

1. Prepare the eggplant by generously sprinkling kosher salt on both sides of the eggplant slices and laying them flat between sheets of paper towel. Let the eggplant sit like this for 30 minutes.

2. Meanwhile, add the olive oil, garlic and hot red pepper flakes to a deep sauté pan or Dutch oven, and then heat the pan over medium heat. Cook gently until the garlic is fragrant. When the garlic is just starting to brown around the edges, add the tomatoes and the ½ teaspoon salt, and bring to a simmer. Simmer for 20 to 30 minutes.

3. Brush any remaining kosher salt off the eggplant slices and brush both sides of the eggplant with oil. Cook the eggplant until tender, either by grilling or by baking for 30 minutes in a 350° F oven. Once cooked, cut the eggplant into large chunks and add to the tomato sauce.

4. Bring a large pot of salted water to a boil. Add the pasta and cook according to the package directions. Drain the pasta and toss with the sauce. Serve with crumbled ricotta salata (a dense, dry ricotta cheese) or grated Parmesan cheese, and chopped fresh parsley or basil.

TIP

Eggplants are known to have a bitter taste. To avoid this, choose small to medium eggplants that are firm, blemish-free and are heavier than you'd expect them to be for their size. Also, choose eggplants that have a shallow circular dimple on the bottom rather than a deeper oblong shaped dimple. The former are males of the species and have fewer bitter seeds. Finally, use the technique of salting the eggplant described above. This helps to draw the bitter juices out of the eggplant before you cook it.

Smoky Tomato and Sausage Fusilli
with Spinach and Black Olives

Fire-roasted tomatoes and smoked paprika work wonders to bring a smoky flavor to this version of a marinara.

SERVES

4 - 6

2 tablespoons olive oil

½ onion, finely chopped (about ½ cup)

1 pound sweet Italian sausage, removed from casing and broken into chunks

2 cloves garlic, sliced

1 teaspoon smoked paprika

pinch hot red pepper flakes

1 (28 ounce) can of fire-roasted diced tomatoes

½ teaspoon salt

1 pound dried fusilli

1 tablespoon butter

5 ounces fresh baby spinach, cleaned

½ cup pitted black olives

½ cup grated Parmesan cheese

1. Heat a deep sauté pan over medium high heat. Add the olive oil and cook the onion until tender and translucent – about 5 to 7 minutes. Add the sausage and cook until no longer pink. Add the garlic, smoked paprika and hot red pepper flakes, and cook for an additional minute.

2. Add the tomatoes and salt to the pan and bring to a simmer. Simmer, partially covered, for 30 to 40 minutes.

3. Bring a large pot of salted water to a boil. Add the fusilli and cook according to the package directions. Drain the fusilli and set aside.

4. While the fusilli is cooking, heat a skillet over medium heat. Add the butter and wilt the spinach gently.

5. Just before serving, stir the spinach and the black olives into the sauce. Season again with salt and freshly ground black pepper. Spoon the sauce over the fusilli, and serve with grated Parmesan cheese at the table.

TIP

Smoked paprika, also known as Pimentón, is what gives this dish its smoky flavor. Smoked paprika is used in a lot of Spanish foods and differs quite distinctly from the more common Hungarian paprika. If you want the smoky flavor in this dish, be sure to use the smoked variety. If you want less of a smoky flavor, just leave the paprika out.

Fettuccine with Tomato Vodka Sauce

Tomatoes contain some flavor components that are only soluble in alcohol, which is why you so often see the two combined. Here, vodka brings out all those great tomato flavors. Simmering the vodka in the sauce is an important step – it boils off all the alcohol so the sauce doesn't have a boozy aftertaste.

SERVES

4 - 6

2 tablespoons olive oil

1 clove garlic, finely chopped

1 (28 ounce) can of diced tomatoes OR 3 cups chopped fresh tomatoes

½ cup vodka

½ cup heavy cream

½ teaspoon salt

freshly ground black pepper

¼ cup chopped fresh parsley or basil

1 pound dried fettuccine

Parmesan cheese, grated (optional)

1. Add the olive oil and garlic to a deep sauté pan or Dutch oven, and then heat the pan over medium heat. Cook gently until the garlic is fragrant, but do not brown.

2. Add the tomatoes and bring to a simmer. Simmer for roughly 30 minutes, stirring occasionally. Add the vodka and simmer for another 20 minutes. Add the heavy cream and simmer for another 10 minutes. Season with salt and freshly ground black pepper. Stir in parsley or basil.

3. Bring a large pot of salted water to a boil. Add the fettuccine and cook according to the package directions. Drain the fettuccine and toss with the sauce. Serve with grated Parmesan cheese if desired.

Linguine with Bacon and Sweet Apple Tomato Sauce

I first saw this prepared by Lidia Bastianich on her PBS television series. I couldn't wait to try it myself. The apple in this marinara sauce is a sweet surprise. To me, bacon just makes it better, but you can leave it out if you like.

1 tablespoon olive oil

6 slices bacon, chopped (1-inch pieces)

½ onion, finely chopped (about ½ cup)

1 clove garlic, finely chopped

1 (28 ounce) can of diced tomatoes OR 3 cups chopped fresh tomatoes

1 Granny Smith apple, peeled, cored and grated (about 1 cup)

¼ to ½ tsp salt

freshly ground black pepper

¼ cup chopped fresh parsley

1 pound dried linguine

Parmesan cheese, grated (optional)

1. Heat a deep sauté pan or Dutch oven over medium heat. Add the olive oil and cook the bacon until the bacon is almost crispy. Remove the bacon with a slotted spoon and set aside. Pour out all but 1 to 2 tablespoons of the bacon fat. Add the onion and cook until translucent and tender, but not brown – about 8 minutes. Add the garlic and cook for another minute.

2. Add the tomatoes and bring to a simmer. Simmer, partially covered, for about 20 minutes, stirring occasionally. Add the grated apple and simmer for another 20 minutes. Season with salt and freshly ground black pepper. Stir in parsley and reserved cooked bacon.

3. Bring a large pot of salted water to a boil. Add the linguine and cook according to the package directions. Drain the linguine and toss with the sauce. Serve with grated Parmesan cheese if desired.

TIP

Make sure you cook the onion until it is very soft and tender before you add the tomatoes to the pot. The tomatoes will inhibit the onions from cooking any further.

Basic Mac 'n' Cheese

When I was a little girl, I used to ask my mother to make boxed macaroni and cheese for me. She refused and always made macaroni and cheese from scratch. At the time, I didn't know how lucky I was. I do now! While it's not my mother's, this version is a really good basic recipe that uses a combination of cheeses.

SERVES

6 - 8

1 pound dried macaroni or other short pasta

Cheese Sauce:

4 tablespoons butter

1 onion, finely chopped (about 1 cup)

6 tablespoons flour

2 teaspoons dried mustard powder

4 cups milk, room temperature

3 cups grated Gruyère or other Swiss cheese

2 cups grated Cheddar cheese

1 cup grated Parmesan cheese

2 teaspoons salt

freshly ground black pepper

Topping:

2 cups breadcrumbs (preferably coarse homemade crumbs)

2 teaspoons fresh thyme leaves, chopped

1 tablespoon chopped fresh parsley

½ teaspoon salt

1. Pre-heat the oven to 350° F.

2. Bring a large pot of salted water to a boil. Add the macaroni and cook according to the package directions. Drain the macaroni and set aside.

3. While the macaroni is cooking, heat a 2- to 3-quart saucepan over medium heat. Melt the butter and cook the onion until translucent and very tender, but not brown. Add the flour and mustard powder and stir, cooking for 2 minutes. Whisk in the milk, stirring constantly to avoid lumps. Stirring regularly, bring the sauce to a boil. Once it has boiled and thickened, remove the pan from the heat and stir in the grated cheeses, salt and pepper.

4. In a large mixing bowl, combine the cooked macaroni and cheese sauce. Transfer to a casserole or baking dish. Combine the topping ingredients and spread the mixture on top of the macaroni. Cook in a 350° F oven for 30 to 40 minutes.

Recipe Explained!

● As one of America's most popular comfort foods, there are hundreds of recipes for macaroni and cheese out there. It seems everyone has an opinion on what makes a perfect mac 'n' cheese – some like it with a lot of sauce, while others prefer a stiffer and drier version that can be scooped. There's no right or wrong way to make the dish. Adjust the recipe to suit your own taste. If you want the casserole to be drier rather than soupy, just add less sauce or leave it in the oven a little longer.

● This recipe starts with onions cooked in butter. These add great flavor to the dish. It is very important to cook the onions until they are very tender and soft. Once they are added to the cheese sauce, they will not have any more cooking time, and you don't want to have crunchy onions in the finished dish.

● Using whole milk will make the sauce richer and more decadent, but you can substitute low-fat or nonfat milk, as you like. Three cheeses are combined in this sauce. Gruyère is an excellent melting cheese with a relatively mild flavor. It gives the sauce good

body. Cheddar has a stronger flavor, but one that is very amenable to all tastes. If you love Cheddar, choose an old sharp version for this dish. Finally the Parmesan adds a nutty flavor with a salty finish.

● It is entirely acceptable to stop the recipe after the cheese sauce and pasta have been combined, but the crunchy breadcrumb topping adds an interesting texture to the meal. Some people like to add a layer of fresh tomato slices before sprinkling on the breadcrumbs. Delicious!

Lobster Mac 'n' Cheese

This is a pretty "rich" mac 'n' cheese – one you won't make everyday – but it is great for a special occasion.

½ pound dried macaroni or other short pasta

Cheese Sauce:

2 tablespoons butter

½ onion, finely chopped (about ½ cup)

1 clove garlic, peeled and smashed

2 tablespoons flour

3 cups milk, room temperature

¼ teaspoon freshly grated nutmeg

⅛ teaspoon hot red pepper flakes

½ teaspoon lemon zest, finely chopped

½ teaspoon salt

2 cups grated Gruyère or other Swiss cheese

1 cup grated Parmesan cheese

2 to 3 cooked lobster tails (5 to 6 ounces each), shelled and meat chopped into bite-sized pieces

Topping:

1 cup breadcrumbs (preferably coarse homemade crumbs)

1 teaspoon fresh thyme leaves, rough chopped

1 tablespoon chopped fresh parsley

¼ teaspoon salt

1. Pre-heat the oven to 350° F.

2. Bring a large pot of salted water to a boil. Add the macaroni and cook according to the package directions. Drain the macaroni and set aside.

3. While the macaroni is cooking, heat a 2- to 3-quart saucepan over medium heat. Melt the butter and cook the onion and garlic until translucent and very tender, but not brown. Add the flour and stir, cooking for 2 minutes. Whisk in the milk, stirring constantly to avoid lumps. Stirring regularly, bring the sauce to a boil and then reduce the heat to low. Season the sauce with nutmeg, hot red pepper flakes, lemon zest and salt. Remove the pan from the heat and stir in the grated cheeses.

4. In a large mixing bowl, combine the cooked macaroni, lobster meat and cheese sauce. Transfer to a casserole or baking dish. Combine the topping ingredients and spread the mixture on top of the macaroni. Cook in a 350° F oven for 30 to 40 minutes.

TIP You can buy pre-cooked lobster tails or cook them yourself. Cook the lobster tails either by boiling in salted water for 2 to 3 minutes, or by baking in a 450° F oven for 8 to 9 minutes. If you choose to bake your lobster tails (my preference), cut the top of the shell down the center, leaving the tail intact. Put your fingers underneath the lobster shell and pull the lobster meat out, letting it rest on the shell. Brush with butter, season with salt, and then bake.

Bacon, Tomato and Green Pea Mac 'n' Cheese

Ahhh bacon! It really does make everything taste better!

1 pound dried macaroni or other short pasta

1½ cups green peas, frozen

1 pint cherry tomatoes, halved (about 2 cups)

Cheese Sauce:

6 slices bacon, chopped (1-inch pieces)

1 onion, finely chopped (about 1 cup)

6 tablespoons flour

2 teaspoons dried mustard powder

4 cups milk, room temperature

3 cups grated Gruyère or other Swiss cheese

2 cups grated Cheddar cheese

1 cup grated Parmesan cheese

2 teaspoons salt

freshly ground black pepper

Topping:

2 cups breadcrumbs (preferably coarse home-made crumbs)

2 teaspoons fresh thyme leaves, chopped

1 tablespoon chopped fresh parsley

½ teaspoon salt

1. Pre-heat the oven to 350° F.

2. Bring a large pot of salted water to a boil. Add the macaroni and cook according to the package directions, adding the peas to the pot for the last 2 minutes of cooking. Drain the macaroni and peas and set aside.

3. While the macaroni is cooking, heat a 2- to 3-quart saucepan over medium heat. Add the bacon and cook until the bacon is almost crispy. Remove the bacon with a slotted spoon and set aside. Add the onion to the pan and cook until translucent and very tender, but not brown. Add the flour and mustard powder and stir, cooking for 2 minutes. Whisk in the milk, stirring constantly to avoid lumps. Stirring regularly, bring the sauce to a boil. Once it has boiled and thickened, remove the pan from the heat and stir in the grated cheeses, salt and pepper.

4. In a large mixing bowl, combine the cooked macaroni and peas, cooked bacon, cherry tomatoes and cheese sauce. Fold everything together and transfer to a casserole or baking dish. Combine the topping ingredients and spread the mixture on top of the macaroni. Cook in a 350° F oven for 30 to 40 minutes.

Primavera Mac 'n' Cheese

Shouldn't there be a mac 'n' cheese to announce the arrival of every new season? I think so! Here we add fresh vegetables to the cheese and pasta. In this recipe, the vegetables are blanched in the pasta-cooking water to save a step. You can sauté the vegetables instead, or use any combination of leftover cooked vegetables you might have on hand.

1 pound dried macaroni or other short pasta

1 bunch broccoli, cut into florets (about 2 cups)

1 bunch asparagus, cut on the bias
 (1-inch pieces; about 2 cups)

1 orange or red bell pepper, chopped
(1-inch pieces; about 1 cup)

1 pint cherry tomatoes, halved (about 2 cups)

Cheese Sauce:

4 tablespoons butter

1 small red onion, finely chopped (about ¾ cup)

6 tablespoons flour

2 teaspoons dried mustard powder

4 cups milk, room temperature

3 cups grated Gruyère or other Swiss cheese

2 cups grated Cheddar cheese

1 cup grated Parmesan cheese

2 teaspoons salt

freshly ground black pepper

Topping:

2 cups breadcrumbs
(preferably coarse homemade crumbs)

2 teaspoons fresh thyme leaves, chopped

1 tablespoon chopped fresh parsley

½ teaspoon salt

1. Pre-heat the oven to 350° F.

2. Bring a large pot of salted water to a boil. Add the macaroni and cook according to the package directions. When there are 4 minutes left in the cooking time, add the broccoli florets and asparagus to the pasta pot. When there are 2 minutes left in the cooking time, add the peppers. Drain the macaroni and vegetables and set aside.

3. While the macaroni is cooking, heat a 2- to 3-quart saucepan over medium heat. Melt the butter and cook the onion until translucent and very tender, but not brown. Add the flour and mustard powder and stir, cooking for 2 minutes. Whisk in the milk, stirring constantly to avoid lumps. Stirring regularly, bring the sauce to a boil. Once it has boiled and thickened, remove the pan from the heat and stir in the grated cheeses, salt and pepper.

4. In a large mixing bowl, combine the cooked macaroni, vegetables, cherry tomatoes and cheese sauce. Transfer to a casserole or baking dish. Combine the topping ingredients and spread the mixture on top of the macaroni. Cook in a 350° F oven for 30 to 40 minutes.

Butternut Squash and Green Apple Mac 'n' Cheese

I like the burst of sweetness that comes with each bite of apple in this version of mac 'n' cheese.

1 pound dried macaroni or other short pasta

2 tablespoons butter

1 medium butternut squash, peeled and diced (½-inch pieces; about 3 cups)

2 Granny Smith apples, peeled, cored and diced (½-inch pieces; about 2 cups)

Cheese Sauce:

4 tablespoons butter

1 onion, finely chopped (about 1 cup)

6 tablespoons flour

2 teaspoons dried mustard powder

4 cups milk, room temperature

3 cups grated Gruyère or other Swiss cheese

2 cups grated Cheddar cheese

1 cup grated Parmesan cheese

2 teaspoons salt

freshly ground black pepper

Topping:

2 cups breadcrumbs (preferably coarse home-made crumbs)

2 teaspoons fresh thyme leaves, chopped

1 tablespoon chopped fresh parsley

½ teaspoon salt

1. Pre-heat the oven to 350° F.

2. Bring a large pot of salted water to a boil. Add the macaroni and cook according to the package directions. Drain the macaroni and set aside.

3. While the macaroni is cooking, heat a skillet or sauté pan over medium high heat. Add the butter and cook the butternut squash until almost tender – about 6 to 8 minutes. Add the apple and continue to cook for another 2 minutes. Set aside.

4. Heat a 2- to 3-quart saucepan over medium heat. Melt the butter and cook the onion until translucent and very tender, but not brown. Add the flour and mustard powder and stir, cooking for 2 minutes. Whisk in the milk, stirring constantly to avoid lumps. Stirring regularly, bring the sauce to a boil. Once it has boiled and thickened, remove the pan from the heat and stir in the grated cheeses, salt and pepper.

5. In a large mixing bowl, combine the cooked macaroni, squash and apples and cheese sauce. Transfer to a casserole or baking dish. Combine the topping ingredients and spread the mixture on top of the macaroni. Cook in a 350° F oven for 30 to 40 minutes.

Greek Pasta Salad

I love having this pasta in the summer when tomatoes are at their best. Served at room temperature, it's the kind of pasta that's great to feed a crowd because you never have to worry about keeping it hot.

SERVES

6 - 8

1 pound dried rotini or fusilli

4 to 5 ripe tomatoes, cut into wedges OR 1 pint cherry tomatoes, halved

1 cucumber, peeled and cubed (about 2 cups)

1 half red onion, thinly sliced and soaked in cool water for 10 minutes (about ½ cup)

1 red bell pepper, chopped (about 1 cup)

1 cup of Kalamata olives, pitted and halved

1½ to 2 cups of feta cheese, crumbled or cubed

¼ cup chopped fresh basil or mint

Dressing:

⅓ cup red wine vinegar

1 clove of garlic, crushed

1 teaspoon dried oregano

pinch dried marjoram

salt

freshly ground black pepper

⅔ cup olive oil

1. Bring a large pot of salted water to a boil. Add the rotini and cook according to the package directions. Drain the rotini and set aside.

2. Combine tomatoes, cucumber, red onion, red pepper and olives in a large mixing bowl and set aside.

3. Prepare the dressing by whisking together the red wine vinegar, garlic, oregano, marjoram, salt and pepper. Whisk in the olive oil. Set aside.

4. Assemble the salad by adding the cooked rotini to the vegetables, then toss in the feta cheese and add as much dressing as you like (you may have some dressing left over).

5. Finally, toss in the fresh basil or mint, and season with salt and pepper. Serve at room temperature in a serving bowl or over a bed of greens on a large platter

TIP Soaking onions after they have been sliced or chopped is a great way to make them less pungent and more palatable if they are not going to be cooked. Soak or rinse the raw onions in cold water and then dry well with paper towel before adding them to the dish.

Pasta with Fresh Tomato, Brie and Basil

This pasta is lovely and simple and simply lovely. There is no sauce to prepare, but by tossing everything together as soon as the pasta has been drained, the Brie melts and coats the noodles beautifully, forming a sauce of its own. It's a perfect summer meal.

SERVES

4

1 pound dried pasta

2 vine-ripened tomatoes, chopped (about 2 cups)

4 to 6 ounces Brie cheese, cut into thin strips (1½-inch long, rind included)

16 to 20 leaves of fresh basil, thinly sliced

salt

freshly ground black pepper

extra virgin olive oil, as needed

1. Bring a large pot of salted water to a boil. Add the pasta and cook according to the package directions. Drain the pasta and return the pasta to the hot pasta pot.

2. As soon as you drain the pasta, immediately toss it with the tomatoes, Brie and basil. Season to taste with salt and lots of freshly ground fresh black pepper. Add extra virgin olive oil to lubricate the pasta and serve immediately.

You can use American or French Brie for this pasta. French Brie has a lower fat content than American Brie, but both would melt perfectly. Whichever you choose, do make it a good quality Brie, since it is the primary ingredient for the sauce in this pasta recipe.

Farfalle with Ham, Asparagus and Goat Cheese

Goat cheese and lemon zest add a little tang to this cream sauce for pasta. This dish is also very nice with fresh cherry tomatoes thrown in at the last minute.

SERVES

6

1 pound dried farfalle

2 tablespoons butter

2 shallots, thinly sliced

1 bunch asparagus, sliced on the bias (¼-inch slices)

1½ to 2 cups heavy cream

3 to 4 ounces goat cheese, crumbled or cut into chunks

5 to 6 ounces Black Forest ham, thinly sliced (½ inch slices; about 1 cup)

1½ teaspoons lemon zest

½ cup grated Parmesan cheese

salt

freshly ground black pepper

3 tablespoons chopped fresh parsley

1. Bring a large pot of salted water to a boil. Add the farfalle and cook according to the package directions.

2. While the farfalle is cooking, heat a sauté pan or skillet over medium heat. Add the butter and cook the shallots and asparagus for 5 minutes. Add the heavy cream and simmer together for 5 minutes. Add the goat cheese and stir until the cheese melts.

3. Drain the farfalle and return it to the hot pasta pot. Pour the sauce over the farfalle and toss in the ham, lemon zest and Parmesan cheese. Season with salt and lots of freshly ground pepper and sprinkle with parsley.

TIP

In Europe, any ham labeled "Black Forest" must have been produced in the Black Forest in Southwestern Germany. This regulation is not enforced in North America, however. Traditionally, Black Forest ham is cured with juniper, coriander, garlic, salt and pepper and then cold smoked over fir or pine branches. It has a sweet, smoky flavor and a dark rind. You can substitute regular ham or prosciutto in this recipe if need be.

Meats and Poultry

The recipes that follow are organized by cooking method, rather than by the type of meat or poultry. Learn how to braise, sauté, pan-fry, roast, pan-roast, pot-roast, make a pan sauce, create a pocket for stuffing, and build a perfect burger or meatloaf. Once you understand a technique, you will be able to apply it to so many different foods. Learn the basics and then let your creativity flow.

Basic Stuffed Chicken Breasts
with Spinach and Feta Cheese

Stuffing a chicken breast is an easy way to dress it up, and elevate simple chicken to dinner party status. I prefer to make a real pocket in the chicken, rather than butterflying the breast wide open or wrapping the chicken around the stuffing. Tucked into a pocket, the stuffing won't leak out during the cooking process.

1 (10 ounce) package frozen spinach, thawed and drained

1 cup Feta cheese, crumbled

½ teaspoon freshly ground black pepper

4 boneless chicken breasts (with skin on or off)

1 tablespoon olive oil

salt

freshly ground black pepper

1. Pre-heat the oven to 350° F.

2. Prepare the filling: Squeeze as much liquid as possible from the thawed spinach. Rough chop the spinach and combine it in a mixing bowl with the Feta cheese and the ½ teaspoon of freshly ground black pepper.

3. Prepare the chicken breasts: Place a chicken breast on a cutting board and press down on the chicken breast with one hand to keep it stabilized. Make an incision about 1-inch long in the fattest side of the breast. Make a pocket by moving the knife up and down inside the chicken breast, taking care not to poke through either the top or the bottom, or the other side of the breast. The pocket should be about 3-inches long, but the opening should only be about 1-inch. If this is too difficult, you can make the incision longer, but you will have to be more careful when cooking the chicken breast since this will expose more of the stuffing. Repeat for each chicken breast.

4. Once you have created the pockets in the chicken breasts, use your fingers to stuff the filling into each pocket, spreading the mixture as far in as you can.

5. Heat an oven-safe skillet or sauté pan over medium-high heat. Add the olive oil and brown the chicken breasts on both sides – about 3 to 4 minutes per side, seasoning with salt and pepper. Transfer the skillet to the oven and finish cooking the chicken breasts – about 8 minutes, or until an instant read thermometer registers 165° F in the fattest part of the chicken, as well as in the stuffing.

6. Remove the skillet from the oven and let the chicken breasts rest on a cutting board for a couple of minutes. Slice the chicken on the bias and plate the slices fanned out.

The Keys to Stuffing

● The key to stuffing any meat successfully is to create a pocket that holds in the stuffing, and doesn't allow it to fall out during the cooking process. The procedure in these recipes describes how to make a true pocket for the stuffing. Keeping the opening in the meat very small, while making a large pocket for the stuffing is critical. If you make too large an opening, you can use toothpicks or trussing twine to secure the pocket.

● Any mixture of ingredients can be combined to form a stuffing. Try to include something that will add moisture, like cheese, mushrooms, or leafy greens. If you use a breadcrumb stuffing, be sure to moisten it with stock or an egg. It is best to pre-cook any ingredients that will lose much of their volume before stuffing them into a chicken breast or pork chop. Otherwise, you'll be left with much less stuffing than you'd anticipated.

● Season the stuffing with salt and pepper, unless the ingredients are inherently salty themselves. For instance, the Feta cheese in the basic recipe makes the stuffing salty enough without adding extra salt.

● Finally, make sure the stuffing is in small pieces so that you can stuff it through the small opening and into the pocket.

● Once stuffed, start by searing the meat on the stovetop in order to get good color on the outside. Transferring it to the oven once both sides are brown will help cook the meat and stuffing evenly, without losing moisture.

● Check the finished dish with a thermometer not just in the thickest part of the meat, but also in the stuffing. The stuffing was in contact with the raw meat from the beginning, so you need to cook the stuffing to the same degree of doneness as the meat.

● Remember to slice stuffed chicken breasts before serving them. They look so elegant fanned out on the plate. Stuffed pork chops are a little more rugged and are not the right shape to be sliced very easily. They should be served whole with a sharp steak knife.

Stuffed Chicken Breasts
with Prosciutto, Asparagus and Fontina Cheese

Prosciutto and asparagus are a classic combination and make a very pretty stuffing for this chicken when you slice it and fan it out on the plate.

4 slices prosciutto

12 stalks asparagus

1 cup grated Fontina cheese

¼ teaspoon freshly ground black pepper

4 boneless chicken breasts
(with skin on or off)

1 tablespoon olive oil

salt

freshly ground black pepper

1. Pre-heat the oven to 350° F.

2. Prepare the filling: Blanch the asparagus in boiling water for 3 minutes. Once cool, slice the asparagus into ¼-inch slices on the bias. Slice the prosciutto into thin strips. Combine the prosciutto, asparagus and Fontina cheese in a mixing bowl, and add the ¼ teaspoon of freshly ground black pepper.

3. Prepare the chicken breasts: Place a chicken breast on a cutting board and press down on the chicken breast with one hand to keep it stabilized. Make an incision about 1-inch long in the fattest side of the breast. Make a pocket by moving the knife up and down inside the chicken breast, taking care not to poke through either the top or the bottom, or the other side of the breast. The pocket should be about 3-inches long, but the opening should only be about 1-inch. If this is too difficult, you can make the incision longer, but you will have to be more careful when cooking the chicken breast since this will expose more of the stuffing. Repeat for each chicken breast.

4. Once you have created the pockets in the chicken breasts, use your fingers to stuff the filling into each pocket, spreading the mixture as far in as you can.

5. Heat an oven-safe skillet or sauté pan over medium-high heat. Add the olive oil and brown the chicken breasts on both sides – about 3 to 4 minutes per side, seasoning with salt and pepper. Transfer the skillet to the oven and finish cooking the chicken breasts – about 8 minutes, or until an instant read thermometer registers 165° F in the fattest part of the chicken, as well as in the stuffing.

6. Remove the skillet from the oven and let the chicken breasts rest on a cutting board for a couple of minutes. Slice the chicken on the bias and plate the slices fanned out.

 TIP Prosciutto is actually Italian for "ham", but in most instances, it refers to a thinly sliced dry-cured ham, as opposed to a cooked ham. Prosciutto has a great flavor and a salty finish. Consequently, there is no need to season the filling with more salt. Prosciutto can be found at most deli counters these days, but it has a relatively high price. Sliced ham would be a good substitute in this recipe.

Stuffed Chicken Breasts
with Apricots, Leeks and Goat Cheese

The sweet-tart flavor of the apricots is a nice surprise inside these chicken breasts.

2 small leeks, cleaned and sliced (½-inch slices)

2 teaspoons olive oil

10 dried apricots, chopped

4 ounces goat cheese, crumbled

salt

¼ teaspoon freshly ground black pepper

4 boneless chicken breasts (with skin on or off)

1 tablespoon olive oil

salt

freshly ground black pepper

1. Pre-heat the oven to 350° F.

2. Prepare the filling: Heat a skillet over medium heat. Add the olive oil and cook the leeks until tender – about 4 to 5 minutes. Transfer the leeks to a mixing bowl and let them cool. Once cool, add the apricots and goat cheese and mix well, seasoning with salt and pepper.

3. Prepare the chicken breasts: Place a chicken breast on a cutting board and press down on the chicken breast with one hand to keep it stabilized. Make an incision about 1-inch long in the fattest side of the breast. Make a pocket by moving the knife up and down inside the chicken breast, taking care not to poke through either the top or the bottom, or the other side of the breast. The pocket should be about 3-inches long, but the opening should only be about 1-inch. If this is too difficult, you can make the incision longer, but you will have to be more careful when cooking the chicken breast since this will expose more of the stuffing. Repeat for each chicken breast.

4. Once you have created the pockets in the chicken breasts, use your fingers to stuff the filling into each pocket, spreading the mixture as far in as you can.

5. Heat an oven-safe skillet or sauté pan over medium-high heat. Add the olive oil and brown the chicken breasts on both sides – about 3 to 4 minutes per side, seasoning with salt and pepper. Transfer the skillet to the oven and finish cooking the chicken breasts – about 8 minutes, or until an instant read thermometer registers 165° F in the fattest part of the chicken, as well as in the stuffing.

6. Remove the skillet from the oven and let the chicken breasts rest on a cutting board for a couple of minutes. Slice the chicken on the bias and plate the slices fanned out.

TIP

Bright orange dried apricots have been treated with sulphur-dioxide to keep their vibrant color. Darker orange dried apricots are naturally dried. Both will have the same bright taste.

Pork Chops
with Apple, Bacon and Pecan Cornbread Stuffing

If you can't get your hands on cornbread for this stuffing, substitute regular coarse breadcrumbs.

3 slices of bacon, chopped (¼-inch pieces)

2 apples, peeled, cored and chopped (¼-inch pieces)

¼ cup pecans, toasted and chopped

½ cup crumbled cornbread (or coarse breadcrumbs)

salt

freshly ground black pepper

4 center cut pork chops, at least 1-inch thick

1 tablespoon olive oil

½ shallot, finely chopped (about 2 tablespoons)

1 clove garlic, minced

1 teaspoon chopped fresh thyme

½ cup chicken stock

1. Pre-heat the oven to 350° F.

2. Prepare the filling: Cook the bacon in a skillet until almost crispy. Transfer the bacon (along with some of the bacon fat) to a mixing bowl and toss with the apples, pecans and cornbread. Season with the salt and pepper and mix well.

3. Prepare the pork chops: Place the pork chop on a cutting board and press down on the chop with one hand to keep it stabilized. Make an incision about 3-inches long in the side of the chop. Make a pocket by moving the knife up and down inside the pork chop, taking care not to poke through either the top or the bottom of the chop. Repeat for each pork chop.

4. Once you have made the pockets in the chops, use your fingers to stuff the filling into each pocket, filing the pockets as full as you can.

5. Heat an oven-safe skillet or sauté pan over medium-high heat. Add the olive oil and brown the pork chops on both sides – about 3 to 4 minutes per side, seasoning with salt and pepper. Transfer the skillet to the oven and finish cooking the pork chops – about 8 minutes, or until an instant read thermometer registers 155° F in the thickest part of the pork, as well as in the stuffing.

6. Remove the skillet from the oven and let the pork chops rest on a cutting board while you make the pan sauce. Return the skillet to the stovetop (remember the handle of the skillet will still be very hot and you will need to use an oven mitt) and add the shallots, garlic and fresh thyme. Stir with a wooden spoon to pick up any brown bits on the bottom of the skillet. Cook for about 1 to 2 minutes and then add the chicken stock. Let this simmer and reduce for a few minutes and then pour over the pork chops to moisten.

TIP

Make your own breadcrumbs by chopping up stale bread by hand or pulsing it in a food processor until it is as coarse or as fine as you would like it. Store in the freezer in a sealed bag.

Pork Chops
with Dried Cherry Breadcrumb Stuffing

You can't slice these pork chops and fan them out on a plate because of the bone in the meat. For a pretty presentation, make a larger opening when stuffing the pork chop. That way the stuffing is visible when you serve the pork chop whole.

1 cup dried cherries

½ cup port wine

1 teaspoon fresh thyme leaves

1 cup coarse breadcrumbs

1 egg, lightly beaten

salt

freshly ground black pepper

4 bone-in center cut pork chops, at least 1-inch thick

1 tablespoon olive oil

2 tablespoons chopped shallot

1 clove garlic, minced

½ cup chicken stock

1 tablespoon butter

1. Pre-heat the oven to 350° F.

2. Prepare the filling: Soak the dried cherries in the port wine until they are soft – about 20 minutes. Drain the cherries, reserving the port wine. Give the cherries a rough chop and combine in a bowl with the thyme, breadcrumbs and egg. Season with salt and pepper and mix well.

3. Prepare the pork chops: Place a pork chop on a cutting board and press down on the chop with one hand to keep it stabilized. Make an incision about 3 inches long in the side of the chop opposite the bone. Make a pocket by moving the knife up and down inside the pork chop, taking care not to poke through either the top or the bottom of the chop. Repeat for each chop.

4. Once you have made the pockets in the chops, use your fingers to stuff the filling into each pocket, filling the pocket as full as you can.

5. Heat an oven-safe skillet or sauté pan over medium-high heat. Add the olive oil and brown the pork chops on both sides – about 3 to 4 minutes per side, seasoning with salt and pepper, and being cautious to keep as much of the stuffing inside the chop as possible. Transfer the skillet to the oven and finish cooking the pork chops – about 8 minutes, or until an instant read thermometer registers 155° F in the thickest part of the pork, as well as in the stuffing.

6. Remove the skillet from the oven and let the pork chops rest on a cutting board while you make the pan sauce. Return the skillet to the stovetop (remember the handle of the skillet will still be very hot and you will need to use an oven mitt) and add the shallots and garlic. Stir with a wooden spoon to pick up any brown bits on the bottom of the skillet. Cook for 1 to 2 minutes and then add the reserved port wine and chicken stock. Let this simmer and reduce for a few minutes and then turn off the heat and add the butter. Season to taste with salt and pepper again, and pour the sauce over the pork chops.

TIP For a silky smooth sauce, strain the reduced liquid in step 6 before adding the butter and seasoning with salt and pepper. Just a touch of this flavorful sauce on each chop is sufficient.

Basic Chicken Cacciatore

Cacciatore, which translates as "hunter-style", is a popular braised dish prepared with tomatoes, mushrooms, and herbs. It is a perfect example of braising – cooking partially covered in liquid, in a covered pot, at low heat for a relatively long period of time, often after preliminary browning.

1 to 2 tablespoons olive oil

1 (4 pound) chicken,
cut into 8 pieces left on the bone

1 onion, chopped

2 cloves garlic, minced

½ teaspoon dried oregano

½ teaspoon dried thyme

1 bay leaf

½ cup red wine

½ cup chicken stock

1 (28 ounce) can diced tomatoes,
or 3 cups fresh chopped tomatoes

8 ounces mushrooms (any variety),
quartered or cut into bite-sized pieces

2 teaspoons finely chopped fresh rosemary

1. Heat a large sauté pan or Dutch oven over medium-high heat for 2 to 3 minutes. Add one tablespoon of the olive oil. Season the chicken pieces with salt and pepper, and brown the chicken in batches until well browned on all sides, adding more oil as necessary. Once the chicken pieces are nicely browned, remove them to a side plate and set aside. Pour off and discard most of the fat that has accumulated in the pan.

2. Add the onion to the pan and cook until tender – about 5 minutes. Add the garlic, oregano, thyme and bay leaf and continue to cook for an additional minute. Pour in the red wine and deglaze the pan, scraping up any brown bits on the bottom of the pan. Let the wine simmer for 4 to 5 minutes and then add the chicken stock. Let this simmer for another 2 to 3 minutes.

3. Add the tomatoes and return the chicken to the pan. Cook over low heat, covered, for 45 minutes.

4. While the chicken is braising, heat a skillet over medium-high heat. Add 1 tablespoon of olive oil and cook the mushrooms until they are brown and tender. Toss in the rosemary. Stir the mushrooms into the cacciatore just before serving.

5. Serve over egg noodles or rice and accompany with a green salad.

Braising Simplified

Braising is a simple and satisfying cooking method. Tough, cheaper cuts of meat are ideal for braising, as cooking them at low heat over a long period of time makes them tender. Braising also fills the house with fantastic aromas of whatever you happen to be cooking. There are some important points to consider when braising.

● **Choice of meat**. It makes more sense to braise tougher pieces of meat, although you are not restricted to these cuts. Traditionally, a tough rooster might have been selected for chicken cacciatore. Today, roosters are hard to come by (!), but you can certainly select a tougher, larger chicken for this recipe. If you're braising beef, good cuts to choose are: top blade roast, chuck eye roast, seven bone roast, shanks, short ribs, brisket or ribs.

● **Braising liquid.** The meat that you are braising should be partially covered in liquid, but not submerged. This liquid will eventually become the sauce for the meat, so make sure it is full of flavor. It will take flavor from the meat you are cooking, but it should also provide flavor of its own. Liquids often used to braise foods are: wine, beer, stocks, fruit juices, or tomatoes.

● **Temperature**. Braising requires a low temperature. A low temperature is important because the goal of braising is to break tough collagen in the meat into silky smooth gelatin, which happens at 140° F. If you use too high a heat to braise, the exterior of the meat will dry out before the inside of the meat has time to reach this critical temperature.

● **Time.** Braising takes time. Believe it or not, you can end up with dry meat when you're braising if you don't cook it for long enough. While the collagen is breaking down into gelatin, the muscle fibers of the meat contract and squeeze out moisture. This flavors the sauce, but it dries out the meat. After time, however, the muscle fibers relax and re-absorb liquid. Don't cut the braising time short.

● **Other ingredients.** Vegetables often make up part of a braised meat dish. Vegetables, however, cook much faster than meats so add them near the end of the cooking time so they don't turn to mush. Sometimes, it is nice to cook the vegetables separately to seal in their flavor and then add them to the braised dish at the very end.

● **Sauce.** As mentioned above, the braising liquid will become the sauce for the finished dish. If the braising liquid is not tasty enough, let the meat rest and simmer the liquid a little longer to reduce the sauce. The flavors will concentrate, and the liquid will thicken.

Caribbean Chicken
with Rice

I used to hate this dish. Seriously. As a child, Pelau (as it was known in my family) was almost the only dinner I didn't want to eat – but of course, I did anyway. Years later, as an adult, I took a recipe from my Auntie Grace, who is a brilliant cook and tried it again. Today I really like it! Funny, how that happens.

Marinade:

2 bunches green onions

4 cloves garlic

1 teaspoon dried thyme

½ Habanero (or Scotch Bonnet)
pepper, seeds removed
OR 1 Jalapeño pepper, seeds included

2 limes, juiced

¼ cup soy sauce

¼ cup teriyaki sauce

2 onions, cut into wedges

2 cloves garlic, crushed

1 (3 to 4 pound) chicken,
cut into 8 pieces left on the bone

2 tablespoons canola or vegetable oil

¼ cup sugar

¼ cup tomato ketchup

1 tablespoon dried oregano

3½ cups water

salt

2 cups converted rice (not instant)

1 tablespoon chopped fresh parsley

1. Prepare the marinade. Combine the green onions, 4 cloves of garlic, thyme, Habanero pepper and lime juice in a blender and purée until smooth and bright green. Transfer to a large bowl or container. Add the soy sauce, teriyaki sauce, onion wedges and crushed garlic cloves. Marinate the chicken in this mixture for 2 hours to overnight in the refrigerator.

2. Heat a Dutch oven over medium high heat. Add the vegetable oil and sugar and let the sugar brown, stirring and watching carefully. Don't let the sugar burn, but let it turn a nice brown color. Remove the chicken from the marinade and carefully add it to the Dutch oven. The chicken will spit a fair amount when you do this, and the sugar may seize up temporarily. Cook the chicken, turning to brown it on all sides.

3. Remove the chicken pieces from the Dutch oven and set aside. Add the left over marinade, ketchup and oregano to the pan and stir well. Simmer for 3 to 4 minutes. Add the water and bring the mixture to a simmer. Taste the liquid and season with salt if needed. Add the rice and stir well.

4. Return the chicken pieces to the Dutch oven and reduce the heat to keep the liquid at a very slow simmer. Cover and cook until the rice is tender – about 20 minutes. Garnish with fresh parsley.

Moroccan Braised Chicken Thighs
with Apricots and Olives

The spices, apricots and olives in this recipe dress chicken up in a whole new outfit! It's nice to have a new outfit now and again, isn't it?

2 tablespoons olive oil, divided

8 skinless bone-in chicken thighs
(or 4 skinless chicken legs)

salt

freshly ground black pepper

1 onion, chopped (½-inch pieces)

1 carrot, sliced on the bias (½-inch slices)

2 cloves garlic, minced

½ teaspoon ground cinnamon

½ teaspoon ground cumin

¼ teaspoon turmeric

⅛ teaspoon ground cayenne pepper

½ teaspoon ground coriander

6 ounces beer
(a fruity ale is good – apricot ale is even better!)

½ cup raisins

16 dried apricot halves, halved again

½ cup green olives, pitted

1 (28 ounce) can diced tomatoes

1 cup chicken stock

2 tablespoons chopped fresh parsley

1. Heat a large sauté pan or Dutch oven over medium-high heat for 2 to 3 minutes. Add one tablespoon of the olive oil. Season the chicken pieces with salt and pepper, and brown the chicken in batches until well browned on all sides, adding more oil as necessary. Once the chicken pieces are nicely browned, remove them to a side plate and set aside. Pour off and discard most of the fat that has accumulated in the pan.

2. Add the onion and carrot to the pan and cook until tender – about 3 minutes. Add the garlic and dried spices and continue to cook for another minute. Pour in the beer and deglaze the pan, scraping up any brown bits on the bottom of the pan. Let the beer simmer for 4 to 5 minutes. Return the chicken to the pan and then add the raisins, apricots, olives, tomatoes and chicken stock. Let this simmer, covered, for 45 to 60 minutes. Season to taste with salt and pepper.

3. Serve over couscous or rice, garnish with the chopped fresh parsley and accompany with a green salad.

TIP Dried spices and dried herbs are best kept in small quantities in a cool dark place, and used within 6 months of purchase. Dried spices and dried herbs should always be used at the start of cooking, while fresh herbs should be added at the end of cooking for the best flavor. If substituting dried herbs for fresh herbs, use a 1:4 ratio of dried to fresh.

Orange Braised Beef Short Ribs

Braising in orange juice creates an interesting sauce for serving with the beef.

2 tablespoons olive oil

4 pounds beef short ribs

salt

freshly ground black pepper

1 onion, chopped

1 rib celery, chopped

2 cloves garlic, minced

3 sprigs fresh thyme

1 bay leaf

½ cup white wine

1½ cups orange juice

2 tablespoons soy sauce

2 tablespoons chopped fresh chives

1. Pre-heat a large sauté pan or Dutch oven over medium-high heat. Add the olive oil. When the oil is hot and almost smoking, season the short ribs with salt and pepper and sear them in batches, until browned on all sides – about 15 minutes per batch.

2. Once the ribs are nicely browned, remove them to a side plate and set aside. Pour off and discard the fat that has accumulated in the pan. Add the onion and celery and cook for 2 to 3 minutes. Add the garlic, thyme and bay leaf and continue to cook for another minute.

3. Add the wine and deglaze the pan, scraping up any brown bits on the bottom of the pan. Let the wine simmer and reduce until it has almost entirely disappeared. Add the orange juice and soy sauce and bring the mixture back to a simmer. Return the browned short ribs to the pan, reduce the heat to very low and cover the pan with a tight-fitting lid.

4. Let the ribs simmer on very low heat, or cook in the oven at 300° F, for roughly 5 hours. The meat should be so tender that it falls off the bone. Remove the ribs from the pan and set aside, loosely covered with foil. Increase the heat under the pan and reduce the braising liquid until it has thickened slightly and is almost syrupy like a glaze. Return the ribs to the pan and turn them to coat in this sauce.

5. Serve the ribs over smashed potatoes, spoon a little sauce on top and garnish with chives. The sauce can also be strained if you prefer a smooth finish.

TIP Short ribs got their name because they are taken from the short plate of beef, not because they are short. There are two ways to cut short ribs. "English Style" cuts the meat parallel to the bone, so one bone is covered with meat (as seen here). "Flanken Style" cuts across three or four of the rib bones, creating a piece of meat that has three or four little bones in it. Either cut is good for this recipe.

Braised Country Style Ribs
with Apples and Sweet Potatoes

Country-style ribs are not really ribs at all. They are cut from the front end of the loin near the shoulder of the pork. With more meat and less fat than true ribs, country-style ribs are actually more like pork chops.

2 tablespoons olive oil

3 pounds country style ribs
(also known as pork shoulder ribs)

salt

freshly ground black pepper

1 onion, chopped

1 rib celery, chopped

2 cloves garlic, minced

1 teaspoon dried thyme

1 bay leaf

3 cups apple cider

3 cups chicken stock

2 tablespoons brown sugar

6 medium sweet potatoes, peeled and chopped
(1- to 2-inch chunks)

4 Granny Smith apples, peeled, cored
and cut into 6 wedges each

2 tablespoons chopped fresh parsley

6 sprigs fresh thyme

1. Pre-heat a large sauté pan or Dutch oven over medium-high heat. Add the olive oil. When the oil is hot and almost smoking, season the ribs with salt and pepper and sear them in batches, until browned on all sides – about 15 minutes per batch.

2. Once the ribs are nicely browned, remove them to a side plate and set aside. Pour off and discard the fat that has accumulated in the pan. Add the onion and celery and cook for 2 to 3 minutes. Add the garlic, thyme and bay leaf and continue to cook for another minute.

3. Add the apple cider and deglaze the pan, scraping up any brown bits on the bottom of the pan. Let the cider simmer for 5 to 10 minutes. Add the chicken stock and return the browned short ribs to the pan. Reduce the heat to very low and cover the pan with a tight-fitting lid.

4. Let the ribs simmer on very low heat, or cook in the oven at 300° F, for at least 1½ hours. Add the brown sugar, sweet potatoes and apples to the pan and continue to simmer for another 35 minutes. At this point, the meat should be so tender that it falls off the bone. Remove the ribs from the pan and set aside, covered with foil. Spoon the fat off the surface of the sauce, or pour the sauce into a gravy separator, returning the de-fatted juices to the pan. Increase the heat under the pan and reduce this braising liquid slightly. Season to taste with salt and pepper. Stir in the fresh parsley.

5. Serve with rice or cornbread and garnish with fresh thyme sprigs.

Basic Chicken Marsala

Chicken Marsala is a delightful dish that you can pull together in a matter of minutes. It may not sound like a quick weeknight meal, but it is. That is one of the things that is so appealing about sautéing and making a pan sauce – it takes no time at all.

4 boneless skinless chicken breasts

salt

freshly ground black pepper

½ cup flour

2 tablespoons olive oil

3 tablespoons butter, divided

8 ounces mushrooms
(white button or brown mushrooms), sliced

1 clove garlic, minced

1 tablespoon fresh sage leaves, finely chopped

1 cup sweet Marsala wine
(Fine Marsala, with minimal aging
would be a good choice)

½ cup chicken stock

2 tablespoons chopped fresh parsley

1. Pre-heat the oven to the lowest temperature possible – usually around 170° F.

2. Using a meat pounder, pound the chicken breasts until they are about ½-inch thick. Alternatively, you can slice the chicken breasts in half horizontally so that they become two flat chicken cutlets. Season the chicken with salt and pepper, and then lightly dredge each breast in the flour, shaking off any excess.

3. Heat a large skillet over medium-high heat. Once the skillet is hot, add 1 tablespoon of the olive oil and 1 tablespoon of the butter to the skillet. Place the chicken in the skillet, reduce the heat to medium and brown well on both sides – about 2 minutes per side. Brown the chicken in batches if necessary, rather than over-crowding the skillet. Transfer the browned chicken to a platter, cover with aluminum foil, and place it in the oven to keep warm.

4. Add the remaining olive oil to the skillet. Cook the mushrooms in the skillet until nicely browned and tender – about 2 minutes, tossing occasionally. Add the garlic and the sage leaves and continue to cook for another minute.

5. Add the Marsala wine to the skillet and bring to a simmer. Deglaze the skillet, scraping up any brown bits on the bottom of the skillet. Reduce the wine by half – about 3 minutes. Add the chicken stock and continue to simmer for another 3 to 4 minutes. Remove the skillet from the heat and finish with the remaining 2 tablespoons of butter and stir in the parsley. Season the sauce to taste with salt and pepper. Return the chicken and any juices to the skillet and turn to coat all the pieces with the sauce. Serve immediately.

Classic Sautéing

- Chicken Marsala is a classic Italian dish, and a perfect example of sautéing meat and making a pan sauce.

- First of all, the chicken or meat pieces should be as close to an even thickness as possible. To accomplish this, either pound the meat thin with a meat pounder, or slice the chicken in half horizontally, creating two chicken pieces per breast. I prefer slicing chicken because then each person gets two pieces of chicken, which feels more generous.

- The meat must be dry before it goes in the pan. If it is moist or wet on the surface, it will not brown properly. Dredging the meat in flour will remove any residual moisture.

- I use oil and butter in this recipe because I want the flavor of butter, but also want to use a higher temperature. The olive oil can withstand a higher temperature without burning. Using butter and olive oil together gives me the best of both worlds.

- When sautéing the meat, do not over-crowd the pan. Overcrowding will also inhibit browning. It is better to brown the meat in batches than to overcrowd the pan.

- The next step is critical. After browning the meat in the pan, you need to deglaze the pan and incorporate the flavor of the meat into the pan sauce. Deglazing means to remove the browned bits on the bottom of the pan by adding a liquid or acidic in-gredient. This is easy enough as long as the brown bits on the bottom of the pan have not burned. For this reason, reduce the heat to medium once the meat is in the pan. This will help prevent burning the browned bits, also known as the fonds. If you think the fonds are getting too brown before you're ready to make the pan sauce, pour in your deglazing liquid right away. Once you've deglazed and salvaged the fonds, you can pour out the liquid and proceed with the recipe, adding the liquid again at the right step. This way, you won't have lost any of the flavor of the fonds.

- Finally, finishing the sauce with a little butter is a classic step in sauce-making. In French kitchens, it is called "monter au beurre". The only thing you want to do here is to melt the butter into the sauce, but not to have it separate and make the sauce greasy. Adding the butter should be the last thing you do. Remove the pan from the heat and stir in the butter. Season to perfection and enjoy!

Chicken Cutlets
with Oranges and Sweet Peppers

With bright flavors, this is a fresh and vibrant dish. It's perfect for late summer, or all year round. Serve it over rice to soak up the delicious sauce.

SERVES

4

4 boneless skinless chicken breasts

salt

freshly ground black pepper

2 tablespoons olive oil

½ red onion, sliced (about ½ cup)

1 carrot, sliced on the bias (¼-inch slices)

½ red bell pepper, sliced

½ yellow bell pepper, sliced

1 clove garlic, minced

½ cup orange juice

½ cup chicken stock

2 oranges, peeled and segmented
(see TIP for instructions)

2 tablespoons butter

2 tablespoons chopped fresh parsley

1. Pre-heat the oven to the lowest temperature possible – usually around 170˚ F.

2. Using a meat pounder, pound the chicken breasts until they are about ½-inch thick. Alternatively, you can slice the chicken breasts in half horizontally so that they become two flat chicken cutlets. Season the chicken with salt and pepper.

3. Heat a large skillet over medium-high heat. Once the skillet is hot, add the olive oil. Place the chicken in the skillet, reduce the heat to medium and brown well on both sides – about 2 minutes per side. Brown the chicken in batches if necessary, rather than over-crowding the skillet. Transfer the browned chicken to a platter, cover with aluminum foil, and place it in the oven to keep warm.

4. Add the onion, carrot and red and yellow pepper slices to the skillet and cook for 4 to 5 minutes. Add the garlic and continue to cook for another minute. Pour in the orange juice and bring the mixture to a simmer for 3 to 4 minutes. Add the chicken stock and continue to simmer, scraping up any brown bits on the bottom of the skillet, until the liquid has reduced by half – about 4 minutes.

5. Add the orange segments to the skillet and heat through – 30 seconds. Remove the skillet from the heat and stir in the butter to thicken the sauce. Add the parsley and season to taste with salt and pepper. Return the browned chicken to the skillet and coat in the sauce. Serve immediately.

TIP
To segment an orange, start by cutting off both ends of the orange. Then cut the peel away from the flesh with a paring knife, making a curved slice down from one end to the other. Carefully cut in between the membranes of the segments to loosen the orange segments from the orange. Do this over a small bowl, to collect the juice that drips out.

Turkey Cutlets
with Reisling and Cranberries

Sometimes I use fresh cranberries for this pan sauce along with some brown sugar to sweeten them, but only when cranberries are in season. Dried sweetened cranberries work fine and are available all year long.

1 to 1½ pounds turkey cutlets

salt

freshly ground black pepper

¼ cup flour

1 tablespoon olive oil

2 to 3 tablespoons butter, divided

1 shallot, sliced

½ cup dried sweetened cranberries

½ cup Reisling wine

½ cup chicken stock

1 tablespoon chopped fresh tarragon

1. Pre-heat the oven to the lowest temperature possible – usually around 170° F.

2. Season the turkey with salt and pepper, and then lightly dredge each cutlet in the flour, shaking off any excess.

3. Heat a large skillet over medium-high heat. Once the skillet is hot, add the olive oil and 1 tablespoon of the butter to the pan. Place the turkey in the skillet, reduce the heat to medium and brown well on both sides – about 2 minutes per side. Brown the turkey cutlets in batches if necessary, rather than over-crowding the pan. Transfer the browned turkey to a platter, cover with aluminum foil, and place it in the oven to keep warm.

4. Add the shallot to the skillet and cook for just 1 minute.

5. Add the cranberries and Reisling and bring to a simmer. Reduce the liquid by half – about 3 minutes. Add the chicken stock and continue to simmer for another 3 to 4 minutes. Remove the pan from the heat and finish with the remaining 1 to 2 tablespoons of butter and the tarragon. Season to taste with salt and pepper. Pour this sauce over the turkey cutlets immediately and serve.

TIP Some Reisling wines are dry, but many are sweet. Either will work in this recipe. Which should you use? Whichever you'd like to enjoy in a glass once you've used ½ cup for this recipe!

Pork Medallions
with Madeira and Olives

I like using pork tenderloin to make medallions. It ensures a tender and lean piece of pork, and it takes just a second to pound tenderloin slices into nice sized medallions.

SERVES

4

1 pork tenderloin (about 1 pound)

salt

freshly ground black pepper

2 tablespoons olive oil

½ shallot, minced

1 clove garlic, minced

¼ cup pitted green olives, sliced

½ cup Madeira wine

½ cup chicken stock

2 tablespoons butter

2 tablespoons chopped fresh parsley

1. Pre-heat the oven to the lowest temperature possible – usually around 170° F.

2. Prepare the pork medallions. Remove the silver skin (the silver membrane found on part of the exterior of the tenderloin) by running a sharp knife underneath it and cutting it off the meat. Slice the tenderloin into 1-inch slices. Pound these slices gently with a meat pounder until they are approximately ¾-inch thick. Season the pork medallions with salt and pepper.

3. Heat a large skillet over medium-high heat. Once the skillet is hot, add the olive oil and sear the pork in batches for about 1½ to 2 minutes per side. Remove the pork and place on a platter, covered with aluminum foil, in the oven to keep warm.

4. Reduce the heat to medium and add the shallots, garlic and olives to the skillet. Cook for 1 minute, scraping up any brown bits on the bottom of the skillet.

5. Add the Madeira wine to the skillet and bring to a simmer. Reduce the wine by about half – about 3 minutes. Add the chicken stock and continue to simmer for another 3 minutes. Remove the skillet from the heat and stir in the butter and parsley. Season to taste with salt and pepper. Pour this sauce over the pork immediately and serve.

TIP

Madeira is a Portuguese fortified wine, named after the Madeira Islands where it is made. There is no need to buy the most expensive Madeira to cook with (in fact, you shouldn't), but don't be tempted to buy "cooking Madeira", which like all cooking wines has salt added to it. The tradition of adding salt to cooking wines came from a time when the master of the house would add salt to wine kept in the kitchen to keep the cooking staff from drinking it. There's no good reason to add salt now, and there's no reason to use cooking wine either.

Pork Medallions
with Picatta Sauce

Picatta is a versatile Italian pan sauce made with lemons and capers. It's a great sauce to have in your repertoire because you can pair it with chicken, pork, veal, fish or seafood.

1 pork tenderloin (about 1 pound)

salt

freshly ground black pepper

¼ cup all purpose flour

2 tablespoons olive oil

½ lemon, sliced

½ shallot, minced

1 clove garlic, minced

1 cup chicken stock

¼ cup fresh lemon juice (about 2 lemons)

3 tablespoons capers, drained and rinsed

3 tablespoons butter

2 tablespoons chopped fresh parsley

1. Pre-heat the oven to the lowest temperature possible – usually around 170° F.

2. Prepare the pork medallions. Remove the silver skin (the silver membrane found on part of the exterior of the tenderloin) by running a sharp knife underneath it and cutting it off the meat. Slice the tenderloin into 1-inch slices. Pound these slices gently with a meat pounder until they are approximately ¾-inch thick. Season the pork medallions with salt and pepper. Lightly dredge the pork in the flour and shake off any excess.

3. Heat a large skillet over medium-high heat. Once the skillet is hot, add the olive oil and sear the pork in batches for about 1½ to 2 minutes per side. Remove the pork and place on a platter, covered with aluminum foil, in the oven to keep warm.

4. Reduce the heat to medium, add the lemon slices to the skillet and brown lightly. Then, add the shallots and garlic to the skillet and cook for another minute, taking care not to burn the drippings in the skillet. Add the chicken stock and simmer, scraping up any brown bits on the bottom of the skillet, until the liquid has reduced by half – about 8 minutes.

5. Add the lemon juice and capers to the skillet and continue to simmer for another 2 minutes. Remove the skillet from the heat and stir in the butter to thicken the sauce. Add the parsley and season to taste with salt and pepper. Return the pork medallions and any juices to the skillet and turn to coat all the pieces in the sauce. Serve immediately.

 Capers are the un-blossomed flower buds of a bush native to the Mediterranean. You can purchase them salted or pickled. Either way, give them a rinse before you use them.

Basic Pan-Fried Chicken

Pan-frying is the cooking method that falls in between sautéing and deep-frying. Where sautéing uses minimal oil and deep-frying submerges the food in oil, pan-frying uses significant oil, but does not coat the food completely.

1 chicken (approximately 4 pounds), cut into 8 pieces left on the bone

2 cups buttermilk

1½ cups flour

2 teaspoons salt

2 teaspoons paprika

2 teaspoons cayenne pepper

1 pound shortening (2 cups)

1. Cut the chicken into 8 pieces and then submerge them in the buttermilk. A zipper sealable plastic bag works well for this. Let the chicken soak in the buttermilk in the refrigerator for at least one hour, or even overnight.

2. Mix the flour, salt, paprika and cayenne in another zipper sealable bag. Put four chicken pieces in the bag and shake around to coat. Remove from the bag, shaking off any excess flour, and let the chicken rest on a wire rack at room temperature. Repeat with the remaining four pieces of chicken.

3. Heat the shortening in a 12-inch heavy-bottomed sauté pan. Bring the shortening to about 350° F. You can use a deep-frying or candy thermometer to measure the temperature of the shortening. Otherwise, just dip a part of one piece of chicken in the oil when you think it is ready – the oil should bubble rapidly around the chicken.

4. Place the chicken pieces in the oil and cover with a lid. Reduce the heat slightly and cook for 8 to 10 minutes. Then, remove the lid and flip the chicken pieces over. Cook for another 10 minutes uncovered. When the chicken is done, drain the chicken on a clean wire rack and serve.

Pan-Frying – Crispy, Moist and Tasty

● Pan-fried meats should be crispy, moist and tasty. They should not be greasy or dry, and they must of course, be cooked properly on the inside.

● In order for the chicken or meat to have a crispy exterior, it needs a good coating. The pan-fried chicken is soaked in buttermilk because buttermilk is thick and allows the flour coating to adhere well. Buttermilk is also acidic and adds flavor to the chicken coating. Some people add a few dashes of hot sauce to the buttermilk for a little bite of spicy flavor with fried chicken.

● The flour or coating for pan-fried meats must be well seasoned. This is the only seasoning that the meat gets while it is cooking, so be sure to add any herbs and spices that you want to the coating, and of course, don't forget the salt.

● Using shortening to pan-fry has a couple of advantages. First and foremost, shortening is odorless, so it will minimize the smell for which frying is notorious. Secondly, it is solid at room temperature, so when the time comes to dispose of your frying fat, it is easier to throw away than liquid oil.

● The temperature of the cooking fat is very important. Having a candy or deep-frying thermometer is a handy investment. If you don't have one, however, you can test the oil in a couple of different ways. You can dip a small piece of the meat or the handle of a wooden spoon into the fat and if you see bubbles immediately form around the meat or the spoon handle – the fat is ready. Of course, using an electric skillet will take the guesswork out of temperature-taking completely. Fat at the right temperature will sear your foods properly, rather than be absorbed by the food. The right temperature makes all the difference between delicious crispy chicken and greasy chicken.

● Once the chicken is in the fat, let the fat come back to temperature and then turn the heat down a little, and keep the temperature around 300° F. Reducing the temperature a little will ensure that the inside of the chicken cooks before the exterior burns.

● Covering the chicken for the first half of cooking traps steam in the pot and helps to cook the chicken that is not currently submerged in the fat. Leaving the lid off for the second half of cooking allows the steam to escape, thereby preventing a soggy cooked crust.

● Draining cooked chicken on paper towel makes the bottom of the chicken soggy. Try to drain the chicken on a wire rack, where all parts of the chicken are exposed to the air.

Honeybell Hazelnut Chicken
with Honeybell Sauce

Honeybells are a cross between a Dancy tangerine and a Duncan grapefruit. They are extraordinarily sweet and juicy, and are also known as Tangelos. They are only available and in season for a short while in January and February. If you want to make this dish at some other time of the year, just substitute oranges.

SERVES

4

2 eggs, lightly beaten

1 Honeybell, zest and juice (or 2 oranges), divided

½ cup Panko breadcrumbs

¼ cup hazelnuts, finely chopped

½ teaspoon salt

freshly ground black pepper

4 boneless skinless chicken breasts

¼ cup all purpose flour

½ cup vegetable oil

½ shallot, finely chopped

½ teaspoon fresh thyme leaves, finely chopped

2 tablespoons butter, room temperature

1. Combine the eggs and half the Honeybell juice in a shallow dish. In another shallow dish, or a zipper sealable plastic bag, combine the breadcrumbs, hazelnuts, Honeybell zest, salt and pepper. Lightly dredge each chicken breast in the flour, then dip into the egg mixture, and then coat the chicken breasts with the breadcrumb mixture. Place the coated chicken breasts on a wire rack at room temperature.

2. Heat a medium skillet over medium to medium-high heat. Add the vegetable oil to the skillet and heat until bubbles form around the handle of a wooden spoon when inserted into the oil, or your candy/deep-frying thermometer registers 350° F.

3. Carefully place the chicken breasts in the oil and cook until browned on both sides and cooked through (the chicken should be firm to the touch) – about 6 minutes per side. Remove the chicken to a resting plate and cover loosely with foil.

4. Drain off almost all the oil and return the skillet to the stovetop. Add the shallot and the fresh thyme and sauté for 1 to 2 minutes. Add the remaining half of the Honeybell juice and bring to a simmer. Turn the heat off the skillet and stir in the butter. Season to taste again with salt and pepper. Pour the sauce over the chicken breasts and serve immediately.

TIP

Many people get confused about proper breading technique, thinking that the meat should be dipped in egg first, then flour, then breadcrumbs. The correct way to bread is to start by coating the meat in flour. The flour absorbs any liquid on the surface of the meat and actually allows the egg to adhere to the meat better. Then the egg acts as the "glue" for the breading.

Breaded Pork Chops
with Quick Apple Sauce

"Pork chops and apple sauce" – I can hear you saying that now, just the same way Peter Brady said it on the Brady Bunch. Whether he was imitating James Cagney, Humphrey Bogart, or WC Fields is surprisingly a subject of much debate. The only thing we're certain of is that it was followed by "Ain't that swell?" Yes, it is, Peter!

4

4 thick pork chops, with or without bone (¾-inch thick)

2 cups buttermilk

1½ cups Panko breadcrumbs

1 teaspoon salt

¼ teaspoon garlic powder

1 teaspoon dried thyme

½ cup vegetable oil

1 tablespoon butter, divided

2 Granny Smith apples, cut into chunks

¼ teaspoon cinnamon

1 tablespoon brown sugar

½ cup apple cider, or natural apple juice

¼ cup chicken stock

1 tablespoon chopped fresh parsley

1. Submerge the pork chops in the buttermilk. A zipper sealable bag works well for this. Let the pork soak in the buttermilk in the refrigerator for at least one hour, or even overnight.

2. Mix the breadcrumbs, salt and spices in another zipper sealable bag. Place the pork chops in the bag and shake to coat. Remove the chops from the bag and let them rest on a wire rack.

3. Heat the oil in a 12-inch heavy-bottomed sauté pan. Bring the oil to about 350° F. You can use a deep-frying or candy thermometer to measure the temperature of the oil. Otherwise, the oil is ready when bubbles form around the handle of a wooden spoon inserted into the oil.

4. Fry the pork chops in the oil until nicely browned on both sides – about 8 to 10 minutes per side or until an instant read thermometer registers 155° F in the center of the pork chop. Remove the chops to a resting plate, loosely tent with foil and proceed to make the apple sauce.

5. Drain the oil out of the pan. Add half the butter and the apples to the pan. Cook over medium-high heat for 3 to 4 minutes, or until they just start to brown. Add the cinnamon and brown sugar and cook for another minute or two.

6. Pour in the apple cider and scrape the bottom of the pan with a wooden spoon to loosen any brown bits. Bring the mixture to a simmer and reduce for a minute. Add the chicken stock and simmer again. Remove the pan from the heat and stir in the remaining butter and the parsley. Season the sauce to taste with salt and pepper. The sauce should be chunky rather than soupy. Serve with the pork chops.

Parmesan Crusted Chicken
with White Wine Cream Sauce

Take away the sauce and cut the chicken into strips before you bread it, and this makes a wonderful kid-friendly meal. When I made this for my young friends, Jack and Meredith, Jack proclaimed that he didn't like it, and then proceeded to eat everything on his plate!

¼ cup flour

2 eggs, lightly beaten

½ cup Panko breadcrumbs

½ cup grated Parmesan cheese

½ teaspoon salt, plus more to season the sauce

freshly ground black pepper

4 boneless skinless chicken breasts

½ cup vegetable oil

½ shallot, finely chopped

1 clove garlic, minced

½ teaspoon fresh thyme leaves, finely chopped

1 bay leaf

½ cup white wine

½ cup heavy cream

1. Pre-heat the oven to the lowest temperature possible – probably around 170° F.

2. Place the flour and eggs in two separate shallow dishes. In another shallow dish, or a zipper sealable plastic bag, combine the breadcrumbs, Parmesan cheese, salt and pepper. Lightly dredge each chicken breast in the flour, then dip into the egg mixture, and then coat the chicken breasts with the breadcrumb mixture. Place the coated chicken breasts on a wire rack.

3. Heat a medium skillet over medium to medium-high heat. Add the vegetable oil to the skillet and heat until bubbles form around the handle of a wooden spoon when inserted into the oil, or your candy/deep-frying thermometer registers 350° F.

4. Carefully place the chicken breasts in the oil and cook until browned on both sides and cooked through (the chicken should be firm to the touch) – about 6 minutes per side. Remove the chicken to a clean wire rack and keep the chicken warm while you make the pan sauce by placing the wire rack in the oven.

5. Drain off almost all the oil and return the skillet to the stovetop. Add the shallot, garlic, the fresh thyme and bay leaf and sauté for 1 to 2 minutes. Add the white wine and bring to a simmer. Reduce for 2 to 3 minutes. Add cream and simmer again for 3 minutes. Season to taste with salt and pepper. Remove the bay leaf and pour a small amount of sauce over the chicken breasts and serve the remainder of the sauce at the table.

Chicken Fried Steak

Chicken fried steak's name refers to its similarities to fried chicken. Both have a breaded exterior, both are pan-fried, and both are Southern comfort foods.

1 cup buttermilk

1 cup + 2 tablespoons flour, divided

1 teaspoon salt

freshly ground black pepper

¼ teaspoon garlic powder

4 tenderized round steaks
(about 5 to 6 ounces each; ½-inch thick)

1 pound shortening (2 cups)

2 teaspoons fresh thyme leaves

1 cup milk, room temperature

1. Pre-heat the oven to 170° F.

2. Pour the buttermilk into a shallow bowl. Combine 1 cup flour, salt, pepper and garlic powder and then divide the mixture between two shallow bowls.

3. Heat the shortening in a 12-inch heavy-bottomed sauté pan. There should be about ½-inch of fat on the bottom of the pan. Heat the fat to 350° F measuring with a candy/deep-frying thermometer, or when bubbles form around the handle of a wooden spoon when inserted into the fat.

4. When the shortening is hot, dip the tenderized steaks one at a time into the first batch of seasoned flour, into the buttermilk and then into the second batch of seasoned flour, and then gently place them into the pan. Fry for 2 to 3 minutes per side. Remove and drain steaks on a wire rack. Keep the steaks warm while you make the gravy by placing the wire rack in the oven.

5. Drain all but 1 tablespoon of the shortening out of the pan. Add the 2 tablespoons of flour to the pan, along with the fresh thyme. Cook for 2 minutes and then add the milk to the pan. Whisk vigorously while the mixture comes to a boil and thickens. Season with salt and freshly ground black pepper. Pour the gravy into a pitcher or gravy boat for serving. Serve the chicken fried steaks with mashed potatoes and gravy.

TIP

Tough steaks need to be tenderized. In other words, they need to have their muscle fibers softened or broken up. One method is to pound the meat with a meat pounder, sandwiching the meat between two layers of plastic wrap to keep things tidy. You could also score the surfaces of the meat with a sharp knife, cutting against the grain of the meat. A blade tenderizing tool is my preferred method, however. With its several sharp knives that are pushed into the meat, tenderizing this way is very easy.

Basic Roast Chicken

Oh a roast chicken! There is something magical about a simple roast chicken. A word to the wise – when you're roasting a chicken, roast two. It takes no extra time, very little extra energy, and leftover chicken can be used in so many ways.

SERVES

4

1 (4 pound) chicken

2 tablespoons canola, vegetable or olive oil or melted butter

1 tablespoon coarse sea salt or kosher salt

1 to 2 teaspoons freshly ground black pepper

1 lemon, halved

3 to 4 cloves garlic, smashed

½ small onion, peeled

water, beer, wine or chicken stock
(for the bottom of the roasting pan)

1. Pre-heat the oven to 425° F.

2. Clean the chicken by removing the giblets and any extra fat inside the cavity, rinsing with water and drying thoroughly with a paper towel.

3. Sprinkle the salt and pepper inside the cavity of the chicken. Squeeze the lemon over the chicken and inside the cavity. Stuff the squeezed lemon halves into the cavity with the garlic and half an onion. Brush the chicken liberally all over with the oil, and sprinkle salt and pepper over the entire exterior of the chicken.

4. Place the chicken on a rack in a roasting pan and pour enough liquid (water, beer, wine or chicken stock) into the roasting pan to cover the bottom. This will prevent the chicken drippings from evaporating and at the end you'll have a base for a gravy or sauce.

5. Roast at 425° F for 15 minutes and then turn the oven down to 350° F. Continue to roast for another 60 to 75 minutes, or until an instant read thermometer in the inner thigh meat registers 165° F. Let the chicken rest for 5 minutes and then carve and serve. If you like, strain the drippings and serve them as a simple sauce with the chicken. Alternately, use the drippings to make gravy for the chicken.

Classic Roast Chicken

It seems everyone has a method for cooking roast chicken. Some cooks start at a high temperature and then drop the temperature down. Others start it low and increase the heat for the end of cooking. Some start the chicken breast facing down in the pan, moving it to its back later on. Others start with a thigh facing down and rotate the bird at intervals. Some baste regularly. Others are not baster-believers. There are many ways to roast a chicken, but let's keep it simple.

● A perfect roast chicken has crispy brown skin, moist meat, and thigh meat that is cooked without the breast meat being dry. I have found that one of the best ways to achieve these goals is to use a vertical chicken roaster (pictured on page 88). This is a roaster where the chicken actually sits on a cylinder filled with liquid. The chicken roasts sitting up, and the liquid inside the cylinder creates a steamy environment inside the chicken, helping to keep the breast meat moist while the thighs cook fully. Because all exterior surfaces of the chicken are exposed to the hot dry air, the skin becomes beautifully brown and crispy.

● If you don't have a vertical chicken roaster, you can still make a good roast chicken. The chicken must sit on some sort of a rack in the roasting pan. A rack allows the air to circulate around the entire chicken, helping it to cook uniformly. If you don't have a roasting rack, you can use whole carrots and celery stalks, building a grate upon which the chicken can sit.

● Start by seasoning the bird with good flavors – lemon juice, garlic, herbs, onions – and then be sure to coat the skin of the chicken with either oil or butter. This will brown the skin as well as crisp it. Don't be shy with the salt. Salt will draw moisture out of the skin and help it crisp up. The salt sprinkled in the cavity of the chicken is the only seasoning the chicken meat will get, so be generous.

● I don't truss chickens when I roast them. Trussing, or tying the legs and wings to the chicken body, keeps the thighs from getting the heat they need to cook more quickly.

● Placing some liquid in the bottom of the roasting pan is an important step. The liquid catches the drippings, without letting them burn on the bottom of the pan. This keeps your kitchen from getting smoky and also provides you with juices when the chicken has finished roasting. The liquid also creates a moist environment for roasting, and makes it easier to clean the roasting pan at the end of the night. Check the liquid throughout roasting, replenishing it if it starts to evaporate.

● I like to start the chicken at a higher temperature to get the roasting process started. Then drop the temperature so that the skin of the chicken doesn't get too dark before the meat has fully cooked.

● Basting the chicken makes it more difficult to get a crispy skin, unless you baste with butter. I don't baste my roast chickens. I find the skin on the breasts gets crispy all by itself, as long as you've brushed it with oil or butter at the beginning.

● Finally, try not to overcook the chicken. Try to catch the chicken when the thigh meat registers just 165° F. If it goes much over that temperature, the breast meat will be overcooked and dry. One trick to help with this is to slice open the skin attaching the thigh to the body for the last 5 minutes of roasting. This allows the hot air to directly hit the inner thigh.

Jerk Spiced Roast Chicken

Jerk is a Jamaican way of cooking meats, where meats are marinated and then slowly grilled over allspice, or pimentón wood. There are four key ingredients to a jerk marinade: Habanero or Scotch Bonnet peppers, allspice, green onions and thyme. Don't worry, there's no need to build a fire pit with allspice wood in your backyard for this recipe. All the jerk flavor will come from the marinade.

1 (4 pound) chicken

Spice Rub:

1 teaspoon brown sugar

1 teaspoon ground allspice

1 teaspoon dried thyme

½ teaspoon ground ginger

½ teaspoon ground cinnamon

¼ teaspoon ground nutmeg

3 cloves garlic

4 green onions, roughly chopped

1 Habanero pepper (leave the seeds in if you want a lot of spice)

1 tablespoon coarse sea salt or kosher salt

1 tablespoon vegetable oil

juice of 1 lime

water, beer, wine or chicken stock
(for the bottom of the roasting pan)

1. Clean the chicken by removing the giblets and any extra fat inside the cavity, rinsing with water and drying thoroughly with a paper towel.

2. Prepare the spice rub by combining all the ingredients for the rub in a food processor and puréeing. Rub this mixture all over the chicken, inside the cavity as well as all over the skin. (You may want to use plastic gloves or a re-sealable plastic bag to do this, since the mixture will be very spicy and can burn your hands.) Let the chicken rest in the refrigerator for half an hour to 4 hours.

3. Pre-heat the oven to 425° F. Place the chicken on a rack in a roasting pan and pour enough liquid (water, beer, wine or chicken stock) into the roasting pan to cover the bottom. This will prevent the chicken drippings from evaporating and burning.

4. Roast at 425° F for 15 minutes and then turn the oven down to 350° F. Continue to roast for another 60 to 75 minutes, or until an instant read thermometer in the inner thigh meat registers 165° F. Let the chicken rest for 5 minutes and then carve and serve.

TIP

The name allspice might lead you to believe that it is a mix of different spices. It is actually the dried unripe fruit of the pimentón tree, native to the Caribbean, Mexico and Central America. Allspice berries resemble large peppercorns and are a key ingredient in Caribbean and Middle Eastern cuisines. Buy allspice in whole berries when possible, and grind them just before using for the most flavor.

Summer Ale Chicken
with Caramelized Onions

I created this recipe specifically for a vertical chicken roaster, where the beer steams the inside of the chicken while it roasts, and the onions can caramelize around the outside of the chicken. Here I've adapted that recipe by pouring some of the beer into the chicken cavity and caramelizing the onions separately.

SERVES

4

1 (4 pound) chicken

Spice Rub:

1 tablespoon vegetable oil

2 tablespoons brown sugar

2 tablespoons paprika (not smoked paprika)

1 teaspoon dry mustard powder

1 teaspoon chili powder

2 tablespoons coarse sea salt or kosher salt

2 teaspoons coarsely ground black pepper

1 to 2 bottles summer ale

1 tablespoon vegetable oil

3 to 4 sweet onions, sliced

1 bay leaf

4 sprigs fresh thyme

salt

freshly ground black pepper

1. Clean the chicken by removing the giblets and any extra fat inside the cavity, rinsing with water and drying thoroughly with a paper towel. Rub the outside of the chicken with vegetable oil.

2. Prepare the spice rub by combining 1 tablespoon of oil, the brown sugar, paprika, mustard powder, chili powder, salt and pepper. Rub this mixture all over the chicken, inside the cavity as well as all over the skin. You'll be left with more rub than you need for this recipe, but you'll lose a fair amount in the process of rubbing it on the chicken. Be sure to throw away any spice rub that doesn't make it onto the chicken to avoid cross contamination. Let the chicken rest in the refrigerator for half an hour to 4 hours.

3. Pre-heat the oven to 425° F. Place the chicken on a rack in a roasting pan, pour enough beer into the roasting pan to cover the bottom of the pan and pour the remainder of the beer inside the chicken cavity.

4. Roast at 425° F for 15 minutes and then turn the oven down to 350° F. Continue to roast for another 60 to 75 minutes, or until an instant read thermometer in the inner thigh meat registers 165° F. Let the chicken rest for 5 minutes and then carve and serve.

5. While the chicken is roasting, heat a large skillet or sauté pan over medium to medium-low heat. Add 1 tablespoon of oil, onions, bay leaf and thyme, and cook slowly, stirring every once in a while. As the onions start to brown, give the skillet a stir, and reduce the heat to low. The onions will take about an hour to caramelize properly. Season to taste with salt and pepper. When the chicken has come out of the oven, pour the drippings from the cavity of the chicken into the onions and stir well. Serve the onions along with the chicken.

Chipotle Orange Roast Chicken

This chicken gets very dark on the outside because of the dark spice rub. Beneath the spicy skin, there's very moist chicken inside.

1 (4 pound) chicken

Spice Rub:

1 tablespoon chipotle peppers in adobo sauce, seeded and minced

1 tablespoon adobo sauce (from the peppers above)

1 tablespoon orange zest

1 teaspoon ground cumin

1 tablespoon brown sugar

1 tablespoon coarse sea salt or kosher salt

1 orange, halved

water, beer, wine or chicken stock
(for the bottom of the roasting pan)

1. Clean the chicken by removing the giblets and any extra fat inside the cavity, rinsing with water and drying thoroughly with a paper towel.

2. Prepare the spice rub by combining the chipotle peppers, adobo sauce, orange zest, cumin, brown sugar and salt. Rub this mixture all over the chicken, inside the cavity as well as all over the skin. (You may want to use plastic gloves or a re-sealable plastic bag to do this, since the mixture will be very spicy and can burn your hands.) Let the chicken rest in the refrigerator for half an hour to 4 hours.

3. Pre-heat the oven to 425° F. Stuff the cavity of the chicken with the orange halves. Place the chicken on a rack in a roasting pan and pour enough liquid (water, beer, wine or chicken stock) into the roasting pan to cover the bottom. This will prevent the chicken drippings from evaporating and burning.

4. Roast at 425° F for 15 minutes and then turn the oven down to 350° F. Continue to roast for another 60 to 75 minutes, or until an instant read thermometer in the inner thigh meat registers 165° F. Let the chicken rest for 5 minutes and then carve and serve.

Five-Spice Roast Chicken

This is one of my favorite roast chicken recipes. The spice rub gives just enough flavor and interest to the chicken.

1 (4 pound) chicken

1 to 2 tablespoons canola or vegetable oil

2 tablespoons coarse sea salt or kosher salt

1 teaspoon Chinese five-spice powder

water, beer, wine or chicken stock
(for the bottom of the roasting pan)

1. Clean the chicken by removing the giblets and any extra fat inside the cavity, rinsing with water and drying thoroughly with a paper towel.

2. Prepare the spice rub by simply combining the salt and the five-spice powder. Rub or brush the oil over the chicken and then sprinkle the spice and salt mixture all over the chicken, inside the cavity as well as all over the skin. Let the chicken rest in the refrigerator for half an hour to 4 hours.

3. Pre-heat the oven to 425° F. Place the chicken on a rack in a roasting pan and pour enough liquid (water, beer, wine or chicken stock) into the roasting pan to cover the bottom. This will prevent the chicken drippings from evaporating and burning.

4. Roast at 425° F for 15 minutes and then turn the oven down to 350° F. Continue to roast for another 60 to 75 minutes, or until an instant read thermometer in the inner thigh meat registers 165° F. Let the chicken rest for 5 minutes and then carve and serve.

TIP You can purchase Chinese five-spice powder, or you can make your own with the following: 2 teaspoons toasted Szechuan peppercorns, 3 teaspoons toasted fennel seed, 6 star anise, ½ teaspoon ground cloves and 1 teaspoon ground cinnamon. Combine all ingredients in a blender or spice grinder and grind to a powder. Store in an airtight container.

Basic Pot Roast

Pot roast is another American comfort food. In this version, the vegetables that braise with the roast for the full cooking time will be very soft at the end. Some people like the vegetables this way. If you're not one of those people, remove the vegetables from the braising liquid just before you add the potatoes and mushrooms to the pot.

2 ½ to 3 pound boneless chuck roast

salt

freshly ground black pepper

1 tablespoon vegetable oil

1 onion, cut into wedges

3 carrots, sliced (1-inch slices)

2 stalks celery, sliced (½-inch slices)

1 cup red wine

1 cup beef stock

2 to 3 sprigs of fresh thyme

1 bay leaf

2 cups button mushrooms, quartered

4 large white or red-skinned potatoes, quartered or 12 fingerling potatoes left whole

1. Pre-heat the oven to 325° F.

2. Heat a Dutch oven or casserole pan with a lid over medium heat. Season the roast on all sides with salt and pepper. Add the vegetable oil to the pot and brown the roast on all sides – about 10 to 12 minutes. Then, remove the roast to a resting plate.

3. Add the onion, carrots and celery to the pot and cook for 3 to 4 minutes. Pour in the red wine and using a wooden spoon, scrape up any brown bits that have formed on the bottom of the Dutch oven. Add the beef stock to the Dutch oven, along with the thyme and bay leaf. Bring the mixture to a boil and then reduce the heat to a simmer. Return the roast to the Dutch oven and cover.

4. Transfer the Dutch oven to the oven and cook for 3 hours, turning the roast over half way through cooking. After 3 hours, add the mushrooms and potatoes to the pot and continue to cook for another 30 minutes.

5. Remove the pot roast from the oven. Transfer the roast and vegetables to a resting plate and loosely cover with foil. Place the pot on the stovetop and bring the liquid to a simmer. Reduce the liquid by half. If thicker gravy is desired, mix 1 tablespoon of softened butter with 1 tablespoon of flour and whisk this paste into the liquid. Season to taste with salt and pepper and spoon the liquid and vegetables over the roast.

Pot Roast Tips

A pot roast is a form of braising, and so the same cooking principles apply. In my opinion, the only thing that distinguishes a pot roast is that it involves one large chunk of meat, rather than smaller pieces. When you braise smaller pieces of meat, it is called a stew.

When braising, there are a number of points to consider and these can be seen on page 98. Here, we'll focus on the equipment needed to properly make a pot roast. All you need is a good braising pot!

A Dutch oven is the traditional pot used for braising. A Dutch oven was originally a cast iron cooking pot with thick walls and a tight-fitting lid. Historically, the Dutch made very good cast iron pots, and exported these pots to England and beyond. Early cooks found them incredibly useful and versatile and referred to them as Dutch ovens. Indeed, they loved their cast iron Dutch ovens so much there are actually records of the pots being passed down through generations and left in wills to children. Dutch ovens could be put directly in a fire and used as ovens or as braising vessels. Some versions had feet to raise the pot up above the coals. Many countries make cast iron today, and have renamed their versions of these cooking pots. You'll see references to French ovens, braisers, cocottes or casserole pans. Regardless of their names, all of these pots perform the same function.

A cast iron Dutch oven has all the qualities of a good pot for braising. It has thick walls in order to retain and conduct the heat evenly over a long period of time – ideal for pot-roasting.

A good braising pot must also have a tight-fitting lid. The lid must trap the steam because the steam cooks the meat that is not submerged in the braising liquid. If the pot you are using does not have a tight-fitting lid, cover the pot with aluminum foil first and then place the lid on top to make a tight seal.

It is also important for the pot to be safe for use on both the stovetop and in the oven. The flavor of a pot roast is enhanced if the meat is browned first on the stovetop before the braising liquid is added. While it is possible to brown the meat in one pot and then transfer all the ingredients to a pot for the oven, it creates more pots to clean and you lose the flavors from the browning pot. While pot roasts can be cooked entirely on the stovetop, it is easier to maintain the low cooking temperature required in an oven at 300˚ to 325˚ F.

With the right pot and an understanding of the rules of braising – the choice of meat, the braising liquid, the temperature and time required – you have everything you need to make a great pot roast.

Pork Loin Braised in Milk

Braising meat in milk is an Italian technique. The acid in the milk helps to tenderize the pork, and the flavor of the pork in the milk makes a delicious sauce. Traditionally, the milk curds are served with the pork. This recipe veers from that tradition by straining the milk curds and making a gravy.

2 slices of bacon, chopped

2½ to 3 pound boneless pork loin

6 cloves garlic, sliced

2 sprigs fresh rosemary, plus more for garnish

salt

freshly ground black pepper

1 onion, cut into wedges

2 teaspoons dried thyme

1 bay leaf

4 cups whole milk

1 tablespoon butter

1 tablespoon flour

pinch ground nutmeg

½ teaspoon lemon zest, very finely chopped

1. Pre-heat the oven to 325° F.

2. Heat a Dutch oven or casserole pan with a lid over medium heat. Add the bacon and cook until crispy. Remove the bacon with a slotted spoon and reserve. While the bacon is cooking, make several small incisions into the roast at random intervals, and push a slice of garlic and a few leaves of rosemary into each incision. Once you remove the bacon from the Dutch oven, season the roast on all sides with salt and pepper and brown the roast on all sides in the bacon fat – about 10 to 12 minutes. Remove the roast to a resting plate.

3. Add the onion, thyme and bay leaf to the Dutch oven and cook for 2 to 3 minutes. Pour in the milk and using a wooden spoon, scrape up any brown bits that have formed on the bottom of the pan. Bring the mixture to a boil and then reduce the heat to a simmer. Return the roast to the Dutch oven and cover with a tight-fitting lid.

4. Transfer the pan to the oven and cook for 2 hours, rotating the roast once after 1 hour.

5. Remove the Dutch oven from the oven. Transfer the roast to a resting plate and loosely cover with foil. Place the Dutch oven on the stovetop and bring the liquid to a simmer. Reduce the liquid by half – about 20 minutes. At this stage, the sauce will have golden lumps of milk and will not look pretty. (Traditionally, this sauce would be reduced further and served lumpy, with very little liquid left.) Strain the sauce, discard the curds and set the liquid aside.

6. Melt the butter in a small saucepan. Add the flour and whisk, cooking for 2 minutes. Pour the strained sauce into the saucepan and bring to a boil to thicken. Season the sauce to taste with salt, freshly ground black pepper, pinch of ground nutmeg and lemon zest. Slice the pork roast into ½-inch slices and place on a platter. Spoon the sauce over the sliced roast and garnish with the reserved bacon pieces and sprigs of rosemary.

Chicken in a Pot
with Tomatoes and Fennel

Here we "pot roast" a whole chicken, resulting in a fall-off-the-bone dinner. Use a stewing chicken if you can find one. It has more flavor and the pot-roasting method will ensure it is tender.

6 slices bacon, chopped

1 (5 to 6 pound) stewing or roasting chicken

salt

freshly ground black pepper

1 onion, cut into wedges

3 carrots, sliced
(1- to 2-inch slices; about 2 cups)

2 stalks celery, sliced
(1- to 2-inch slices; about 1 cup)

1 clove garlic, smashed

1 cup white wine

1 (14½ ounce) can diced tomatoes

1 cup chicken stock

2 to 3 sprigs of fresh rosemary

1 bay leaf

2 bulbs fennel, cut into wedges

Fennel fronds (greens)

1. Pre-heat the oven to 300° F.

2. Heat a Dutch oven or casserole pan with a lid over medium heat. Cook the bacon until almost crispy. Remove the bacon with a slotted spoon and reserve. Pour out much of the fat, but leave at least 1 tablespoon in the pot.

3. Season the chicken well on all sides with salt and pepper. Brown the chicken in the Dutch oven on all sides – about 10 to 12 minutes. Remove the chicken to a resting plate.

4. Add the onion, carrots and celery to the pot and cook for 5 minutes, until lightly browned. Add the garlic and continue to cook for 30 seconds. Pour in the white wine and using a wooden spoon, scrape up any brown bits that have formed on the bottom of the Dutch oven. Add the tomatoes and chicken stock to the Dutch oven, along with the rosemary and bay leaf. Bring the mixture to a boil and then reduce the heat to a simmer. Return the chicken to the Dutch oven and cover with a tight-fitting lid. Transfer the Dutch oven to the oven and cook for 45 minutes.

5. Remove the Dutch oven from the oven and add the fennel wedges, scattering them around and on top of the chicken. Return the cooked bacon to the Dutch oven and continue to cook, covered in the oven, for another 45 minutes.

6. Once the chicken has reached an internal temperature of 165° F, transfer the chicken to a resting plate and loosely tent with foil. Place the Dutch oven on the stovetop and bring the liquid to a simmer. Reduce slightly to concentrate flavors. Carve the chicken into 8 pieces and arrange on a serving platter. Season the liquid to taste with salt and pepper and spoon the broth and vegetables over the carved chicken, garnishing with the feathery fronds of the fennel.

TIP
Chickens become tougher but more flavorful as they age. You can find broiler/fryer chickens, roasting chickens, or stewing chickens in the grocery store. Broiler/fryer chickens weigh up to 3 ½ pounds, roasting chickens weigh up to 5 pounds, and stewing chickens are over 5 pounds. Their name tells you the best cooking method to use. The easiest way to remember which is older and which is younger besides using the weight is alphabetically – the further along in the alphabet, the older the chicken.

Pot Roast Leg of Lamb
with Oranges and Honey

This recipe is for people who like their lamb cooked all the way through, but still moist.

1 (5 pound) bone-in leg of lamb

salt

freshly ground black pepper

1 tablespoon olive oil

1½ onions, halved and sliced

3 cloves garlic, smashed

1 cup red wine

½ cup orange juice

1 orange, sliced (peel left on), plus another for garnish

1 bay leaf

3 whole cloves

1 cinnamon stick

2 to 3 sprigs fresh rosemary, plus more for garnish

3 tablespoons honey

2 tablespoons soy sauce

1. Pre-heat the oven to 300° F.

2. Heat a Dutch oven or casserole pan with a lid over medium heat. Season the lamb well on all sides with salt and pepper. Add the oil to the Dutch oven and brown the lamb in the pot on all sides – about 10 to 12 minutes. Remove the lamb and set aside.

3. Add the onions to the Dutch oven, and cook for 5 minutes, until starting to brown. Add the garlic and continue to cook for another minute. Add the red wine and using a wooden spoon, scrape up any brown bits that have formed on the bottom of the Dutch oven. Add the orange juice, along with the orange slices, bay leaf, cloves, cinnamon stick and rosemary. Bring the mixture to a boil and then reduce the heat to a simmer. Return the lamb to the Dutch oven, turning it a couple of times to cover all surfaces with the liquid. Cover with a tight-fitting lid and transfer the Dutch oven to the oven and cook for 2½ hours, basting with the juices in the pot every once in a while, and turning the lamb once after 1¼ hours.

4. Combine the honey and soy sauce in a small saucepan, melting the honey to combine well with the soy. Remove the Dutch oven from the oven and pour the honey-soy glaze over the lamb. Return the Dutch oven to the oven and continue to cook, uncovered, for another 30 to 60 minutes, or until the lamb is tender to a fork.

5. Once the lamb is tender, transfer it to a resting plate and loosely cover with foil. Strain the braising liquid into a fat separator. Pour the de-fatted juice from the fat separator into a gravy boat. Slice the lamb and arrange the slices on a serving platter. Spoon some of the broth over the top, garnishing with more orange slices and rosemary sprigs if desired.

TIP

An oval shaped Dutch oven works well for this recipe because it fits the shape of a leg of lamb better than a round casserole. Whatever pan you decide to use, make sure the leg of lamb will fit inside before you start.

Brandy Braised Beef Roast
with Beets, Carrots and Horseradish Cream

Simmering this pot roast on the stovetop for the duration of its cooking time frees up the oven to roast vegetables to accompany it. The beets turn the braising liquid a wonderful red, and then the horseradish cream on your plate makes the sauce pink. After you add the carrots, all those colors combine to make this the prettiest pot roast I've ever seen!

2½ to 3 pound boneless chuck roast

salt

freshly ground black pepper

1 tablespoon vegetable oil

1 onion, cut into wedges

1 cup brandy

1 cup beef stock

2 to 3 sprigs of fresh thyme

1 bay leaf

6 beets (red and yellow if available)

5 large carrots, peeled and chopped (2-inch pieces)

2 tablespoons olive oil, divided

1 teaspoon chopped fresh thyme

1 clove garlic, minced

1 tablespoon chopped fresh parsley

For the Horseradish Cream Sauce:

1 tablespoon lemon juice

½ cup crème fraîche (or sour cream)

2 tablespoons prepared horseradish

1. Heat a Dutch oven or casserole pan with a lid over medium heat. Season the roast on all sides with salt and pepper. Add the vegetable oil to the Dutch oven and brown the roast on all sides – about 10 to 12 minutes. Remove the roast to a resting plate.

2. Add the onion to the Dutch oven and cook for 3 to 4 minutes. Pour in the brandy and using a wooden spoon, scrape up any brown bits that have formed on the bottom of the Dutch oven. Add the beef stock to the Dutch oven, along with the thyme and bay leaf. Bring the mixture to a boil and then reduce the heat to a simmer. Return the roast to the Dutch oven and cover. Simmer on the stovetop at the very lowest heat possible for 3 to 3½ hours, turning the roast once after 1½ hours.

3. While the pot roast is simmering, pre-heat the oven to 400° F. Scrub any dirt off the beets, but leave the skins on. Place the beets in a shallow oven-safe pan and drizzle with olive oil. Season with salt and pepper and add ¼ cup of water to the pan (the water will help the skins come off more easily after roasting). Cover with a lid or aluminum foil, and transfer the pan to the oven for 30 to 45 minutes (depending on the size of the beets). The beets won't be completely tender, but will be starting to get tender. When cool enough to handle, peel the beets by scraping them with a paring knife and slice them into wide wedges.

4. Toss the carrots with 1 tablespoon of olive oil, thyme, garlic, salt and freshly ground black pepper and spread out on a baking sheet. Toss the peeled beets with the remaining tablespoon of olive oil, salt and freshly ground black pepper and transfer them to the same baking sheet as the carrots. Roast in the 400° F oven for 40 minutes or until tender.

5. Make the horseradish cream sauce. In a small bowl, combine the lemon juice, crème fraîche and horseradish. Mix well and season with salt and freshly ground black pepper. Set aside to serve with the finished pot roast. Remove the pot roast from the oven. Transfer the roast to a resting plate and loosely tent with foil. Strain the braising liquid into a fat separator and return the de-fatted juice to the Dutch oven. Bring the liquid to a simmer, and reduce the liquid by half. Season to taste with salt and pepper. Slice the pot roast and transfer to a serving platter. Scatter the roasted beets and carrots around the roast and pour the reduced sauce over the top. Sprinkle chopped parsley over everything and serve with the horseradish cream.

TIP
If thicker sauce is desired, whisk in a *beurre manié*. A *beurre manié* is a mix of butter and flour. Mix 1 tablespoon of softened butter with 1 tablespoon of flour and whisk this paste into the braising liquid after the liquid has reduced.

Basic Pan Roasted Strip Steak
with Red Wine Pan Sauce

Pan roasting is a great technique to learn. It's quick, efficient and produces great results, whether you're cooking chicken, pork, duck, or beef.

1 tablespoon olive or vegetable oil

4 boneless strip steaks
(or rib-eye or sirloin steaks),
at least 1-inch thick

salt

freshly ground black pepper

1 large shallot, finely chopped (about ½ cup)

2 teaspoons chopped fresh thyme

2 cloves garlic, minced

½ cup red wine

1 cup beef stock

¼ cup heavy cream

1 tablespoon chopped fresh parsley

1. Pre-heat the oven to 450° F.

2. Heat a large oven-safe skillet or sauté pan over medium-high heat. Add olive oil to the skillet. Place the steaks in the skillet, season them with salt and freshly ground black pepper and cook without turning for 4 minutes. Flip the steaks, season again and transfer the skillet to the oven to cook for another 4 minutes for medium rare, 5 minutes for medium, or longer for well done.

3. Once the desired degree of doneness has been reached, remove the steaks to a plate and let them rest while you make the pan sauce.

4. Transfer the skillet to the stovetop. (Remember to use an oven mitt as the handle of this skillet will be very hot.) Add the shallot to the skillet and cook for a minute or two. Add the thyme and garlic and continue to cook for another 30 seconds. Pour in the red wine and deglaze the skillet by scraping off any brown bits that have accumulated on the bottom of the pan with a wooden spoon. Let the wine simmer for a minute or two. Add the beef stock and simmer to reduce the liquid to ½ cup. Turn off the heat and add the cream and parsley. Season to taste with salt and pepper.

5. Slice the steaks if desired, or serve whole with the sauce drizzled on top.

Restaurant Style Pan Roasting

Pan roasting is a popular cooking method in restaurants for good reason — it is a very efficient way to get a nicely seared exterior and evenly cooked interior on any piece of meat or poultry. Pan roasting uses high heat to cook and brown the meat — starting on the stovetop and finishing in a hot oven. The stovetop allows you to brown the exterior of the meat well. Then the oven heat helps to cook the interior evenly before the outside gets too brown or dried out. Another advantage to pan roasting is that by transferring the pan to the oven, you have time to complete other parts of the meal or clean up the kitchen a little.

The first step is to be sure you have the right pan. You will need a skillet or sauté pan that is oven-safe up to 450° F.

Then, select an appropriate cut of meat. Meat and poultry cuts that are suitable for pan roasting need to be at least 1-inch thick. Cuts that are thinner than 1-inch can be cooked fully on the stovetop and won't improve with time in the oven. The best meats for pan roasting are relatively lean and tender. Chicken breasts, duck breasts, and thick pork chops are all good candidates for pan roasting. In the beef category, the leanest and most tender steak is filet mignon. Other cuts like top sirloin, ribeye, T-bone, New York strip, or Porterhouse are a little less lean, but more flavorful, and also make great pan roasted steaks.

Pre-heat the pan you are using. This is a critical part of searing any food. Putting meat into a cold pan will not give you good color on the steak. Instead it will draw out moisture and dry out the meat.

Season the meat immediately before you sear it, or even after you put it in the pan. Salt will draw out moisture onto the surface of the meat and will therefore inhibit browning.

Resist the urge to flip the meat too soon. Meat needs a little time in the pan to form a crust and brown. If you try to flip the meat and it appears a little stuck, it is definitely too soon to turn it. Leave it for another minute and then try again.

Learn to check the degree of doneness with your finger rather than cutting the meat or poking a meat thermometer into it. A raw piece of meat will feel squishy and soft, like the center of your cheek. As the meat cooks, it becomes firmer to the touch. A medium piece of beef will feel more like your nose, and a well-done piece of beef will feel like your forehead. You might have to start learning by using an instant read thermometer to gauge your success.

Resting the meat is as important as seasoning the meat. After cooking, let the meat sit for 5 minutes before you cut into it. This will result in a juicier interior. If the muscle fibers are tense when you cut into them, they will squeeze out all the juice. Letting them relax solves this problem. However, remember to account for carry-over cooking. The temperature inside the steak will continue to rise about 5° F while it rests. So, pull your meat out of the pan 5° F under the desired temperature or desired degree of doneness.

You don't have to make a pan sauce when pan roasting but it's an easy thing to do while the meat rests.

Roasting Chart

The temperatures that correspond to the different degrees of doneness in meat and poultry.

Beef and Lamb:		Chicken:	Pork
Rare	120° F	Always aim for a final temperature of **165°F**	Aim for **155°** or **160° F**
Medium rare	135° F		
Medium	150° F		
Medium well	160° F		
Well-done	170° F		

Pan Roasted Chicken Breast
with Mushrooms

Airline breasts – skin-on chicken breasts with the wing still attached –are perfect for this dish and make a pretty presentation.

SERVES

4

1 tablespoon olive or vegetable oil

4 boneless chicken breasts, skin on

salt

freshly ground black pepper

2 cups brown mushrooms, quartered OR shiitake mushrooms, stems removed and halved

2 cloves garlic, minced

½ teaspoon chopped fresh thyme

½ cup white wine

½ cup chicken stock

2 tablespoons butter

½ lemon to squeeze

1 tablespoon chopped fresh parsley

1. Pre-heat the oven to 425° F.

2. Heat a 12-inch oven-safe skillet or sauté pan over medium-high heat. Add olive oil to the skillet. Place the chicken in the skillet, skin side down, season with salt and pepper and brown for 3 to 5 minutes. Turn the chicken over and toss the mushrooms in around the chicken. Transfer the skillet to the oven to cook for another 15 minutes, or until the internal temperature of the chicken reaches 165° F.

3. Once cooked through, remove the chicken to a plate, loosely cover with foil and let it rest while you make the pan sauce.

4. Drain off and reserve any liquid that might have accumulated in the skillet, leaving the mushrooms in the skillet. Transfer the skillet to the stovetop. (Remember to use an oven mitt as the handle of this skillet will be very hot.) Add the garlic and thyme, and cook for 30 seconds. Pour in the white wine and deglaze the pan by scraping off any brown bits that have accumulated on the bottom of the skillet with a wooden spoon. Let the wine simmer for 2 to 3 minutes. Add the chicken stock and any reserved liquid from before and simmer to reduce the liquid to ½ cup. Turn the heat off and add the butter, a squeeze of lemon juice and parsley. Season to taste with salt and pepper. Slice the chicken breasts on the bias and spoon the sauce over the top.

Filet Mignon
with Blue Cheese Crust

No need to go to a steakhouse for a delicious steak anymore! Filet mignon is not inexpensive, but for a special occasion it's a nice choice. Of course, this recipe could also be made with a different cut, like sirloin or ribeye instead.

½ cup crumbled blue cheese

¼ cup Panko breadcrumbs

1 teaspoon chopped fresh parsley

½ teaspoon fresh thyme leaves, plus sprigs for garnish

1 tablespoon olive or vegetable oil

4 (6 to 8 ounce) filet mignon steaks

salt

freshly ground black pepper

1. Pre-heat the oven to 450° F.

2. Combine the blue cheese, breadcrumbs, parsley and thyme in a small bowl.

3. Heat a large oven-safe skillet or sauté pan over medium-high heat. Add olive oil to the skillet. Place the steaks in the skillet, season them with salt and freshly ground black pepper and cook without turning for 4 minutes. Flip the steaks, season again and top each steak with the blue cheese and breadcrumb mixture. Transfer the skillet to the oven to cook for another 4 minutes for medium rare, 5 minutes for medium, or longer for well done.

4. Once the desired degree of doneness has been reached, remove the steaks to a plate and let them rest for 5 minutes before serving with thyme sprigs as garnish.

TIP
These steaks are delicious served with the same red wine pan sauce from the Basic Pan Roasted Strip Steak recipe on page 133.

Pan Roasted Pork Chops
with Cognac and Prunes

If you turned your nose up at the title of this recipe, change the last word to "Dried Plums" and give it a try.

SERVES

4

½ cup cognac

1 cup pitted dried prunes (about 6 ounces)

1 tablespoon olive or vegetable oil

4 rib pork chops (1-inch thick)

salt

freshly ground black pepper

1 large shallot, finely chopped (about ½ cup)

2 cloves garlic, minced

½ teaspoon chopped fresh rosemary, plus sprigs for garnish

½ cup chicken stock

½ cup heavy cream

1. Pre-heat the oven to 400° F.

2. In a small bowl, combine the cognac and prunes, and let the prunes soak for 20 minutes.

3. Heat a large oven-safe skillet or sauté pan over medium-high heat. Add olive oil to the skillet. Place the chops in the skillet, season with salt and pepper and sear on both sides – 2 minutes per side. Transfer the pan to the oven to cook for another 6 to 7 minutes, or until the internal temperature of the pork reaches 150° F.

4. Once cooked through, remove the chops to a plate and let them rest while you make the pan sauce.

5. Transfer the skillet to the stovetop. (Remember to use an oven mitt as the handle of this skillet will be very hot.) Add the shallot to the skillet and sauté briefly. Add the garlic and rosemary, and continue to cook for another 30 seconds. Pour in the cognac, prunes and chicken stock. (At this point, the cognac might flame up. If it does, simply cover the skillet with a lid until the flames go out and then proceed.) Deglaze the skillet by scraping off any brown bits that have accumulated on the bottom of the skillet with a wooden spoon. Let this mixture simmer for about two minutes. Add the cream and simmer to reduce the liquid to ½ cup. Season to taste with salt and pepper, and pour over the pork chops with rosemary sprigs as garnish.

TIP

Prunes had a negative public image and were known mostly as a digestive aid in North America up until year 2000 when prunes received a little public relations assistance. They were then re-labeled "dried plums", making them more appealing to consumers. Plums destined to become prunes are left on the tree longer to ripen and become very sweet. Store prunes in an airtight container in a cool dark place. Don't like prunes? Try a "dried plum" dipped in melted dark chocolate. That might change your mind!

Pan Roasted Rack of Lamb
with a Pecan Parmesan Crust

The hardest part of cooking a rack of lamb is frenching the bones – in other words, removing the meat, fat and membranes that connect the bones. Luckily, these days, the butcher does that for you, so there's really nothing difficult about it at all!

¼ cup Panko breadcrumbs

¼ cup grated Parmesan Cheese

2 teaspoons chopped fresh rosemary

2 teaspoons chopped fresh oregano

¼ cup finely chopped toasted pecans

½ teaspoon salt

freshly ground black pepper

1 tablespoon olive oil

2 racks of lamb, bones frenched

3 tablespoons Dijon mustard

1 shallot, finely chopped

½ cup red wine

1 cup beef stock

2 tablespoons cold butter

1 tablespoon chopped fresh parsley

salt

freshly ground black pepper

1. Pre-heat the oven to 400° F.

2. Combine the breadcrumbs, Parmesan cheese, rosemary, oregano, pecans, salt and pepper in a small bowl.

3. Heat a large oven-safe skillet over medium-high heat. Add olive oil to the skillet. Season the racks of lamb with salt and pepper on all sides. Sear the lamb in the hot skillet, browning on all sides. Once brown, remove the skillet from the heat. Brush the fat side of the lamb rack with the Dijon mustard and pack on the Parmesan breadcrumb mixture, pressing the breadcrumbs into the lamb with your hands.

4. Transfer the skillet to the oven and roast for 20 to 25 minutes, or until an instant read thermometer reads 140° for medium. Roast for a shorter or longer period of time if you prefer your lamb cooked less or more.

5. Once the desired internal temperature is reached, remove the lamb from the skillet and allow it to rest on a cutting board, covered loosely with aluminum foil.

6. Transfer the skillet to the stovetop. (Remember to use an oven mitt as the handle of this skillet will be very hot.) Add the shallots to the skillet and cook for a minute. Add the red wine to the skillet to deglaze and scrape off any brown bits that have accumulated on the bottom of the skillet with a wooden spoon. Add the beef stock and bring to a simmer. Let this simmer and reduce until ½ cup of liquid remains. Turn the heat off and add the butter, parsley, salt and pepper.

7. Slice the racks of lamb into ribs and arrange on the dinner plates. Pour the reduced liquid (the "jus") over the top just before serving.

 When you put the two lamb racks into the oven, criss-cross the bones of the two racks. This will keep them standing up and allow them to cook evenly.

Basic Stew: Spring Lamb Stew

Lamb shoulder is perfect for a stew since it is tougher than leg or rack of lamb. It is already full of flavor, and the slow cooking makes it tender too.

3 tablespoons olive oil

3 pounds lamb shoulder,
trimmed of fat and cubed (1-inch cubes)

1 teaspoon salt

freshly ground black pepper

1 onion, chopped (about 1 cup)

3 cloves garlic, minced

2 tablespoons flour

1 cup red wine

2 cups chicken stock

½ teaspoon dried rosemary

1 teaspoon dried thyme

1 bay leaf

2 tablespoons Worcestershire sauce

8 small red potatoes,
halved or cut into bite-sized pieces

2 carrots, peeled and sliced on the bias

1 cup pearl onions, defrosted if frozen

1 cup frozen peas

2 tablespoons chopped fresh parsley

1. Pre-heat the oven to 250° F.

2. Heat a large Dutch oven or stockpot over medium heat. Add 1 to 2 tablespoons of olive oil. Working in batches so you don't overcrowd the Dutch oven, brown the lamb cubes, seasoning with salt and pepper – about 5 minutes. Set the browned meat aside.

3. Add the onion to the Dutch oven and cook until browned - about 5 minutes. Add the garlic and cook for another 30 seconds. Sprinkle the onions and garlic with the flour and cook, stirring, for another minute or two. Then add the red wine and deglaze the Dutch oven by scraping up any browned bits on the bottom of the Dutch oven with a wooden spoon. Bring the wine to a boil and let it simmer for a minute or two. Add the stock and return the liquid to a simmer. While this comes back to a simmer, return the browned lamb to the Dutch oven, along with the dried rosemary, dried thyme, bay leaf and Worcestershire sauce. Cover with a tight-fitting lid and transfer the Dutch oven to the oven for one hour.

4. Remove the Dutch oven from the oven and add the potatoes and carrots. Return to the oven for another hour.

5. Meanwhile, heat a skillet on medium-high heat. Add the remaining tablespoon of olive oil and cook the pearl onions until lightly browned.

6. Remove the Dutch oven from the oven and add the browned pearl onions. Return to the oven for another 30 minutes. Stir in the peas and heat through for 3 to 4 minutes. Stir in the parsley and serve.

Distinctive Stews

- A stew, like a pot roast, is a form of braising. There are three main distinctions that distinguish a stew from other braised dishes such as a pot roast.

- Stews contain small, uniformly sized pieces of meat. A pot roast, on the other hand, cooks one large piece of meat and makes it tender.

- A stew also has more liquid than a regular braise. It should not have as much liquid as a soup, but the gravy created in a stew is almost as important as the meat itself. A stew should be served on a plate with something to soak up the gravy, rather than relegated to a bowl.

- Finally, not all stews start by browning the meat first. A blanquette or fricassee is a white stew that has no browning of the meat ahead of time and is usually finished with cream to make a white sauce for the gravy. Aside from those differences, stews follow the same rules as braising and pot-roasting.

1. Use a heavy-bottomed pot with a tight-fitting lid to trap the steam.

2. Use tougher cuts of meat, but make sure they are cut uniformly into smaller pieces for even cooking.

3. Make sure you are adding flavor every time you add an ingredient. This applies to the liquid that you add. Red wine, beer, stock and juice are all good candidates.

4. Cook over a very low heat either on the stovetop or in the oven.

5. Cook for a very long time so that the meat has time to contract and then relax again. In other words, until the meat has become tender.

6. Add other ingredients at different times according to how long they take to cook. Vegetables, which cook faster than the meat, should be added after the stew has already been cooking for a while.

7. Finish the stew by enhancing the sauce. Some stews have a broth-like jus, while others have thickened gravy. Season the sauce before you serve the stew and thicken it if you wish.

Curried Chicken Stew

All that is needed to finish this meal is a bowl of rice. Try spicing up your rice by quickly cooking a cardamom pod, a couple of cloves and a cinnamon stick in oil before adding the rice and stock for a quick rice pilaf.

2 tablespoons vegetable oil

1 onion, chopped (about 1 cup)

1 teaspoon salt

2 teaspoons ground cumin

2 teaspoons ground coriander

1 teaspoon ground turmeric

¼ to ½ teaspoon cayenne pepper
(depending on how spicy you want the stew)

½ teaspoon ground cinnamon

⅛ teaspoon ground cloves

3 cloves garlic, very finely minced or puréed

2 tablespoons grated gingerroot,
grated very finely or puréed

2 pounds chicken, light or dark meat or a
combination of the two, cubed (1½-inch cubes)

1 cup chicken stock

1 can unsweetened coconut milk
(not light coconut milk)

8 small red potatoes, cut into bite-sized pieces

1 cup frozen peas

2 tablespoons chopped fresh cilantro

2 tablespoons toasted slivered almonds
or chopped peanuts

1. Heat a large Dutch oven or sauté pan over medium heat. Add the vegetable oil and cook the onion until tender – about 5 to 6 minutes. In a small bowl, combine the salt, cumin, coriander, turmeric, cayenne pepper, cinnamon and cloves. Add the spice mixture, garlic and ginger to the Dutch oven and cook, stirring, for another minute.

2. Add the cubed chicken, chicken stock and coconut milk to the Dutch oven and bring to a simmer. Add the potatoes, cover and simmer for 20 to 30 minutes.

3. Stir in the peas and heat through for another 10 minutes. Stir in the cilantro and serve with toasted almonds or peanuts.

TIP

You can substitute 2 tablespoons of good quality curry powder instead of the mixed dried spices (cumin, coriander, turmeric, cayenne pepper, cinnamon and cloves).

Pork and Poblano Pepper Stew

Though they can range in intensity, a Poblano pepper is a relatively mild pepper. In its dried form, it is called an Ancho chile pepper. If you want to add more heat to this stew, use two Jalapeño peppers.

1 to 2 tablespoons vegetable oil

3 pounds pork shoulder, trimmed of fat and cubed (1½-inch cubes)

1 teaspoon salt

1 onion, chopped (about 1 cup)

4 Poblano peppers, seeded and chopped

1 Jalapeño pepper seeded and finely chopped

3 cloves garlic, minced

1 teaspoon ground cumin

1 teaspoon dried oregano

3 cups chicken stock

1 (28 ounce) can diced tomatoes

2 (15 ounce) cans cannellini beans, drained

2 tablespoons chopped fresh parsley or cilantro

1. Pre-heat the oven to 250° F.

2. Heat a large Dutch oven or stockpot over medium heat. Add 1 to 2 tablespoons of oil and working in batches so you don't overcrowd the Dutch oven, brown the pork cubes, seasoning with salt – about 5 minutes. Set the browned meat aside.

3. Add the onions, Poblano and Jalapeño peppers to the Dutch oven and cook until tender - about 5 minutes. Add the garlic, cumin and oregano, and cook for another 30 seconds. Add the stock and tomatoes to the Dutch oven and bring the mixture to a boil. Return the pork to the Dutch oven, cover and transfer the Dutch oven to the oven for two hours.

4. Remove the Dutch oven from the oven and add the cannellini beans. Return to the oven for another 30 minutes. Stir in the parsley or cilantro and serve.

White Turkey Chili

This chili is "white" because it contains no tomatoes. White turkey chili is my favorite ski-trip meal every year. I try to make it on the first night of our trip so that after the first day of skiing, all I have to do is heat up a pot, enjoy the aroma throughout the house and sit down to a delicious dinner in front of the television.

1 tablespoon olive oil

3 pounds ground turkey meat, white, dark or a combination of the two

2 yellow onions, chopped (about 2 cups)

2 ribs celery, chopped (about 1 cup)

2 large carrots, chopped (about 1 cup)

2 red bell peppers, chopped (about 2 cups)

2 green bell peppers, chopped (about 2 cups)

2 large cloves garlic, minced

2 teaspoons dried ground cumin

2 tablespoons chili powder

2 (14 ounce) cans white beans, drained

2 (14 ounce) cans chickpeas, drained

1 tablespoon salt

3 cups chicken stock

¼ cup fresh cilantro, chopped (or parsley)

Cheddar cheese, grated

sour cream

green onions, chopped

1. Heat a large Dutch oven or stockpot over medium high heat. Add the olive oil and brown the ground turkey in batches. Set the browned meat aside and reserve. Drain off most of the fat and discard.

2. Return the Dutch oven to the heat and add the onion, celery, carrot, peppers and garlic. Cook together over medium heat until tender – about 6 to 8 minutes.

3. Add the dried cumin and chili powder and stir well to coat all the vegetables in the spices. Continue to cook for 4 to 6 minutes. Return the ground turkey to the Dutch oven and add the white beans, chickpeas and chicken stock. Season with salt and simmer for 45 to 60 minutes.

4. Stir in the fresh cilantro and serve with a choice of garnish – Cheddar cheese, sour cream, and/or green onions.

TIP
Chili powder provides a lot of the flavor in this dish, so get the best quality chili powder you can find. A good chili powder should have at least 80% chile pepper blended with other spices and preferably no added salt or monosodium glutamate.

French Canadian Beef Stew

I'm not exactly sure what makes this recipe French Canadian other than the fact that it has the sweet overtones found in a lot of Québécoise cuisine, and that it was given to me by my favorite French Canadian. French Canadians are experts at warming up with a bowl of stew after a cold winter day, and I can attest this stew works perfectly in that regard.

1 tablespoon olive oil

6 slices of bacon, chopped

2 pounds beef chuck, cubed (1-inch cubes)

1 teaspoon salt

freshly ground black pepper

2 medium leeks, cleaned and sliced
(½-inch slices)

2 carrots, peeled and sliced on the bias
(½-inch slices)

2 turnips, peeled and diced
(1-inch dice)

2 parsnips, peeled and chopped
(½-inch pieces)

2 tablespoons sugar

4 cloves garlic, minced

1 cup red wine

2 cups beef stock

1 teaspoon dried thyme

1 bay leaf

2 tablespoons red currant jelly

8 small red potatoes, halved

6 ripe plum tomatoes

2 tablespoons chopped fresh parsley

1. Pre-heat the oven to 250° F.

2. Heat a large Dutch oven or stockpot over medium heat. Add the olive oil and cook the bacon until crispy. Remove the bacon with a slotted spoon and reserve. Drain most of the fat out of the Dutch oven.

3. Return the Dutch oven to the stovetop and brown the beef cubes in batches, seasoning with salt and pepper. Set the browned meat aside.

4. Add the leeks, carrots, turnips, parsnips and sugar to the Dutch oven and cook until browned - about 5 minutes. Remove the vegetables and set aside.

5. Add the garlic to the Dutch oven and cook for 30 seconds. Then add the red wine and deglaze the Dutch oven by scraping up any browned bits on the bottom of the Dutch oven with a wooden spoon. Bring the wine to a boil and let it simmer for a minute or two. Add the stock and return the liquid to a simmer. While this comes back to a simmer, return the browned beef to the Dutch oven, along with the dried thyme, bay leaf and red currant jelly. Cover and transfer the Dutch oven to the oven for one hour.

6. Remove the Dutch oven from the oven and add the potatoes and tomatoes. Return to the oven for another hour.

7. Remove the Dutch oven from the oven and return the browned vegetables and bacon to the Dutch oven. Return to the oven for another 30 minutes to an hour, or until the beef is tender. Stir in parsley and serve.

Basic Meatloaf

Though the first recipes for meatloaf came from Europe, it has become one of America's best-loved meals.

SERVES

8

1 cup rolled oats or fresh breadcrumbs

½ cup milk

1 tablespoon vegetable oil

1 onion, finely chopped

1 carrot, finely chopped

2 cloves garlic, minced

1 pound ground beef

½ pound ground pork

½ pound ground veal

½ teaspoon dried thyme

½ teaspoon dried oregano

¼ cup finely chopped fresh parsley

2 eggs

1 tablespoon Worcestershire sauce

1 teaspoon salt

½ teaspoon freshly ground black pepper

8 slices of bacon

1. Pre-heat the oven to 350° F.

2. Place the rolled oats and milk in a large mixing bowl and let the oats soak while you prepare the rest of the ingredients.

3. Pre-heat a skillet over medium-high heat. Add the vegetable oil and then cook the onion, carrot and garlic until tender, but not browned – 5 to 6 minutes. Transfer the vegetables to the bowl with the oats and milk.

4. Add the ground meats, thyme, oregano, parsley, eggs, Worcestershire sauce, salt and pepper to the bowl and mix everything together with your hands just until everything is combined. Transfer the mix to a meatloaf pan or baking sheet. If you like a meat loaf with soft sides, leave the mix in the meatloaf pan, ideally one with a perforated bottom and a pan below to catch the drippings. If you prefer a harder crust on the sides of your meatloaf, invert the mix onto a baking sheet. Arrange the bacon slices over the top of the meatloaf, overlapping the slices a little. Tuck the bacon ends into the loaf pan or underneath the free formed loaf.

5. Bake in the oven for 60 to 75 minutes, or until an instant read thermometer registers 160° F in the center of the meat. Let the meatloaf rest and then slice and serve.

Making Flavorful Meatloaf

● Texture and flavor are the two important qualities of a good meatloaf.

● Using a combination of beef, pork and veal provides a meaty flavor without having one flavor dominating. A meatloaf made entirely of beef is very dense and bold in flavor. Pork adds a little subtlety to the beef, and the veal adds a tender quality to the meatloaf.

● Other flavors can be added to a meatloaf in the form of vegetables and spices, but don't go crazy adding too many different flavors to one meatloaf. In this recipe, the vegetables are cooked before mixing them in with the meat. Without pre-cooking, the onions and carrots would be somewhat crunchy in the finished dish.

● Originally, breadcrumbs or cereal were added to meatloaf in order to stretch the meat in tough times. As it turns out, the breadcrumbs serve another purpose. They help bind the meatloaf and make the texture lighter, breaking up the meat a little. The eggs also help to bind the meatloaf.

● The last essential ingredient in a good meatloaf is an ingredient to add moisture. Milk works very well to provide moisture, and softens the oatmeal or breadcrumbs. Chopped fresh mushrooms can also be used for this purpose, as they release their moisture into the meatloaf as they cook.

● When packing the meatloaf, try not to over handle the meat. Packing the meatloaf too much will make it dense and heavy.

● Your last decision is whether to cook the meatloaf in a loaf pan or on a baking sheet. The answer all depends on how you like your meatloaf. Meatloaf cooked on a baking sheet will form a crust around the outside of the loaf, and will take a glaze better than a meatloaf cooked in a loaf pan. If you prefer a meatloaf with a soft exterior, bake it in a loaf pan. A regular loaf pan is not ideal, however, since the meatloaf will collect juices and fat around and on top of the loaf, making it impossible to glaze. There are now specifically designed meatloaf pans that have perforations on the bottom and another pan below to catch the drippings. If you choose to make a meatloaf in a loaf pan, I highly recommend one with a perforated bottom.

● Finally, cook the meatloaf until it just registers 160° F on an instant read thermometer. Then, as with all meats, let it rest. The result will be a juicier meatloaf.

Turkey Mushroom Meatloaf

Mushrooms add moisture to the inside of this meatloaf and then garnish the top for an attractive presentation.

1 cup rolled oats or fresh breadcrumbs

½ cup milk

1 tablespoon vegetable oil

1 onion, finely chopped

1 rib celery, finely chopped

2 cloves garlic, minced

2 pounds ground turkey

4 ounces button mushrooms, very finely chopped (a food processor is perfect for this)

½ teaspoon dried thyme

¼ cup finely chopped fresh parsley

2 eggs

1 tablespoon Worcestershire sauce

1 teaspoon salt

½ teaspoon freshly ground black pepper

1 tablespoon olive oil

4 ounces button mushrooms, sliced

1. Pre-heat the oven to 350° F.

2. Place the rolled oats and milk in a large mixing bowl and let the oats soak while you prepare the rest of the ingredients.

3. Pre-heat a skillet over medium-high heat. Add the vegetable oil and then cook the onion, celery and garlic until tender, but not browned – 5 to 6 minutes. Transfer the vegetables to the bowl with the oats and milk.

4. Add the ground turkey, mushrooms, thyme, parsley, eggs, Worcestershire sauce, salt and pepper to the bowl and mix everything together with your hands. Transfer the mix to a meatloaf pan or baking sheet. If you like a meatloaf with soft sides, leave the mix in the loaf pan, ideally one with a perforated bottom and a pan below to catch the drippings. If you prefer a harder crust on the sides of your meatloaf, invert the loaf pan onto a baking sheet and bake the meatloaf without the loaf pan.

5. Bake in the oven for 60 to 75 minutes, or until an instant read thermometer registers 160° F in the center of the meat. Let the meatloaf rest.

6. While the meatloaf is resting, heat a skillet over medium-high heat. Add the olive oil and cook the sliced mushrooms until tender. Season with salt and pepper and serve the sliced meat loaf with the sautéed mushrooms over the top.

Spicy Italian Meatloaf

Italian sausage spices up this meatloaf, and the tomato slices on top dress it up to be one of the best looking meatloaves I've seen in a long time.

1 cup fresh breadcrumbs
(torn up day old bread is good)

½ cup milk

2 tablespoons olive oil, divided

1 onion, chopped

3 cloves garlic, sliced

1 pound ground beef

½ pound hot Italian sausage,
casings removed and meat broken up

½ pound sweet Italian sausage,
casings removed and meat broken up

½ cup chopped roasted red pepper

½ teaspoon dried basil

½ teaspoon dried oregano

¼ cup finely chopped fresh parsley

2 eggs

1 tablespoon Worcestershire sauce

1 teaspoon salt

½ teaspoon freshly ground black pepper

2 vine-ripened tomatoes, sliced (¼-inch slices)

6 tablespoons tomato ketchup

2 tablespoons brown sugar

1. Pre-heat the oven to 350° F.

2. Place the breadcrumbs and milk in a large mixing bowl and let the bread soak while you prepare the rest of the ingredients.

3. Pre-heat a skillet over medium-high heat. Add 1 tablespoon of olive oil, and cook the onion and garlic until tender but not browned – about 4 to 5 minutes. Transfer the onions and garlic to the bowl with the breadcrumbs and milk.

4. Add the ground beef, sausage meat, roasted red pepper, basil, oregano, parsley, eggs, Worcestershire sauce, salt and pepper to the bowl and mix everything together with your hands just until everything is combined. Transfer the mix to a meatloaf pan or baking sheet. If you like a meatloaf with soft sides, leave the mix in the meatloaf pan, ideally one with a perforated bottom and a pan below to catch the drippings. If you prefer a harder crust on the sides of your meatloaf, invert the loaf pan onto a baking sheet and bake the meatloaf without the loaf pan. Overlap the tomato slices on the meatloaf and drizzle the remaining tablespoon of olive oil on top.

5. Bake in the oven for 60 minutes. Remove the meatloaf from the oven. Quickly combine the ketchup and brown sugar and brush over the tomatoes to glaze the meatloaf. Return the meatloaf to the oven and bake for 15 more minutes, or until an instant read thermometer registers 160° F in the center of the meat. The tomatoes should be roasted and a little brown at the edges. Let the meatloaf rest and then slice and serve.

Meatloaf
with Caramelized Onion and Garlic

By browning the onions and garlic slowly and adding that to the meatloaf mix, you'll create a meatloaf with a different flavor profile. This meatloaf also uses ground turkey instead of ground veal.

1 cup rolled oats or fresh breadcrumbs

½ cup milk

1 tablespoon olive oil

1 tablespoon butter

3 onions, chopped

4 cloves garlic, sliced

½ cup tomato ketchup

2 tablespoons brown sugar

1 tablespoon white vinegar

1 pound ground beef

½ pound ground pork

½ pound ground turkey

½ teaspoon dried thyme

½ teaspoon dried oregano

¼ cup finely chopped fresh parsley

2 eggs

1 tablespoon Worcestershire sauce

1 teaspoon salt

½ teaspoon freshly ground black pepper

1. Pre-heat the oven to 350° F.

2. Place the rolled oats and milk in a large mixing bowl and let the oats soak while you prepare the rest of the ingredients.

3. Pre-heat a skillet over medium to medium-low heat. Add the olive oil and butter, and cook the onion and garlic very slowly, stirring occasionally until well-browned – about 45 minutes. Transfer the onions and garlic to the bowl with the oats and milk.

4. While the onions brown, make the glaze. Combine the ketchup, brown sugar and vinegar in a small saucepan and simmer for a few minutes. Set aside.

5. Add the ground meats, thyme, oregano, parsley, eggs, Worcestershire sauce, salt and pepper to the bowl and mix everything together with your hands. Transfer the mix to a meatloaf pan or baking sheet. If you like a meatloaf with soft sides, leave the mix in the loaf pan, ideally one with a perforated bottom and a pan below to catch the drippings. If you prefer a harder crust on the sides of your meatloaf, invert the loaf pan onto a baking sheet and bake the meatloaf without the loaf pan. Brush the glaze on the top of the meatloaf. Reserve any remaining glaze.

6. Bake in the oven for 60 to 75 minutes, or until an instant read thermometer registers 160° F in the center of the meat. Let the meatloaf rest, and while it rests, heat the remaining glaze and simmer for a minute. Slice the meatloaf and serve with the glaze.

Meatloaf
with Ham and Cheddar Cheese

When you slice into this meatloaf, there's a melted cheese center that's sure to please.

1 cup rolled oats or fresh breadcrumbs

½ cup milk

1 tablespoon vegetable oil

1 onion, finely chopped

1 carrot, finely chopped

2 cloves garlic, minced

1 pound ground beef

½ pound ground pork

½ pound ground veal

½ teaspoon dried thyme

½ teaspoon dried oregano

¼ cup finely chopped fresh parsley

2 eggs

1 tablespoon Worcestershire sauce

1 teaspoon salt

½ teaspoon freshly ground black pepper

4 slices of ham (¼-inch thick)

6 ounces Cheddar cheese,
sliced (¼-inch thick)

½ cup grated Cheddar
(for the top of the meatloaf)

1. Pre-heat the oven to 350° F.

2. Place the rolled oats and milk in a large mixing bowl and let the oats soak while you prepare the rest of the ingredients.

3. Pre-heat a skillet over medium-high heat. Add the olive oil and then cook the onion, carrot and garlic until tender, but not browned – 5 to 6 minutes. Transfer the vegetables to the bowl with the oats and milk.

4. Add the ground meats, thyme, oregano, parsley, eggs, Worcestershire sauce, salt and pepper to the bowl and mix everything together with your hands. Transfer half the mix to a meatloaf pan. Spread the slices of ham out onto a cutting board, overlapping the slices in a row the same length as your loaf pan. Arrange the sliced cheese on top of the ham slices. Roll the ham and cheese slices together creating a tube the same length as the loaf pan. Place the tube of ham and cheese in the center of the ground meat mixture already in the pan. Fill the pan with the remaining meat, covering the ham and cheese and pack down firmly. If you like a meatloaf with soft sides, leave the mix in the loaf pan, ideally one with a perforated bottom and a pan below to catch the drippings. If you prefer a harder crust on the sides of your meatloaf, invert the loaf pan onto a baking sheet and bake the meatloaf without the loaf pan.

5. Bake in the oven for 60 to 75 minutes, or until an instant read thermometer registers 160° F in the center of the meat, sprinkling grated Cheddar on top of the meat loaf for the last 10 minutes of baking. Let the meat loaf rest and then slice and serve.

Grilled Brined Pork Chops
with Grilled Peaches

With determination to cook the meat all the way through, many people inadvertently overcook pork, and as a result "the other white meat" has a reputation for being dry. Brining pork chops before cooking results in moist meat that browns well on the grill and has a superb flavor.

SERVES

4

Brine:

4 cups water

⅔ cup kosher salt

⅓ cup brown sugar

⅓ cup maple syrup

8 cloves garlic, smashed

2 tablespoons grated fresh gingerroot

6 cloves

1 teaspoon hot red pepper flakes

2 cups ice cubes

4 double-cut bone-in pork chops

vegetable oil

2 tablespoons butter, melted

2 tablespoons balsamic vinegar

4 peaches, halved and stones removed

1. Make the brine by bringing all the brine ingredients except the ice cubes to a boil in a saucepan. After the brine boils and the salt and sugar have dissolved, add the ice cubes to help cool the liquid. Once the brine is cool, add the pork chops and let them marinate in the brine in the refrigerator for 6 to 12 hours.

2. Pre-heat the BBQ grill for at least 10 minutes. The grill is hot enough when you can hold your hand 1 inch above the grill grates for no more than 2 to 3 seconds before you have to pull it away. Remove the pork chops from the brine and pat them dry with paper towels. Brush the chops very lightly with vegetable oil and place on the hottest part of the grill for 2 minutes on each side. Don't season them again with salt. Then, move the chops to a cooler part of the grill and continue to cook for 6 to 8 minutes per side, or until the internal temperature reaches 150° F. Remove the chops from the grill to a resting plate and loosely cover with foil.

3. While the pork chops are resting, mix together the melted butter and balsamic vinegar. Brush the cut surfaces of the peaches with this mixture and then grill the peach halves for 3 to 4 minutes. Turn the peaches over so that the skin sides are down, close the grill and cook for another 2 minutes. Plate the pork chops and serve with the grilled peach halves.

TIP Brining involves marinating meat in a saltwater solution for several hours, which improves the flavor, texture and moisture content of meat through osmosis. Because the brine has a higher concentration of salt than the meat, the saltwater moves from the brine into the meat. Once inside the meat, the salt tenderizes or "denatures" the meat proteins and separates them, creating more room for the brine solution. The result is a tender piece of meat that is full of moisture. Because the brine has other ingredients in it besides salt and water, these ingredients also travel into the meat as well, enhancing the flavor.

Lemon Rosemary Grilled Chicken Breasts

Lemon rosemary grilled chicken is a summer staple for me. You really can get great flavor from just 30 minutes in this marinade, making it a relatively quick weeknight meal.

¼ cup olive oil

2 lemons, zest and juice

2 sprigs fresh rosemary, chopped

2 cloves garlic, chopped

lots of freshly ground black pepper

4 chicken breasts (boneless, but skin on)

salt

1. Combine the olive oil, lemon zest, lemon juice, rosemary, garlic and lots of black pepper together in a sealable zipper style plastic bag or mixing bowl.

2. Add the chicken breasts to the marinade and let them marinate for 30 minutes to 4 hours, refrigerated.

3. Pre-heat the BBQ grill for at least 10 minutes. The grill is hot enough when you can hold your hand 1 inch above the grill grates for no more than 2 to 3 seconds before you have to pull it away. Remove the chicken from the marinade, shaking off any excess marinade, and grill for 6 to 8 minutes per side, seasoning with salt as you grill. The chicken should be firm to the touch and have an internal temperature of 165° F when cooked through.

4. Serve whole or sliced on an angle.

TIP Don't put salt in a marinade, unless you are brining food for several hours. Salt in a marinade will draw moisture out of the meat, making it dry. It is better to simply season with salt just before cooking the meat.

Basic Hamburger

Sometimes nothing can beat a good burger.

1 to 1½ pounds ground beef chuck
(80% lean meat)

½ to 1 teaspoon salt

freshly ground black pepper

1 tablespoon vegetable oil

4 hamburger buns

toppings and condiments

1. Gently mix the beef with the salt and pepper. Divide the meat into 4 equal portions and then form the hamburgers, being careful not to over-handle the meat. One good way to do this is to throw the meat back and forth between your hands like a baseball, packing the meat a little each time you catch it. Flatten the balls into patties, making an indentation with your thumb in the center of each patty.

2a. Stovetop Method: Pre-heat a heavy-bottomed skillet over medium-high heat. When the pan is hot, add the oil and place the patties in the pan. Season with salt and pepper, and cook to the desired degree of doneness (see below), flipping once.

2b. Grill Method: Pre-heat the grill until hot (if using charcoal, coals should be covered with white ash; if using gas, pre-heat for at least 10 minutes). Brush the patties lightly with oil and place burgers on the grill. Season with salt and pepper, and cook to the desired degree of doneness (see below), flipping once.

Cooking Times for Burgers:

Rare – 3 minutes per side
Medium – 5 minutes per side
Well – 6 minutes per side

3. Lightly toast the hamburger buns, either in the oven or on the grill. Place the cooked burger patties on the toasted hamburger buns and serve the burgers with your choice of toppings – tomato ketchup, mustard, relish, mayonnaise, onions, tomatoes, lettuce, mushrooms, etc…

Hamburger Heaven

● A good burger should be tasty, juicy and tender, with a good crust on the outside of the patty. Making a good burger is not difficult, but there are a few simple rules to follow to make sure it is as good as it can be.

● Start with the right meat. If you are making a beef burger, choose ground chuck, which has great flavor and look for 80% lean meat. The fat content is important for a tasty, moist burger. Any more than 20% fat makes the burger greasy, and any less fat will make the burger a little dry.

● Season the meat when you mix the burger meat and again when you cook the patties. Seasoning just the surface of the meat as you cook the patties will make the outside of the burger taste great, but leave the inside of the burger a little bland.

● Mix the meat with additional ingredients gently. Over-handling and over-packing will create a burger patty that is dense and tough. Try packing the meat by tossing it back and forth from one hand to another. This method packs the burger well without over-mixing.

● Shaping the patties is important too. Use your thumb to make an indentation in the center of the burger patty so that it looks something like a donut (with a dent but not a hole). Because the meat puffs up in the center while cooking, the indentation will create a burger that is flat when fully cooked, rather than a round baseball-like burger.

● Cook the burger patties on an outdoor grill or on the stovetop in a hot skillet. A cast iron skillet is perfect for cooking burgers because it retains the heat so well. The grill or skillet must be very hot when you start cooking the burgers. This will give the burger patty a good crust on the outside. Whether you are cooking a burger on a grill or in a skillet, refrain from pressing down on the burger with a spatula when it cooks. This bad habit squeezes the juices out of the burger, which is just a crying shame.

● As with all meats, resting the patties for just a few minutes will result in a juicer burger. Sometimes, preparing all the fixings on your burger bun is all the time you need!

Lamb Burgers
with Olives and Feta

It's a nice change to make a burger out of something other than beef. The lamb, olives, Feta and pita bread give this burger a distinctly Greek flavor. Try adding some tzatziki (cucumber, yogurt, and garlic) or hummus instead of the traditional fixings to complete the Greek theme.

1 tablespoon olive oil

½ onion, finely chopped

2 cloves garlic, minced

1½ pounds ground lamb meat

3 tablespoons fresh parsley, finely chopped

2 teaspoons fresh oregano, finely chopped

⅔ cup black olives, finely chopped

½ cup crumbled Feta cheese

½ teaspoon salt

freshly ground black pepper

1 tablespoon vegetable oil

4 thick pita breads

toppings and condiments

1. Pre-heat a medium skillet over medium-high heat. Add the olive oil and cook the onion until tender, but not browned – about 4 to 5 minutes. Add the garlic and cook for another minute.

2. Transfer the onion and garlic to a mixing bowl and add the ground lamb, parsley, oregano, olives, Feta cheese, salt and pepper. Gently mix the ingredients together.

3. Divide the mixture into 4 equal portions and then form the burgers, being careful not to over-handle the meat. One good way to do this is to throw the meat back and forth between your hands like a baseball, packing the meat each time you catch it. Flatten the balls into patties, making an indentation with your thumb in the center of each patty.

4a. Stovetop Method: Pre-heat a heavy-bottomed skillet over medium-high heat. When the pan is hot, add the oil and place the patties in the pan. Season with salt and pepper, and cook to the desired degree of doneness (see below), flipping once.

4b. Grill Method: Pre-heat the grill until hot (if using charcoal, coals should be covered with white ash; if using gas, pre-heat for at least 10 minutes). Brush the patties lightly with oil and place burgers on grill. Season with salt and pepper, and cook to the desired degree of doneness (see below), flipping once.

Cooking Times for Burgers:
Rare – 3 minutes per side
Medium – 5 minutes per side
Well – 6 minutes per side

5. Lightly toast the pita breads, either in the oven or on the grill. Wrap the burgers with the pita breads and serve the burgers with your choice of toppings – tomato ketchup, mustard, relish, mayonnaise, onions, tomatoes, lettuce, mushrooms, etc… or try tzatziki, or hummus.

 You can grind your own meat for burgers (or meatloaf) using a food processor. Cut the meat into small cubes and chill it well. Then, grind small batches of the meat using the pulse feature on the food processor for 20 to 30 seconds.

Turkey Burgers
with Sun-dried Tomatoes and Basil

A turkey burger is a great burger variation for anyone watching his or her cholesterol or fat intake. I recommend using dark turkey meat for this burger, but you can choose light meat if you prefer.

SERVES

4

1 tablespoon olive oil

½ red onion, finely chopped (about ½ cup)

2 cloves garlic, minced

1 to 1½ pounds ground turkey meat

8 sun-dried tomatoes (in oil), chopped (about ¼ cup)

10 large leaves of fresh basil, chopped

freshly ground black pepper

1 teaspoon salt

1 tablespoon vegetable oil

4 Kaiser buns

4 large leaves of Bibb lettuce

mayonnaise

1. Pre-heat a medium skillet over medium-high heat. Add the olive oil and cook the onion until tender, but not browned – about 4 to 5 minutes. Add the garlic and cook for another minute.

2. Add the ground turkey, sun-dried tomatoes, basil and salt and pepper to the bowl and gently mix the ingredients.

3. Divide the mixture into 4 equal portions and then form the turkey burgers, being careful not to over-handle the meat. One good way to do this is to throw the meat back and forth between your hands like a baseball, packing the meat each time you catch it. Flatten the balls into patties, making an indentation with your thumb in the center of each patty.

4a. Stovetop Method: Pre-heat a heavy-bottomed skillet over medium heat. When the pan is hot, add the vegetable oil and place the patties in the pan. Season with salt and pepper, and cook the patties until cooked through – about 6 minutes per side. An instant read thermometer should read 160° F when fully cooked.

4b. Grill Method: Pre-heat the grill until hot (if using charcoal, coals should be covered with white ash; if using gas, pre-heat for at least 10 minutes). Brush the patties lightly with oil and place them on the grill. Season with salt and pepper, and cook the patties until cooked through – about 5 to 6 minutes per side. An instant read thermometer should read 160° F when fully cooked.

5. Lightly toast the Kaiser buns, either in the oven or on the grill. Serve the burgers with mayonnaise and Bibb lettuce leaves.

For extra flavor, use the oil from the sun-dried tomato jar instead of the vegetable oil to brush the burgers before cooking.

Blue Cheese and Bacon Burgers

You can grill a basic hamburger and top it with cooked bacon and blue cheese, but mixing the toppings right into the burger patty makes it so much easier to eat and enjoy.

8 slices thick center cut bacon, chopped (½-inch pieces)

6 ounces blue cheese, crumbled

1 to 1½ pounds ground beef chuck (80% lean meat)

½ to 1 teaspoon salt

freshly ground black pepper

1 tablespoon vegetable oil

4 hamburger buns

topping and condiments

1. Pre-heat a skillet over medium heat. Add the bacon and cook until almost crispy. Remove the bacon with a slotted spoon and transfer to a mixing bowl.

2. Add the blue cheese, ground beef, salt and pepper to the bowl and gently mix the ingredients.

3. Divide the mixture into 4 equal portions and then form the hamburgers, being careful not to over-handle the meat. One good way to do this is to throw the meat back and forth between your hands like a baseball, packing the meat each time you catch it. Flatten the balls into patties, making an indentation with your thumb in the center of each patty.

4a. Stovetop Method: Pre-heat a heavy-bottomed skillet over medium-high heat. When the pan is hot, add the oil and place the patties in the pan. Season with salt and pepper, and cook to the desired degree of doneness (see below), flipping once.

4b. Grill Method: Pre-heat the grill until hot (if using charcoal, coals should be covered with white ash; if using gas, pre-heat for at least 10 minutes). Brush the patties lightly with oil and place burgers on grill. Season with salt and pepper, and cook to the desired degree of doneness (see below), flipping once.

Cooking Times for Burgers:

Rare – 3 minutes per side
Medium – 5 minutes per side
Well – 6 minutes per side

5. Lightly toast the hamburger buns, either in the oven or on the grill. Place the cooked burger patties on the toasted hamburger buns and serve the burgers with your choice of toppings – tomato ketchup, mustard, relish, mayonnaise, onions, tomatoes, lettuce, mushrooms, etc…

Chicken Chipotle Burgers

Here's another burger that is lighter in fat than traditional beef burgers. The chipotle gives it a little kick and salsa on top is a nice alternative to tomato ketchup.

SERVES

4

1 tablespoon olive oil

½ onion, finely chopped (about ½ cup)

2 cloves garlic, minced

1 to 1½ pounds ground chicken

2 tablespoons chipotle peppers in adobo, finely chopped

2 tablespoons chopped fresh cilantro

2 teaspoons fresh thyme, finely chopped

1 teaspoon salt

4 hamburger buns

topping and condiments

1. Pre-heat a medium skillet over medium-high heat. Add the olive oil and cook the onion and garlic until tender, but not browned – about 4 to 6 minutes. Transfer onion and garlic to a mixing bowl.

2. Add the ground chicken, chipotle peppers, cilantro, thyme and salt to the bowl and gently mix the ingredients.

3. Divide the mixture into 4 equal portions and then form the chicken burgers, being careful not to over-handle the meat. One good way to do this is to throw the meat back and forth between your hands like a baseball, packing the meat each time you catch it. Flatten the balls into patties, making an indentation with your thumb in the center of each patty.

4a. Stovetop Method: Pre-heat a heavy-bottomed skillet over medium heat. When the pan is hot, add the vegetable oil and place the patties in the pan. Season with salt and pepper, and cook the patties until cooked through – about 6 to 7 minutes per side. An instant read thermometer should read 165° F when fully cooked.

4b. Grill Method: Pre-heat the grill until hot (if using charcoal, coals should be covered with white ash; if using gas, pre-heat for at least 10 minutes). Brush the patties lightly with oil and place them on the grill. Season with salt and pepper, and cook the patties until cooked through – about 6 minutes per side. An instant read thermometer should read 165° F when fully cooked.

5. Lightly toast the hamburger buns, either in the oven or on the grill. Serve the burgers with your choice of toppings – tomato ketchup, mustard, relish, mayonnaise, onions, tomatoes, lettuce, mushrooms, etc… or try salsa.

Fish
and
Seafood

We all know we should eat more fish and seafood, but so many are reluctant, perhaps because they don't know how to prepare fish. These fish recipes are quick and easy, and are arranged by cooking technique or classic fish preparation, like Sole à la Meunière or Moules Marinières. All the information you need to sauté, make a pan sauce, steam mussels, grill and cook en papillote is here.

Basic Sole à la Meunière

À la Meunière means in the style of the miller's wife, which explains why this recipe calls for the fish to be dredged in flour before sautéing it. What most people think of when they hear "Meunière", however, is the brown butter lemon sauce that finishes the dish. This recipe is a great example of sautéing a fish and making a quick pan sauce.

½ cup flour

2 teaspoons salt

freshly ground black pepper

4 fillets of sole (about 4 to 5 ounces each)

1 to 2 tablespoons olive oil

5 to 6 tablespoons butter, divided

4 tablespoons lemon juice (about 2 lemons)

1 teaspoon lemon zest

1 tablespoon chopped fresh parsley

1. Pre-heat the oven to its lowest setting – probably around 170° F.

2. Combine the flour, salt and pepper in a shallow dish.

3. Heat a large 10- to 12-inch oven-safe skillet over medium-high heat. While the skillet is heating up, dredge the sole fillets in the flour and shake off any excess flour.

4. Add 1 tablespoon of olive oil and 1 tablespoon of butter to the skillet. As soon as the butter melts and has stopped sizzling, add the fish to the skillet, working in batches so you don't overcrowd the skillet. Cook for 2 minutes and then flip the fish and cook the other side for 2 minutes. Remove the fish from the skillet and place on a plate in the warm oven.

5. If there are any burned bits in your pan, wipe out the skillet and return it to the stovetop over medium heat. Otherwise, just continue in the skillet without wiping it out. Add 4 tablespoons of butter to the pan and let it melt, sizzle, and eventually start to turn brown – about 3 to 4 minutes. As soon as the butter has turned brown, turn the heat off, and add the lemon juice and lemon zest. Add the parsley and swirl the skillet to combine well.

6. Remove the fish from the oven and divide onto plates. Pour the sauce over the fish and serve immediately.

Recipe Explained!

● With seafood, I buy the best quality fish I can, and then do as little to it as possible, letting the true flavor of the fish shine through. Fresh, high quality fish should have a mild fresh odor, not a fishy smell; the flesh should be firm; the skin should be shiny; the gills should be bright red; and the eyes should be bright and clear. If I don't have access to a reliable source for fresh fish, I prefer to buy frozen fish and defrost it in the refrigerator overnight.

● I use oil and butter in this recipe because I want the flavor of butter, but also want to use a higher temperature. The olive oil can withstand a higher temperature without burning. Using butter and olive oil together gives me the best of both worlds.

● I cannot stress how important it is not to overcrowd your skillet. Overcrowding the skillet will prevent the fish from browning properly, and it makes it difficult to flip the fish. Use a large skillet, or work in batches.

● The general rule of thumb when cooking fish is to allow 10 minutes of cooking time for every inch of thickness of the fish fillet or steak. This applies to baking at 400° F, cooking on a stovetop, or grilling. Just remember that in a skillet on the stovetop, or on a grill, you'll need to flip the fish half way through that time.

● Making a pan sauce is the easiest and quickest way to make a sauce to go with whatever you are cooking. The flavor of the food you just finished cooking is already in the skillet and ready to flavor your sauce. The only problem is if the skillet has browned the little bits in the skillet too much, you'll end up incorporating burnt flavors into your pan sauce. To avoid this, check the skillet after you've sautéed the food and before you make the pan sauce. If there are any bits that are too brown or burned, wipe them out of the skillet first. It's better to make a pan sauce in a completely clean skillet with no residual flavors than to have a sauce that tastes burnt.

Sautéed Tilapia
with Lime Butter

Tilapia is a tropical freshwater fish with a mild flavor and white flesh. If you cannot find tilapia, you can substitute red snapper, orange roughy, or any white fish fillet. Simply prepared with a quick lime pan sauce, this is an easy dish to make for someone who is not a born fish-lover.

SERVES

4

4 fillets of tilapia (about 4 to 5 ounces each)

salt

freshly ground black pepper

1 to 2 tablespoons olive oil

2 tablespoons butter, divided

½ shallot, finely chopped

1 sprig fresh thyme

¼ cup white wine

2 tablespoons lime juice (about 3 limes)

1 teaspoon lime zest

1 tablespoon chopped fresh chives

1. Pre-heat the oven to its lowest setting – probably around 170° F.

2. Heat a large 10- to 12-inch oven-safe skillet over medium-high heat. Season the fish with salt and pepper.

3. Add 1 tablespoon of olive oil and 1 tablespoon of butter to the skillet. As soon as the butter melts and has stopped sizzling, add the fish to the skillet, working in batches so you don't overcrowd the fish. Cook for 2 minutes and then flip the fish and cook the other side for 2 minutes. Remove the fish from the skillet and place on a plate in the warm oven.

4. Return the skillet to the heat and add the shallot and thyme sprig. Sauté for 2 minutes, stirring regularly. Add the white wine and bring to a simmer. Simmer for 2 minutes to reduce the wine. Add the lime juice and lime zest and as soon as it comes to a simmer, turn off the heat and swirl in the remaining tablespoon of butter. The point is to not have the butter separate, but to stay emulsified and thicken the sauce.

5. Remove the fish from the oven and divide onto plates. Pour the sauce over the fish, garnish with chopped fresh chives and serve immediately.

If a recipe calls for both zest and juice of a lime, lemon or orange, grate the zest first before you cut the fruit open to juice it.

Seared Scallops
with a Hazelnut Orange Sauce

Scallops are one of my favorite seafood. When cooked properly, they are tender, succulent and delectable. When overcooked, they unfortunately turn rubbery and tough. The cooking time will depend on the size of the scallop, but regardless, it won't be long. When cooked, the scallops will give a little bounce when pressed with your finger.

1½ pounds sea scallops, muscle removed

salt

freshly ground black pepper

1 tablespoon olive oil

1 tablespoon butter

½ cup sherry, vermouth or dry white wine

½ cup fresh orange juice

1 teaspoon orange zest

2 tablespoons chopped fresh green onions

⅓ cup chopped hazelnuts, toasted

1. Heat a large 10- to 12-inch skillet over medium-high heat. Season the scallops with salt and pepper.

2. Add the olive oil and butter to the skillet and sear the scallops for 2 minutes per side, being careful not to overcook. Remove the scallops to a plate and set aside. Drain the oil left in the skillet.

3. Add the sherry and orange juice to the skillet and bring to a simmer. Simmer until the liquid has reduced by half and is somewhat syrupy – about 4 to 6 minutes. Add the orange zest, green onions and the toasted hazelnuts and swirl around to combine.

4. Return the scallops to the skillet and heat through gently while coating with the sauce – about 1 minute. Season again with freshly ground black pepper and more orange zest if desired.

TIP

Many scallops have the muscle used to open and close their shell still attached to them when sold from the market. This muscle becomes tough when cooked and is unpleasant to eat. Simply remove the muscle before cooking by pulling it away from the scallop body and discard.

Sautéed Shrimp
in a Paprika Cream Sauce

For anyone a little nervous about cooking shellfish, shrimp are helpful in the kitchen – they let you know when they are cooked by turning pink.

SERVES

4

1 pound raw shrimp, peeled and deveined

salt

freshly ground black pepper

1 to 2 tablespoons olive oil

2 cloves garlic, smashed

pinch hot red pepper flakes

½ teaspoon paprika

¾ cup white wine

¾ cup heavy cream

1 tablespoon chopped fresh parsley

1. Pre-heat a large 12-inch skillet over medium-high heat. Season the shrimp with salt and pepper.

2. Add 1 tablespoon of olive oil to the skillet and sauté the shrimp until they just turn pink – about 4 minutes. Remove the shrimp to a plate and set aside. Add another tablespoon of olive oil to the skillet and cook the garlic, hot red pepper flakes and paprika until fragrant – about 1 minute. Add the white wine and bring to a simmer. Simmer until the liquid has reduced by half. Add the cream and simmer again for about 2 to 3 minutes.

3. Return the shrimp to the skillet and toss around to coat and warm through. Garnish with the parsley and season again with salt and freshly ground black pepper. Serve over noodles or rice.

Sautéed Mahi-Mahi
with Chipotle Tomato Sauce

This pan sauce is full of flavor and needs a fish that can stand up to it. Mahi-mahi is a firm fish with large flakes, and works nicely with this spicy tomato sauce.

4 fillets of mahi-mahi
(about 1-inch thick and 5 to 6 ounces each)

salt

freshly ground black pepper

2 tablespoons olive oil

2 cloves garlic, sliced

1 tablespoon chopped Chipotle pepper
in adobo sauce

2 Roma tomatoes, diced

1 (14½ ounce) can of crushed tomatoes

2 tablespoons chopped fresh cilantro

1. Pre-heat the oven to the lowest possible setting – probably around 170° F.

2. Heat a large 10- to 12-inch oven-safe skillet over medium-high heat. Season the fish on both sides with salt and pepper.

3. Add 1 tablespoon of the olive oil to the skillet and sear the fish for 3 to 4 minutes per side, browning well, until the fish is firm to the touch. Remove the fish from the skillet and place on a plate in the warm oven.

4. Add another tablespoon of olive oil to the skillet and sauté the garlic and Chipotle pepper for 1 minute. Add the fresh tomatoes and toss. Add the canned tomatoes and bring the mixture to a simmer for 5 minutes.

5. Remove the fish from the oven and divide onto plates. Season the sauce to taste with salt and stir in the cilantro. Spoon the sauce over the fish and serve immediately.

 TIP

The ideal temperature at which to store fish is around 32° F. This is colder than most refrigerators. So, if you don't eat the fish the day you buy it, store it in the bottom of your refrigerator on a bed of crushed ice, or sandwiched between two sheets of freezer gel packs (the latter can be found at large discount retail department stores).

Basic Mussels
Moules Marinières

The hardest part about making mussels for dinner is finding them at the grocery store. Once that's accomplished, they are so easy and quick to prepare, and the payoff is a delicious meal that breaks from routine. Remember to provide your guests with empty bowls for the shells.

SERVES

4

4 pounds mussels

3 tablespoons butter, divided

1 large shallot, finely chopped (about ½ cup)

2 cloves garlic, minced

2 sprigs fresh thyme

1 bay leaf

1½ cups white wine

¼ cup chopped fresh parsley

freshly ground black pepper

1. Clean the mussels by scrubbing them with a brush under running water. Pull off the beard (the whiskery hairs protruding from the shell). Discard any mussels that are broken or that don't close their shells when tapped.

2. Melt the butter in a large 12-inch sauté pan or Dutch oven with a lid. Add the shallots and garlic and cook for just a minute or two, until fragrant. Add the thyme, bay leaf and white wine and simmer for 2 to 3 minutes.

3. Increase the heat to high, add the mussels and cover with the lid. Shake the pan every once in a while and steam the mussels for 3 to 5 minutes until they open.

4. Remove the mussels from the pan with a slotted spoon and place in serving bowls, discarding any mussels whose shells are cracked, broken or did not open during cooking. Remove the bay leaf and thyme sprigs from the steaming liquid and stir in the parsley and black pepper. Remove the pan from the heat and swirl in the remaining butter. Pour this over the mussels and serve immediately with crusty bread or French fries to soak up the tasty liquid.

Recipe Explained!

● The first step in preparing mussels is choosing the right mussels. Purchase mussels from a reputable fishmonger or specialty grocery store. The mussels should be tightly closed and have a fresh, but not fishy smell. I prefer rope-cultured mussels to "wild" mussels. Wild mussels are raised and harvested in a traditional way and therefore have A LOT of sand and grit inside. You will have to soak and rinse them many, many times as well as strain the cooking broth, losing all the tasty broth ingredients like the shallots, garlic, etc.

● Once you've got the mussels home, store them properly. Remove the mussels from the mesh bag they came in, place them in a colander and place that colander in a bowl. Cover the surface of the mussels with crushed ice or ice cubes and then cover with damp paper towels. They will keep this way for a day or two, but it is best to eat them the day you buy them.

● When you're ready to prepare the mussels, rinse and scrub them, and make sure each one is tightly closed. If the shell is open or broken, the mussel is dead and should be discarded. Sometimes there are whiskery strings protruding from the mussel shell. These are the byssal threads, also known as "the beard". Remove these threads, just by pulling them off the shell.

● Steaming is the best way to cook mussels. You can steam them open using only water, but the steaming liquid will become your sauce, so it makes more sense to start with a flavorsome liquid. Sautéing garlic and shallots is the start of that flavorsome liquid. White wine is traditionally used to steam mussels, but you can also use other liquids such as beer or fruit juices. The mussels will release their own liquid when they cook, adding to the flavor of the sauce.

● It takes under 5 minutes to steam mussels. Once the shells are open, they are fully cooked, and cooking them longer will only toughen them. Remove them with a slotted spoon so you can make final adjustments to the sauce. I generally don't add salt to the sauce since the mussels add their own saltiness, but season to taste. Any mussels that have closed or damaged shells after being cooked should be discarded and not eaten.

Mussels
with Curried Coconut Milk and Basil

This recipe calls for green curry paste. If you can't find green curry paste in the international section of your supermarket, substitute a good quality curry powder. It won't be exactly the same, but it will still be tasty.

4 pounds mussels

1 tablespoon vegetable oil

4 shallots, thinly sliced (about 1 cup)

2 cloves garlic, minced

1-inch gingerroot, peeled and finely chopped (about 1 tablespoon)

1 tablespoon green curry paste

2 (13½ ounce) cans unsweetened coconut milk

1 cup clam juice or water

¼ cup chopped fresh basil

2 teaspoons lemon zest

salt

freshly ground black pepper

1. Clean the mussels by scrubbing them with a brush under running water. Pull off the beard (the whiskery hairs protruding from the shell). Discard any mussels that are broken or that don't close their shells when tapped.

2. Pre-heat a large 12-inch sauté pan or Dutch oven over medium heat. Add the oil and cook the shallots, garlic and gingerroot for 2 minutes. Add the curry paste and continue to cook, stirring for another minute. Add the coconut milk and clam juice (or water), bring the mixture to a boil and simmer for 3 minutes.

3. Increase the heat to high, add the mussels and cover with the lid. Shake the pan every once in a while and steam the mussels for 3 to 5 minutes until they open.

4. Remove the mussels from the pan with a slotted spoon and place in serving bowls, discarding any mussels whose shells are cracked, broken or did not open during cooking. Stir in the basil and lemon zest and season with salt and freshly ground black pepper. Pour the broth over the mussels and serve immediately with crusty bread or French fries to soak up the tasty liquid.

 TIP Gingerroot freezes well. If you have too much fresh gingerroot on your hands, peel it (the edge of a teaspoon works well to peel gingerroot), grate it with a microplane grater, roll it into a long tube shape, wrap it in plastic wrap, and freeze it. When you need grated gingerroot again, break off a piece. It thaws quickly and will be ready to use.

Mussels
with Italian Sausage and Tomato

You can substitute fresh chorizo or spicy Italian sausage in this recipe, but I think the sweet Italian sausage allows more of the flavor of the mussels to come through.

4 pounds mussels

1 tablespoon olive oil

1 pound sweet Italian sausage, removed from casing and crumbled

1 small red onion, sliced (about 1 cup)

2 cloves garlic, minced

3 tomatoes, chopped (about 2 to 2½ cups)

1½ cups white wine

¼ cup chopped fresh parsley

freshly ground black pepper

1. Clean the mussels by scrubbing them with a brush under running water. Pull off the beard (the whiskery hairs protruding from the shell). Discard any mussels that are broken or that don't close their shells when tapped.

2. Heat a large 12-inch sauté pan or Dutch oven over medium heat. Add the olive oil and cook the crumbled sausage and red onion until the sausage is just cooked through – about 5 minutes. Add the garlic and cook for just a minute, until fragrant. Add the tomatoes and white wine and simmer for 2 to 3 minutes.

3. Increase the heat to high, add the mussels and cover with the lid. Shake the pan every once in a while and steam the mussels for 3 to 5 minutes until they open.

4. Remove the mussels from the pan with a slotted spoon and place in serving bowls, discarding any mussels whose shells are cracked, broken or did not open during cooking. Stir in the parsley and season with black pepper. Pour the broth over the mussels and serve immediately with crusty bread or French fries to soak up the tasty liquid.

Clams
with Bacon, Beer and Potatoes

Littleneck and cherrystone clams are both hard-shelled quahog clams. Littlenecks are a little smaller, about 7 to 10 clams per pound, while cherrystone are slightly larger. They both are also sometimes referred to as steamer clams.

SERVES

4

4 pounds littleneck or cherrystone clams

4 slices thick-cut bacon, chopped

1 small red onion, sliced (about 1 cup)

1 Serrano (or Jalapeño) pepper, sliced

2 Yukon Gold potatoes or other white potato, diced (1/2-inch dice; about 1½ cups)

2 cloves garlic, sliced

12 ounces beer (a light ale or lager)

½ lemon, juiced

¼ cup chopped fresh parsley

1 tablespoon butter

1. Clean the clams by scrubbing them with a brush under running water. Discard any clams that are broken or that don't close their shells when tapped.

2. Heat a large 12-inch sauté pan or Dutch oven over medium to medium-high heat. Add the bacon and cook for 6 to 8 minutes. Add the red onion, Serrano pepper and potato and cook until the onion is tender – about 6 to 8 minutes. Add the garlic and cook for an additional minute, until fragrant. Add the beer and simmer for 3 minutes.

3. Increase the heat to high, add the clams and cover with the lid. Shake the pan every once in a while and steam the clams for 5 to 7 minutes until they open.

4. Remove the clams from the pan with a slotted spoon and place in serving bowls, discarding any mussels whose shells are cracked, broken or did not open during cooking. Stir in the lemon juice, parsley and butter. Pour the broth over the clams and serve immediately.

TIP

To rid clams of any excess grit and sand, soak them in salty water (1 part salt to 10 parts water) in the refrigerator for up to 2 hours. The clams will filter the water and expel sand and silt. Remove the clams from the water with your hands or a slotted spoon, rather than straining them, so that you leave any expelled sand in the bowl.

Mussels
with Fennel, Tomatoes and Cream

These mussels work really well served over a large bowl of spaghetti. The leftover sauce is a delicious addition to pasta so don't throw any away.

SERVES
4

4 pounds mussels

1 tablespoon olive oil

1 shallot, finely chopped

1 bulb fennel, sliced ¼-inch thick

2 sprigs fresh thyme

2 cloves garlic, minced

3 ripe tomatoes, chopped

1½ cups white wine

½ to 1 cup heavy cream

¼ cup chopped fresh parsley

freshly ground black pepper

1. Clean the mussels by scrubbing them with a brush under running water. Pull off the beard (the whiskery hairs protruding from the shell). Discard any mussels that are broken or that don't close their shells when tapped.

2. Heat a large 12-inch sauté pan or Dutch oven over medium heat. Add the oil and cook the shallots and fennel for 2 minutes. Add the thyme sprigs and garlic and continue to cook, stirring, for another minute. Add the tomatoes and white wine and simmer for 2 to 3 minutes.

3. Increase the heat to high, add the mussels and cover with the lid. Shake the pan every once in a while and steam the mussels for 3 to 5 minutes until they open.

4. Remove the mussels from the pan with a slotted spoon and place in serving bowls, discarding any mussels whose shells are cracked, broken or did not open during cooking. Remove the thyme sprigs from the steaming liquid and add the heavy cream. Simmer for 4 to 5 minutes to reduce the liquid and concentrate flavors. Stir in the parsley and black pepper. Pour the broth over the mussels and serve immediately with crusty bread or French fries to soak up the tasty liquid.

Basic Grilled Fish Fillet or Steak

Keeping it simple really applies to grilling fish. Buy the best quality fish you can, and then do as little to it as possible. You'll find the grilled fish recipes in this book do very little to the fish itself other than season and grill it. These recipes will, however give you ideas on how to add flavor and interest in the form of a sauce or accompaniment.

SERVES

4

4 fillets of fish or fish steaks (6 – 8 ounce each)

2 tablepoons vegetable oil

salt

freshly ground black pepper

vinaigrette or salsa

1. Pre-heat your grill (gas, charcoal or stovetop) until it is hot. It is hot when you can hold your hand 1 to 2 inches off the grate for no more than 2 to 3 seconds before you want to pull it away. Make sure the grill is clean before you cook.

2. Dry the fish well with a paper towel and brush both sides with the vegetable oil. Season the fish well with salt and pepper.

3. Grill the fish for 8 to 10 minutes per inch of thickness (4 to 5 minutes per side), flipping only once.

4. Serve immediately with vinaigrette or salsa on top. Grilled vegetables make a great side dish.

Recipe Explained!

● Grilling fish can be tricky and intimidates many because fish is more fragile than beef or chicken, and is more likely to fall apart on the grill. The first step in overcoming this fear of grilling fish is to select the right variety. Good fish to grill are: tuna, swordfish, salmon, mahi-mahi, red snapper, striped bass, trout and bluefish. Fish that are more challenging to grill include tilapia, sole, flounder or any flaky, thin-fleshed fish.

● Use fish fillets or steaks that are cut evenly. These will cook more uniformly and remain moist. Lightly coat the fish with oil before grilling, rather than trying to oil your grill grate, and make sure that the grill grate is clean and free of any residue. This will help reduce any sticking.

● Once you have the fish on the grill, leave it alone. One of the most common mistakes is trying to move the fish too soon, in which case it is almost guaranteed to tear. Give the fish time to sear and then turn it just once.

● Finally, consider adding flavor to the fish at the end of cooking. A sauce, salsa, glaze or dressing works wonders to enhance what is already a great flavor.

Grilled Tuna Steak
with a Caper Black Olive Salsa

This salsa gives a fantastic burst of flavor on the grilled tuna. It also makes an interesting and zippy crostini topping.

1 cup pitted Kalamata olives, chopped

¼ cup capers, rinsed and roughly chopped

pinch crushed red pepper flakes

1 tomato, finely chopped

2 tablespoons red wine vinegar

¼ cup extra virgin olive oil

3 tablespoons chopped fresh basil

4 tuna steaks (5 to 6 ounces each), about 1-inch thick

2 tablespoons vegetable oil

salt

freshly ground black pepper

1. Pre-heat your grill (gas, charcoal or stovetop) until it is hot. It is hot when you can hold your hand 1 to 2 inches off the grate for no more than 2 to 3 seconds before you want to pull it away. Make sure the grill is clean before you cook.

2. While the grill is pre-heating, prepare the salsa. Combine the chopped olives, capers, pepper flakes, tomato, vinegar, olive oil and basil in a small bowl. Set the salsa aside while you grill the tuna.

3. Dry the tuna steaks well with a paper towel and brush both sides with the vegetable oil. Season the steaks well with salt and pepper.

4. Grill the steaks for 4 to 6 minutes per side, turning the steaks 90 degrees once on each side to create crosshatch grill marks. Four minutes on each side will give you medium-rare tuna with a pink center. If you prefer your tuna well done, simply cook it longer.

5. Serve immediately with a spoonful of salsa on top.

TIP The most common varieties of tuna are bluefin, yellowfin and albacore. Bluefin tuna has a dark red flesh at maturity, is higher in fat and has a stronger flavor. It is the tuna of choice for fresh tuna preparations. Yellowfin (also known as Ahi) has a pale pink colored flesh, a milder flavor and is less expensive than bluefin. Albacore has the lightest colored flesh and the mildest flavor of these three varieties. It is usually sold canned.

Tequila Lime Grilled Shrimp

Just the name of this dish sounds like a party! Shrimp are fun and festive for outdoor gatherings. Here you can marinate the shrimp and skewer them ahead of time. After just a few minutes on the grill, the shrimp are ready to serve and you're ready to join the party yourself.

SERVES

4

½ cup tequila

zest of one lime

¼ cup fresh lime juice

2 cloves garlic, minced

¼ cup cilantro leaves, chopped (plus more for garnish)

⅛ teaspoon hot red pepper flakes

½ cup olive oil

1½ pounds jumbo shrimp, deveined but shells left on (about 32 shrimp)

salt

lime wedges (for serving)

1. Combine the tequila, lime zest, lime juice, garlic, cilantro, red pepper flakes and olive oil in a zipper sealable plastic bag or a mixing bowl. Add the shrimp and mix together to coat all the shrimp in the marinade. Refrigerate and marinate for 30 minutes to as long as 4 hours.

2. Pre-heat a stovetop grill pan or an outdoor grill until you cannot hold your hand 1 to 2 inches above the grilling surface for more than 2 to 3 seconds.

3. Remove the shrimp from the marinade and arrange on skewers. If using wooden skewers, be sure to soak the skewers in water for at least 30 minutes to prevent them from burning over an outdoor grill.

4. Grill the shrimp for 2 to 3 minutes per side, seasoning with salt, or until cooked through but not overcooked. Serve with lime wedges and fresh cilantro leaves if desired.

 TIP When grilling shrimp, it is best to leave the shell on. The shell protects the shrimp from drying out on the grill, and adds more shrimp flavor. Make a slit down the back of the shell in order to devein the shrimp and to allow the marinade to soak into the flesh.

Grilled Salmon
with Teriyaki Glaze

The key to success in this recipe is only putting the teriyaki glaze on after you grill the salmon. Putting it on ahead of time would cause a sticky mess on your grill and make the salmon hard to turn without tearing.

4 teaspoons soy sauce

¼ cup orange juice

3 tablespoons honey

1 clove garlic, minced

½ teaspoon fresh gingerroot, minced

½ teaspoon sesame seeds, toasted

pinch hot red pepper flakes

4 fillets of salmon (5 to 6 ounces each)

vegetable oil

salt

freshly ground black pepper

1. Pre-heat your grill (gas, charcoal or stovetop) until it is hot. It is hot when you can hold your hand 1 to 2 inches off the grate for no more than 2 to 3 seconds before you want to pull it away. Make sure the grill is clean before you cook.

2. While the grill is pre-heating, make the teriyaki glaze. Combine the soy sauce, orange juice, honey, garlic, gingerroot, sesame seeds and red pepper flakes in a small saucepan. Bring to a boil and then simmer gently for 5 minutes to thicken slightly. Set the glaze aside.

3. Dry the salmon well with a paper towel and brush both sides with the vegetable oil. Season the fish well with salt and pepper. Place the flesh side of the salmon face down on the grill. Grill for 3 minutes. Flip the fish and then brush immediately with the teriyaki glaze. Grill for another 3 minutes and then remove. Brush with more glaze before serving.

Grilled Swordfish
with Lemon Walnut Vinaigrette

This swordfish is served with a chunky nut vinaigrette which is also great on grilled asparagus. Asparagus, incidentally would be a very nice accompaniment to this dish.

SERVES

4

1 tablespoon finely chopped shallots

½ teaspoon finely chopped lemon zest

2 tablespoons lemon juice

1 tablespoon olive oil

2 tablespoons walnut oil

¼ teaspoon salt

freshly ground black pepper

¼ cup walnut halves, toasted

4 swordfish steaks (5 to 6 ounces each)

vegetable oil

salt

freshly ground black pepper

1 tablespoon chopped fresh parsley

1. Pre-heat your grill (gas, charcoal or stovetop) until it is hot. It is hot when you can hold your hand 1 to 2 inches off the grate for no more than 2 to 3 seconds before you want to pull it away. Make sure the grill is clean.

2. While the grill is heating, prepare the vinaigrette. Combine the shallots, lemon zest, lemon juice, olive oil, walnut oil, salt and pepper in a bowl. Stir in the walnuts. Set the vinaigrette aside while you grill the swordfish.

3. Dry the fish well with a paper towel and brush both sides with the vegetable oil. Season the fish well with salt and pepper.

4. Grill the steaks for 4 to 5 minutes per side, turning the steaks 90 degrees once on each side to create crosshatch grill marks if desired.

5. Serve immediately with the vinaigrette and some chopped parsley on top.

 When buying swordfish, look at the color of the strip of darker meat in the steak. It should be a cherry red color, rather than brown.

Basic Halibut en Papillote
with Lemon and White Wine

To cook en papillote means to cook in parchment paper. All the ingredients are wrapped up together and the moisture trapped inside steams the fish. It's a perfect way to cook fish that are more delicate and harder to handle. You can even serve the fish in its parchment wrapping, like a present on a plate. Healthy, easy, presents... what's not to love?

4 fillets of halibut (about 6 ounces each)

salt

freshly ground black pepper

1 lemon, sliced

8 sprigs fresh thyme

1 egg white, lightly beaten

4 tablespoons butter

½ cup white wine

1. Pre-heat the oven to 400° F.

2. Cut out 4 large squares of parchment paper – about 13-inches by 15-inches each. Place a fillet of halibut on one half of each piece of paper. Season the fish very well with salt and pepper. Top each fillet with lemon slices and thyme sprigs. Brush the outer rim of the parchment squares with the beaten egg white. Dot each fillet with 1 tablespoon of butter and sprinkle 2 tablespoons of white wine on each piece of fish.

3. Fold up each parchment square by folding one half of the paper over onto the other half and pressing the edges together. Make a series of straight folds on the outer rim of the squares to seal the edges together.

4. Place the four packages of fish onto a baking sheet and bake in the oven for 10 to 12 minutes. The packages should be puffed up and slightly browned when fully cooked. The fish should feel firm to the touch (you can carefully press on the fish through the paper).

5. You can serve these simply with the parchment paper cut open to reveal the insides, have your guests cut open the packages at the table or remove the parchment completely, transferring the tasty insides to a plate.

Recipe Explained!

● The components required to cook fish en papillote are: a nice fillet of fish, some additional ingredients to provide flavor, a liquid to create steam, and (optionally) some fat to enhance the finished sauce. Once you have all your ingredients, the most challenging part of cooking en papillote is making sure the folds you make around the edges are tight enough to hold in the steam. There are a few tricks that help create the tight seal required

● First of all, using an egg white wash helps "glue" the paper edges together. I like to brush the perimeter of the parchment

with egg white before I add any liquid to the package. The egg white wash helps to keep the liquid from running off the paper a little, but more importantly putting the egg white wash on first allows you to fold the edges of the paper immediately after adding the liquid, not giving it time to escape.

● Secondly, overlap each fold of the paper. Make an initial fold on one corner of the parchment, and then start the second fold in the middle of the first fold. (see photos on opposite page) Repeat the folds all the way around the fish and then twist the final fold to help keep it closed.

● You won't be able to see the fish cooking through the parchment, so you have to judge whether the fish is cooked by experience, by touching to feel if the fish is firm and by gauging 10 minutes at 400° F for every inch of fish.

● Once cooked, the sauce has already been prepared in the parchment pouch. If you choose to serve the fish without the parchment, be sure to pour all that juice over the fish before serving.

Salmon en Papillote
with Shallots, Tomatoes and Basil

The pink hue of the salmon and the red tomatoes make this such a pretty package to open. Serve this with a nice room temperature potato salad and perhaps a crisp glass of rosé wine for a delicious summer meal.

SERVES

4

4 fillets of salmon (about 6 ounces each)

salt

freshly ground black pepper

1 shallot, minced (about ¼ cup)

2 cups cherry tomatoes, halved

1 to 2 tablespoons olive oil

4 tablespoons fresh basil, sliced

1 egg white, lightly beaten

1. Pre-heat the oven to 400° F.

2. Cut out 4 large squares of parchment paper – about 13-inches by 15-inches each. Place a fillet of salmon on one half of each piece of paper. Season the fish very well with salt and pepper. Toss the shallot and cherry tomatoes together with the olive oil and divide them among the fillets, placing the tomatoes and shallots right on top of the fish. Sprinkle each fillet with the basil.

3. Fold up each parchment square by first brushing the outer rim of the parchment squares with the beaten egg white, and then fold one half of the paper over onto the other half and press the edges together. Make a series of straight folds on the outer rim of the squares to seal the edges together.

4. Place the four packages of fish onto a baking sheet and bake in the oven for 10 to 12 minutes. The packages should be puffed up and slightly browned when fully cooked. The fish should feel firm to the touch (you can carefully press on the fish through the paper).

5. You can serve these simply with the parchment paper cut open to reveal the insides, have your guests cut open the packages at the table or remove the parchment completely, transferring the tasty insides to a plate.

TIP

Most Atlantic salmon are farmed, whereas the majority of Pacific salmon are wild-caught. Wild-caught salmon are more organic than farm raised salmon, which are sometimes fed antibiotics, chemicals and even dyes to give them a brighter color. Pacific salmon varieties include King (Chinook), Sockeye (Red), Coho (Silver), Pink (Humpback) and Chum (Dog).

Swordfish en Papillote
with Fennel, Potatoes and Black Olives

Swordfish lends itself to any method of preparation. It's great on the grill, but it's just as nice wrapped up and steamed in parchment.

SERVES

4

1 to 2 tablespoons olive oil

1 bulb fennel, thinly sliced

4 to 5 fingerling potatoes, thinly sliced (no thicker than ¼-inch slices)

salt

freshly ground black pepper

4 swordfish steaks (about 5 to 6 ounces each)

16 oil-cured black olives, pitted and roughly chopped

2 tablespoons fresh parsley leaves

4 tablespoons butter

1 egg white, lightly beaten

¼ to ½ cup vermouth (or dry white wine)

1. Pre-heat the oven to 400° F.

2. Heat a large skillet over medium heat. Add olive oil and cook the fennel and potatoes for 6 minutes. Season with salt and pepper and set aside to cool.

3. Cut out 4 large squares of parchment paper – about 13-inches by 15-inches each. Place a swordfish steak on one half of each piece of paper. Season the fish very well with salt and pepper. Arrange the fennel and potatoes on top of the fish. Distribute the black olives and parsley leaves on top, and finish by dotting each fillet with 1 tablespoon of butter. Brush the outer rim of the parchment squares with the beaten egg white. Sprinkle 1 to 2 tablespoons of vermouth over each steak.

4. Fold up each parchment square by folding one half of the paper over onto the other half and press the edges together. Make a series of straight folds on the outer rim of the squares to seal the edges together.

5. Place the four packages of fish onto a baking sheet and bake in the oven for 12 to 15 minutes. The packages should be puffed up and slightly browned when fully cooked. The fish should feel firm to the touch (you can carefully press on the fish through the paper).

6. You can serve these simply with the parchment paper cut open to reveal the insides, have your guests cut open the packages at the table or remove the parchment completely, transferring the tasty insides to a plate.

Red Snapper en Papillote
with Mango, Corn and Lime

Red Snapper is one of the most popular white fish. It has a firm flesh and a sweet, nutty flavor that stands up to this mango-corn salsa. The salsa is also excellent served raw with grilled red snapper.

SERVES

4

1 to 2 tablespoons olive oil

½ red onion, finely chopped (about ½ cup)

½ Jalapeño pepper, finely chopped

½ red bell pepper, finely chopped

1 cup fresh corn kernels

2 mangoes, peeled and chopped (about 1 cup)

salt

freshly ground black pepper

4 fillets of red snapper (about 5 to 6 ounces each)

½ cup fresh lime juice

1 egg white, lightly beaten

1. Pre-heat the oven to 400° F.

2. Heat a skillet over medium heat. Add the olive oil and cook the red onions, Jalapeño and red pepper for 2 to 3 minutes. Remove the skillet from the heat and stir in the corn and mango. Season with salt and pepper.

3. Cut out 4 large squares of parchment paper – about 13-inches by 15-inches each. Place a fillet on one half of each piece of paper. Season the fish very well with salt and pepper. Top each fillet with the corn and mango mixture. Brush the outer rim of the parchment squares with the beaten egg white. Sprinkle 2 tablespoons of lime juice over each fillet.

4. Fold up each parchment square by folding one half of the paper over onto the other half and press the edges together. Make a series of straight folds on the outer rim of the squares to seal the edges together.

5. Place the four packages of fish onto a baking sheet and bake in the oven for 10 to 12 minutes. The packages should be puffed up and slightly browned when fully cooked. The fish should feel firm to the touch (you can carefully press on the fish through the paper).

6. You can serve these simply with the parchment paper cut open to reveal the insides, have your guests cut open the packages at the table or remove the parchment completely, transferring the tasty insides to a plate.

Trout en Papillote
with Orange Butter and Asparagus

Trout can be served whole or as fillets. Since a normal portion is one trout per person, this recipe uses whole trout, but fillets can be substituted if you prefer.

1 to 2 tablespoons olive oil

1 leek, cleaned and thinly sliced

12 stalks of asparagus, sliced on the bias (1½-inch long slices)

2 green onions, sliced

2 tablespoons coarse orange zest

salt

freshly ground black pepper

1 orange, sliced

4 whole trout, cleaned

2 teaspoons butter

½ cup white wine

1 egg white, lightly beaten

1. Pre-heat the oven to 400° F.

2. Heat a skillet over medium heat. Add the olive oil cook the leeks for 2 minutes. Add the asparagus and continue to cook for 2 minutes. Toss in the green onions, orange zest, salt and pepper and remove the skillet from the heat. Set aside and let cool.

3. Cut out 4 large squares of parchment paper – about 13-inches by 15-inches each. Arrange a layer of orange slices on one half of each piece of paper – about 3 slices per paper. Place a trout on the orange slices on each piece of paper. Season the fish very well with salt and pepper both inside and out. Fill the cavity of each trout with the leek and asparagus mixture, dot the filling with 1 teaspoon of butter and sprinkle 1 tablespoon of wine inside each trout. Close up the cavity of the trout.

4. Fold up each parchment square by first brushing the outer rim of the parchment squares with the beaten egg white, and then fold one half of the paper over onto the other half and press the edges together. Make a series of straight folds on the outer rim of the squares to seal the edges together.

5. Place the four packages of fish onto a baking sheet and bake in the oven for 12 to 15 minutes. The packages should be puffed up and slightly browned when fully cooked. The fish should feel firm to the touch (you can carefully press on the fish through the paper).

6. You can serve these simply with the parchment paper cut open to reveal the insides, have your guests cut open the packages at the table or remove the parchment completely, transferring the tasty insides to a plate.

Baked Salmon with Horseradish Crust

When feeding a crowd, it is easier to prepare one large portion of something than to prepare several individual portions. This preparation of salmon is very easy and yet it looks impressive when presented whole and served at the table.

SERVES

8 – 12

1 side Pacific wild salmon (about 3 to 4 pounds)

salt

freshly ground black pepper

1 (6 ounce) jar prepared horseradish

2 tablespoons whole grain mustard

2 lemons, zest and juice

2 cloves garlic, minced

½ cup chopped fresh parsley

2 cups Panko breadcrumbs (for more info on Panko breadcrumbs, see page 207)

3 tablespoons olive oil

2 teaspoons salt

freshly ground black pepper

1. Pre-heat the oven to 400˚ F.

2. Place the salmon, skin side down, on a greased baking sheet, or a baking sheet lined with parchment paper.

3. Season the salmon with salt and freshly ground black pepper. Then spread the horseradish on top, covering the whole salmon.

4. Combine the remaining ingredients in a small bowl. Spread the mixture over the top of the salmon and press down lightly with your hands, adhering the mixture to the salmon using the horseradish as "glue". Transfer the salmon to the oven and bake for 20 minutes or until the fish feels firm to the touch.

5. Cut into portions and serve warm or at room temperature.

TIP Any leftover salmon from this recipe can be flaked and made into a delicious salmon salad.

Vegetables

For too long, vegetables have been an afterthought of the home cook! In this section, you'll learn which vegetables are suited to different cooking techniques, which additional ingredients you'll need to cook the vegetables properly, and the basic rules for sautéing, braising, roasting, grilling or making a gratin with vegetables. Make a vegetable your first thought today!

Basic Sautéed Vegetables

To sauté means:
To cook quickly, over high heat, in a small amount of fat.

Good vegetables to sauté:

Onions

Peppers

Summer Squash (Zucchini, Yellow…)

Winter Squash (Butternut, Pumpkin…)

Carrots

Potatoes

Mushrooms

Spinach and other dark greens (Kale, Chard…)

Asparagus

Cauliflower, Broccoli, Broccoli Rabe and Brussels Sprouts

Other ingredients needed:

Fat for cooking but just enough to cook in – not swim in! Use a fat with a high smoke point (the temperature at which an oil starts to smoke). Vegetable, canola, grapeseed, peanut, or even olive oils are good for sautéing. You can use butter to sauté, but you won't be able to use as high a heat, since butter burns quickly. If you want the flavor of butter, add it at the end of cooking so that you don't run the risk of burning your vegetables.

Additional flavor at the end of cooking. Adding fresh herbs, brown sugar, nuts, or acidic ingredients like citrus juice or vinegar can add a burst of flavor.

Seasoning. Adding salt will cause the vegetables to release liquid. This liquid will inhibit browning. If you want to brown your vegetables when you sauté them, season them with salt only at the end of cooking.

Rules for sautéing vegetables:

Almost always pre-heat the pan before adding the oil or the vegetables. Keep the pan on the heat for at least 1 to 2 minutes before adding the ingredients. Occasionally, ingredients like garlic or hot red pepper flakes are heated up in a cold pan, but usually the pan must be pre-heated before adding any ingredient and ultimately a hot pan will be a necessity while sautéing.

Never overcrowd the pan. In order for the vegetables to cook evenly, they must all make contact with the pan. When you overcrowd a pan, moisture accumulates in the pan because it can't evaporate. Moisture inhibits browning, so overcrowding will prevent the vegetables from acquiring any color.

Toss the vegetables while they cook. To sauté means "to jump" in French, and that's exactly what the vegetables should do in the pan – jump around. If you're not comfortable tossing the vegetables by flipping the pan, simply toss them around with a spoon.

Equipment needed:

A large skillet with sloped sides

Sautéed Broccoli Rabe
with Garlic and Feta

Also known as rapini, broccoli rabe has a stem with spiked leaves and little buds that look like broccoli. Despite its name, broccoli rabe is more closely related to turnips than to broccoli. Sometimes you'll even hear it called turnip broccoli. Look for bright green leaves that are crisp and not wilted or yellowing.

SERVES

4

2 bunches broccoli rabe

1 tablespoon olive oil

2 cloves garlic, sliced

⅛ teaspoon hot red pepper flakes

¼ teaspoon salt

⅓ cup crumbled Feta cheese

1. Prepare the broccoli rabe by pulling the leaves and florets away from the central stem or core into smaller sections. Cut off and discard any very thick stems.

2. Add the olive oil, garlic and hot red pepper flakes to a very large skillet and heat over medium heat. (Adding the garlic and olive oil before heating the pan allows a gentler flavor of the garlic and pepper flake to be released.) Just as the garlic starts to color, add the broccoli rabe and season with salt. Sauté until it starts to turn limp – about 4 to 6 minutes. The liquid released from the broccoli rabe should be enough to prevent the garlic from burning.

3. If you like your vegetables very tender, add a couple tablespoons of water to the skillet to help it steam.

4. When the broccoli rabe is tender to your liking, turn it out into a serving dish and crumble the Feta cheese over the top.

TIP Rinse broccoli rabe under cold water to clean it before cooking. Shake most of the water off. The remaining droplets of water will help the broccoli rabe steam and wilt.

Sautéed Zucchini
with Lemon and Mint

Although zucchini can grow to be several feet in length, smaller zucchini have more flavor and are less fibrous. You can find green zucchini, yellow zucchini or round globe zucchini and any variety would work nicely in this recipe.

SERVES

4

2 teaspoons olive oil

2 medium zucchini, halved lengthwise and sliced (¼-inch slices)

1 clove garlic, minced

1 lemon, zest and juice

2 tablespoons chopped fresh mint

¼ teaspoon salt

freshly ground black pepper

1. Heat a large skillet over medium-high heat for a minute. Add the olive oil and sauté the zucchini until lightly browned and just tender – about 4 to 5 minutes.

2. Add the garlic and lemon zest and toss for a minute or two, or until the garlic becomes fragrant. Remove the skillet from the heat, add the lemon juice and mint, and season with salt and pepper.

Sautéed Cauliflower
with Toasted Pine Nuts and Golden Raisins

Sautéing is such a nice change from the standard preparation of boiling or steaming cauliflower. Once you've tried it, it might quickly become your favorite way to serve cauliflower.

SERVES

4

¼ cup pine nuts

1 head cauliflower

2 to 3 tablespoons olive oil, divided

1 clove garlic, minced

¼ cup golden raisins

½ teaspoon salt

freshly ground black pepper

2 tablespoons chopped fresh parsley

1. Pre-heat the oven to 350° F. Spread the pine nuts out on a baking sheet and toast in the oven until lightly browned – about 10 minutes – and set aside.

2. Prepare the cauliflower: Remove any outer leaves and slice the head into quarters. Slice the quarters about ½-inch thick. Some of the florets will fall apart at this point. Don't worry about that. The important thing is that all the pieces of cauliflower are no more than ½-inch thick.

3. Heat a large skillet over medium to medium-high heat. Add 1 tablespoon of the olive oil and sauté the cauliflower in batches until tender and lightly browned – about 3 to 4 minutes. Do not overcrowd the skillet, or you will have a difficult time browning the cauliflower. Transfer the cooked cauliflower to a bowl until all the cauliflower is done.

4. After the last batch of cauliflower has been sautéed, add another tablespoon of olive oil to the pan. Add the pine nuts, garlic and raisins and cook for just a minute. Return the cauliflower to the skillet, season with salt and freshly ground black pepper, and toss everything together to re-heat. Add the parsley and serve.

TIP

All the members of the Brassica family (cabbage, broccoli, cauliflower, etc.) tend to release unpleasant odors if cooked for too long – generally over 5 minutes. Try to keep the cooking time for these vegetables to less than 5 minutes when possible. If you add a bay leaf to the pan while cooking, these odors are lessened. Remember to remove the bay leaf before serving.

Sautéed Butternut Squash
with Sage and Cinnamon

I love the flavors of butternut squash and sage together, and the sweet squash combined with the cinnamon is a perfect pairing. A tasty variation of this recipe is to continue cooking the squash and other ingredients until very soft, and then purée everything with a little cream.

SERVES

4

1 tablespoon olive oil

6 leaves fresh sage

1 butternut squash, peeled and chopped (1-inch cubes; about 3 cups)

½ teaspoon ground cinnamon

½ teaspoon salt

freshly ground black pepper

1 tablespoon butter

1. Heat a large skillet over medium to medium-high heat. Add the olive oil and fry the sage leaves for 30 to 60 seconds. The sage leaves should curl a little and smell quite fragrant. Remove the sage leaves, give them a rough chop and set aside.

2. Add the butternut squash to the skillet and sauté until tender to a knifepoint – about 6 minutes. Toss in the cinnamon, salt and pepper and continue to sauté for another 1 to 2 minutes. Finish by returning the fried sage leaves and tossing in the butter, swirling the skillet until the butter melts. Serve as a side dish, or try this recipe tossed with cooked pasta and some extra olive oil.

Basic Braised Vegetables

To braise means:
To cook slowly for a long period of time, over low heat, partially covered in liquid and in a covered pot.

Good vegetables to sauté:

Bitter Greens (kale, chard, collard greens, endive, radicchio)

Onions

Fennel

Celery

Tomatoes

Green Beans

Cabbage

Brussels Sprouts

Carrots

Other ingredients needed:

Braising liquid. You can use water or any flavorful liquid. Chicken or vegetable stocks are common, but you can also use juices (orange, apple, tomato), wine, beer, coconut milk, etc.

Additional Flavor. Often, additional flavor is added at the beginning of the cooking process, by starting with an ingredient like bacon, garlic, hot red pepper flakes, anchovies, etc. You can also add a burst of flavor at the end of cooking by adding citrus juice, grated or crumbled cheese, etc.

Seasoning. Always season your braised vegetables with salt at the end of cooking. Vegetables and the liquid in which they are cooking will reduce during the cooking process. Seasoning at the end helps prevent over-salting.

Rules for braising vegetables:

Don't add too much liquid. There should be just enough liquid to help the vegetables cook, but it should almost disappear by the time the cooking is over.

The heat should never be higher than medium.

Browning first adds flavor and color to the finished dish.

The vegetables should be covered with a lid for the majority of the cooking time.

Understand that green vegetables will not keep their bright green color when braised, but they will be delicious.

Equipment needed:

A sauté pan or stockpot with a lid

Maple Glazed Carrots

This dish is a variation on braising. In this recipe, the carrots do not get covered in the cooking process because the goal is to have the liquid evaporate and create a glaze.

SERVES

4

2 tablespoons butter, divided

6 medium carrots, peeled and sliced on the bias (½-inch slices; about 3 cups)

¼ cup maple syrup

½ teaspoon salt

freshly ground black pepper

water (about ½ cup)

1 tablespoon fresh chives, chopped

1. Heat a large skillet over medium to medium-high heat. Add 1 tablespoon of the butter and sauté the carrots for just 2 to 3 minutes.

2. Add the remaining tablespoon of butter, maple syrup, salt and pepper and just enough water to partially cover the carrots. Cook over high heat for 8 minutes. The water will evaporate and reduce, leaving a glaze. Once the water has evaporated, toss the carrots to distribute the glaze evenly, and continue to cook until the carrots are tender. Toss in the chopped chives and serve.

TIP

When buying carrots, choose carrots with bright, feathery green tops. This is a sign that the carrots are fresh. Cut the green tops off the carrots before storing them at home, however, because the greens will pull moisture from the root and cause the carrot to wilt prematurely.

Braised Green Beans
with Tomatoes

The beans will lose their bright color in this recipe, but they will be delicious.

1 tablespoon olive oil

1 onion, chopped (about 1 cup)

1 clove garlic, minced

1½ pounds green beans, tough ends trimmed

1 (28 ounce) can diced tomatoes

2 teaspoons fennel seed, crushed (optional)

½ teaspoon salt

freshly ground black pepper

1. Heat a large sauté pan or stockpot over medium heat. Add the olive oil and cook the onion until it softens – about 5 minutes. Add the garlic and continue to cook for another minute.

2. Add the green beans, tomatoes, fennel seed (if using) and salt and bring to a simmer. Cover and cook for 30 minutes, stirring occasionally.

3. Season with salt and freshly ground black pepper and serve.

TIP

The tough end of a green bean can be fibrous and unpleasant to eat. Simply trim off the top ¼-inch of the beans, leaving the pretty curly tail on the other end.

Braised Cabbage
with Bacon and Garlicky Breadcrumbs

Cabbage alone may not excite your family, but start with some bacon and end with crunchy garlicky crumbs and you might get their attention! This dish takes a while to prepare, but you can get plenty of other tasks accomplished while it cooks in the oven.

SERVES

6 – 8

1 tablespoon olive oil

2 slices bacon, chopped (1-inch pieces)

½ white onion, sliced (about ½ cup)

2 carrots, sliced on the bias (½-inch slices)

pinch hot red pepper flakes

1 medium head of green cabbage,
cut into wedges (about 1½ pounds)

½ teaspoon salt

freshly ground black pepper

¼ cup chicken stock

6 ounces Ciabatta or Italian bread
(about 3 to 4 slices)

3 tablespoons butter

1 clove garlic, sliced

1. Pre-heat the oven to 350° F.

2. Heat a large oven-safe sauté pan or Dutch oven over medium heat. Add the olive oil and cook the bacon until it starts to turn a little crispy. Add the onions and carrots with the hot red pepper flakes, and cook for 6 to 7 minutes. Add the cabbage wedges to the pan and tuck them down underneath the onions and carrots. Season with salt and pepper and pour in the chicken stock. Cover with a tight-fitting lid and transfer the pan to the oven for 1½ hours, or until the cabbage is tender.

3. While the cabbage is braising, process the bread in a food processor to make coarse crumbs (you should have about 3 cups of crumbs). Melt the butter in a small saucepan with the garlic slices. Simmer very gently for 2 to 3 minutes. Toss the breadcrumbs in a large bowl with the garlic and melted butter, season with salt and pepper and toast in the oven until golden brown and crispy – about 10 to 15 minutes. It is nice if the breadcrumbs are warm when you serve them, so prepare them near the end of the braising time.

4. Serve the cabbage in a serving dish with the garlicky breadcrumbs sprinkled over the top.

Braised Caramelized Fennel

Fennel is one of Italy's most popular vegetables. With a texture similar to celery, and a flavor reminiscent of licorice, fennel can really add interest to a meal. It is delicious served with seafood as well as with hearty sausages or meats.

1 tablespoon olive oil

2 to 3 bulbs fennel, stalks removed and cut into wedges, feathery fronds reserved for garnish

½ cup white wine

1 tablespoon balsamic vinegar

3 sprigs fresh thyme

½ teaspoon salt

freshly ground black pepper

1. Heat a large sauté pan over medium heat. Add the olive oil and brown the fennel wedges on both sides – about 4 to 5 minutes.

2. Add the white wine, balsamic vinegar and fresh thyme sprigs. Cover and braise on low to medium-low heat for 30 to 40 minutes.

3. Remove the thyme sprigs. Season with salt and pepper and serve, garnishing with the feathery fennel fronds if desired.

TIP Try sprinkling on some orange zest at the end for a fresh finish.

Basic Potato Gratin

Whether you call it Gratin Dauphinois or scalloped potatoes, there are few vegetable dishes as heart-warming as a potato gratin. It is a beautiful oven-to-table dish, which is sure to please everyone. Who doesn't like a potato gratin?

2 to 2½ cups half and half, divided

2 cloves of garlic, smashed flat

½ teaspoon salt

freshly ground black pepper

¼ teaspoon ground nutmeg

2 pounds potatoes (about 6), peeled and sliced (⅛-inch slices)

1 cup grated Parmesan cheese

1 tablespoon butter, cut into small cubes

1. Combine 1½ cups of half and half with the garlic in a shallow oven-safe skillet or gratin pan and bring to a simmer on the stovetop. Simmer for 15 minutes. Season with the salt, pepper, and nutmeg.

2. Remove the pan from the heat and add the sliced potatoes, separating the slices and pressing them into the cream to ensure they are all distributed evenly. Add enough of the remaining half and half to just cover all the potatoes. Top with the Parmesan cheese, dot with butter, and transfer the pan to the oven.

3. Bake in the oven for 50 to 60 minutes, or until the potatoes are tender and nicely browned on top.

Sweet Potato and Apple Gratin

This is a nice change from a standard potato gratin. The sweet apple is a nice surprise underneath the first layer of potatoes, and the sweet potato gives a little color to what is usually a pale dish.

2 to 2½ cups half and half, divided

2 cloves of garlic, smashed flat

½ teaspoon salt

freshly ground black pepper

¼ teaspoon ground nutmeg

2 pounds sweet potatoes (about 6), peeled and sliced (⅛-inch slices)

1 pound Granny Smith apples (about 3), peeled, cored and cut (¼-inch slices)

½ cup Panko breadcrumbs (or regular breadcrumbs)

½ cup grated Parmesan cheese

1 tablespoon butter, cut into small cubes

1. Pre-heat the oven to 400° F.

2. Combine 1½ cups of half and half with the garlic in a shallow oven-safe skillet or gratin pan and bring to a simmer on the stovetop. Simmer for 15 minutes. Season with the salt, pepper and nutmeg.

3. Remove the pan from the heat and add a layer of the sliced sweet potatoes, separating the slices and pressing them into the cream to ensure they are all distributed evenly. Add a layer of the apples and distribute evenly. Repeat with the sweet potatoes and apples until you have run out of ingredients, ending with a layer of sweet potatoes. Add enough of the remaining half and half to just cover all the sweet potatoes. Top with the Parmesan cheese and Panko breadcrumbs, dot with butter and transfer the pan to the oven.

4. Bake in the oven for 60 to 70 minutes, or until the sweet potatoes and apples are tender and nicely browned on top.

TIP

Panko breadcrumbs are Japanese breadcrumbs. They have a coarser, lighter, crispier texture and almost look like flakes. If you can't find Panko breadcrumbs, you can substitute regular breadcrumbs or toasted and crushed saltine crackers.

Cauliflower and Broccoli Gratin

This recipe makes a lot of food, but it was written to use a whole head of cauliflower and a whole bunch of broccoli. It can easily be halved and baked in one dish.

SERVES

8 - 12

1 large head cauliflower, broken into large florets (about 2 pounds)

1 large bunch broccoli, broken into large florets (about 1½ pounds)

¼ cup butter

¼ cup flour

4 cups milk

1 cup grated Cheddar cheese

1 cup grated Parmesan cheese

2 teaspoons salt

1 teaspoon freshly ground black pepper

¼ cup Panko breadcrumbs (or regular breadcrumbs)

1. Pre-heat the oven to 375° F.

2. Bring a large pot of salted water to a boil. Blanch the cauliflower in the boiling water for 6 to 8 minutes, or until tender. Transfer the blanched cauliflower to a colander with a slotted spoon and immediately run cold water over the cauliflower to stop the cooking process. In the same pot, blanch the broccoli in the boiling water for 3 to 5 minutes, or until tender. Transfer the broccoli into the same colander as the cauliflower with a slotted spoon, and immediately run cold water over the vegetables again to stop the cooking process.

3. Heat a medium sized saucepan over medium heat. Melt the butter and, once melted, add the flour to the pan. Stir well to coat all the flour with butter and cook for 2 minutes over medium heat. Whisk the milk into the saucepan and bring the mixture to a boil. Reduce the heat to a simmer and simmer for 3 to 4 minutes. Remove the pan from the heat and add the cheeses, stirring until all the cheese has melted. Season with salt and pepper.

4. Arrange the drained blanched broccoli and cauliflower into two 2-quart baking dishes in an attractive manner with the tops of the florets facing up. Pour the cheese sauce over the top of each dish.

5. Cover the top of each dish with the breadcrumbs and then bake in the oven for 20 to 30 minutes.

Leek and Parmesan Gratin

I do love leeks! This is a beautiful gratin dish without all the cream of the other gratin recipes.

3 large leeks, halved lengthwise, cleaned, and sliced into logs (2½-inches long)

1 tablespoon butter

1 tablespoon olive oil

⅔ cup chicken stock

¼ cup coarse breadcrumbs

¼ cup grated Gruyère cheese

¼ cup grated Parmesan cheese

salt

freshly ground black pepper

1. Pre-heat the oven to 425° F.

2. Heat an oven-safe sauté pan or gratin pan over medium-high heat. Add the butter and olive oil and brown the leeks in the pan, cut side down. They should fit relatively tightly together in the pan. Turn the leeks over and season with salt and pepper. Add enough chicken stock to barely cover the leeks. Cover the pan with a lid and lower the heat to a simmer. Braise the leeks for 50 minutes or until tender to a knifepoint.

3. Remove the lid and increase the heat. Cook until almost all the liquid has disappeared.

4. Combine the breadcrumbs and cheeses and sprinkle this mixture on top of the leeks. Transfer the pan to the oven and bake until the cheese has melted and is light brown in color – about 20 minutes.

Creamy Spinach Gratin

Creamed spinach is such a treat. Here creamed spinach gets baked with crumbs and cheese on top. If you don't want to use fresh spinach or don't have it on hand, you can substitute frozen spinach.

3 pounds fresh baby spinach

1 tablespoon olive oil

½ onion, finely chopped (about ½ cup)

2 cloves of garlic, smashed flat

1½ cups half and half

½ teaspoon salt

freshly ground black pepper

¼ teaspoon ground nutmeg

½ cup grated Parmesan cheese

½ cup Panko breadcrumbs
(or regular breadcrumbs)

1. Pre-heat the oven to 425° F.

2. Pre-heat a large sauté pan or stockpot over medium heat. Wash the spinach well and shake off any excess water – although a few drops left on the spinach is a good thing. Working in batches, place the spinach in the pan and cover with a lid. Let the spinach wilt for just a minute or two, tossing with tongs periodically. Transfer the wilted spinach to a colander and let it cool. When it has cooled enough to handle, squeeze out as much excess water from the spinach as possible. Roughly chop and set aside.

3. Return the sauté pan or stockpot to the stove and heat over medium-high heat. Add the olive oil and sauté the onion until translucent – about 5 minutes. Add the smashed garlic cloves and cook for another 2 to 3 minutes. Add the half and half and bring to a simmer on the stovetop. Simmer gently for 15 minutes. Remove from the heat. Season with the salt, pepper and nutmeg. Add the spinach to the pot and stir to combine.

4. Transfer the mixture to a 1-quart baking dish or gratin pan, and top with both the Parmesan cheese and breadcrumbs.

5. Bake in the oven for 30 minutes, or until the gratin is bubbling and nicely browned on top. If the gratin is browning too quickly, loosely tent with aluminum foil.

TIP

One pound of fresh spinach = 1 cup of cooked spinach = 5 ounces frozen spinach. You can substitute 3 (5-ounce) packages of frozen spinach for the fresh spinach in this recipe.

Basic Roasted Vegetables

To roast means:
To cook by surrounding the food with dry heat, usually in an oven.

Good vegetables to roast:

Onions

Garlic

Potatoes

Beets

Carrots

Turnips

Tomatoes

Eggplant

Peppers

Mushrooms

Summer Squash (zucchini, yellow, etc…)

Winter Squash (butternut, acorn, etc…)

Brassica (cauliflower, broccoli, Brussels sprouts, etc…)

Other ingredients needed:

A fat to coat the vegetables. This helps prevent the vegetables from drying out, helps to brown the vegetables and adds flavor (depending on what fat you use).

Additional flavor. Dried herbs can be tossed with the vegetables before roasting to add flavor. At the end of the roasting process, adding a little meat or chicken broth, or tossing in some fresh herbs, vinegar, citrus juice, or a grating of Parmesan cheese are also good ways to add flavor.

Seasoning. Always season your vegetables with salt. When roasting, you should season the vegetables at the beginning of the cooking process. Roasting pulls moisture out of vegetables and concentrates their flavor. The salt will help.

Rules for roasting vegetables:

You can roast at a high temperature (400° F) or slow roast at a low temperature (200° F). High heat roasting gives a crispier exterior and browns foods. Low temperature roasting concentrates flavors over a longer period of time. Unless that time is very long, there will be very little crisping or browning of foods.

Never cover food with a lid when roasting. Covering traps steam and the food inside will not have a crisp exterior. Suddenly, you'll be braising!

Cut vegetables into uniform sizes so that everything cooks evenly.

Mix vegetables together that have similar roasting times Otherwise, start with the longest cooking vegetable and add other vegetables in order of how long they will take to cook. The more dense the vegetable, the longer it takes to cook.

Keep vegetables in a single layer when roasting, rather than piling them up.

Toss once. About half way through cooking, give the vegetables a turn so that all sides of the vegetables are exposed to the same heat.

Equipment needed:

A roasting pan or large rimmed baking sheet.

Roasted Red Potatoes
with Rosemary

Roasted potatoes are a classic that can be served with breakfast, lunch or dinner.

2 pounds small red-skinned potatoes, cut into bite-sized pieces

2 to 3 tablespoons olive oil

1 teaspoon salt

freshly ground black pepper

4 cloves garlic, smashed

2 sprigs fresh rosemary, finely chopped, plus more for garnish

½ lemon

1. Pre-heat the oven to 425° F.

2. Bring a large pot of salted water to a boil. Cut the potatoes into even chunks and par-boil the potatoes for 5 minutes. Drain and toss the potatoes with the olive oil, salt, pepper, smashed garlic cloves and rosemary. Spread out into a single layer on a baking sheet, being careful not to overcrowd the pan.

3. Roast for 40 minutes, or until the potatoes are nicely browned, crispy, but tender inside. Shake the pan halfway through to redistribute the potatoes.

4. Squeeze half a lemon over the potatoes as soon as they come out of the oven and serve with more fresh rosemary sprigs as garnish.

TIP You can also use large red skinned potatoes for this, cut into wedges for a different look.

Slow Roasted Tomatoes
with Garlic and Herbs

If you have the time to spend on this recipe, these tomatoes will fill your home with a wonderful aroma. The slow roasting concentrates the sugars in the tomatoes, and they are so delicious it will spoil you for tomatoes prepared any other way.

MAKES ROUGHLY

40 tomato halves

4 pounds Roma tomatoes

4 cloves garlic, minced

¼ to ½ cup olive oil

coarse or kosher salt

freshly ground black pepper

1 tablespoon chopped fresh thyme

2 teaspoons finely chopped fresh rosemary (optional)

1. Pre-heat the oven to 225° F.

2. Cut the Roma tomatoes in half and spread out on a baking sheet, cut side up.

3. Drizzle the olive oil generously all over the tomatoes and toss the tomatoes a little to distribute the oil evenly. Sprinkle the minced garlic and chopped herbs over the top and season well with kosher salt and black pepper.

4. Roast for about 5 to 6 hours (yes, 6 hours). Longer is better in this recipe, but if you have to take the tomatoes out early, it's not a disaster.

5. Serve tossed in a pasta dish, spread on crostini or as an accompaniment to chicken, meat or fish.

6. Store in a jar, covered in a little olive oil, in the refrigerator and do your best not to snack on them constantly!

TIP This is best done in the late summer when the tomatoes are at their best. The low heat of the oven will not heat your house up too much, but start early and avoid the peak heat of the day.

Roasted Wild Mushrooms
with Olive Oil and Thyme

As mushrooms lose their moisture they become rubbery. Using high heat to roast them quickly reduces the moisture loss and the olive oil helps prevent the mushrooms from drying out. Roasting these mushrooms on a cedar plank on your outdoor grill would be spectacular.

SERVES

6 – 8

2 pounds mushrooms, any combination of crimini, shiitake, or chanterelles

⅓ cup olive oil

1 teaspoon coarse or kosher salt

freshly ground black pepper

2 tablespoons chopped fresh thyme leaves (or 2 teaspoons dried)

sprigs of fresh thyme, for garnish

1. Pre-heat the oven to 475° F.

2. Prepare the mushrooms: See tip below on washing mushrooms. Remove the tough stems from the shiitake and chanterelle mushrooms. Quarter or halve the mushrooms so they are roughly the same size. Toss all the mushrooms in a large bowl with the olive oil, salt, pepper and fresh thyme. Spread out into a single layer on a baking sheet, being careful not to overcrowd the pan.

3. Roast for 15 minutes, or until the mushrooms are nicely browned, crispy, but tender inside. Shake the pan halfway through to redistribute the mushrooms. Serve with more fresh thyme sprigs as garnish.

TIP

To wash mushrooms or not to wash mushrooms? Good question. Some believe that washing mushrooms causes them to absorb too much water. However, several cooks and food scientists have proven this theory untrue in recent years. The mushrooms actually absorb very little water. Washing mushrooms does leave the mushroom with a wet surface area, but this evaporates quickly in high heat. I compromise – I wash dirty mushrooms; I don't wash clean mushrooms!

Stuffed and Roasted Acorn Squash

All of these flavors, piled high in an acorn squash really capture the essence of autumn. This is a very generous vegetable side dish or a vegetarian main course.

3 acorn squash, halved and seeds removed

3 to 4 thick slices of Italian bread

6 slices of bacon, chopped

1 onion, finely chopped (about 1 cup)

2 ribs celery, chopped (about 1 cup)

1 clove garlic, minced

½ teaspoon dried rubbed sage

½ cup raisins

½ cup chopped pecans, toasted

1 to 2 tablespoons chopped fresh parsley

½ teaspoon salt

freshly ground black pepper

½ cup vegetable or chicken stock

1. Pre-heat the oven to 400° F.

2. Season the cut side of the acorn squash with salt and pepper and place on a baking sheet cut side down. Roast until tender – about 45 minutes.

3. Meanwhile, using a food processor, process the bread slices into coarse breadcrumbs. Set aside.

4. Heat a skillet over medium heat. Add the bacon and cook until crispy. Remove the bacon and set aside. Add the onion and celery to the pan and cook until tender – about 8 minutes. Add the garlic and cook for another minute. Transfer to a mixing bowl.

5. Add the cooked bacon, sage, raisins, pecans, parsley and bread-crumbs to the bowl with the onions and toss well. Season with salt and pepper, and moisten with the stock, tossing again to combine.

6. When the squash is tender, remove the baking sheet from the oven and turn the squash halves over to expose the cut side. Fill each cavity with the stuffing mixture, heaping it as high as you can.

7. Roast in the oven for another 8 to 10 minutes, or until the stuffing is nicely toasted. Serve one-half squash per person.

Brussels Sprouts
with Bacon and Balsamic Reduction

I feel that Brussels sprouts are vegetables that we only come to appreciate in adulthood. I'm not sure how that appreciation develops, but serving the Brussels sprouts with bacon and sweet balsamic vinegar is sure to speed up the process!

SERVES

4 – 6

4 slices bacon, chopped (½-inch pieces)

1½ pounds Brussels sprouts, halved

4 shallots, peeled and cut into wedges

¼ teaspoon salt

freshly ground black pepper

½ cup balsamic vinegar

Parmesan cheese (a block)

1. Pre-heat the oven to 400° F.

2. Heat an oven-safe skillet over medium heat. Add the chopped bacon and cook until the bacon is almost crispy. Remove the bacon with a slotted spoon and set aside.

3. Add the Brussels sprouts and shallots to the skillet, season with salt and pepper and toss. Cook for a minute or two. Deglaze the skillet by adding ¼ cup of water and then transfer the skillet to the oven. Roast in the oven for 20 minutes, or until the sprouts are tender.

4. Meanwhile, simmer the balsamic vinegar over low heat until it has reduced by half and becomes syrupy – about 8 minutes.

5. Remove the sprouts from the oven and toss with the reserved bacon. Serve in a bowl or platter. Drizzle the balsamic reduction over the top and garnish with peelings of Parmesan cheese.

TIP

Pre-made balsamic reduction is readily available in gourmet stores. Pick some up and skip step 4.

Basic Grilled Vegetables

To grill means:
To cook directly on a metal grate over or under radiant heat, as in over a fire or open flame, under a broiler, or on an indoor grill pan.

Good vegetables to grill:

Onions

Mushrooms

Asparagus

Eggplant

Summer Squash (zucchini, yellow)

Peppers

Scallions

Endive

Radicchio

Corn on the cob

Other ingredients needed:

Fat. Though you don't absolutely need a fat to grill, it will give the vegetables a nicer color and flavor if you brush them with an olive oil before grilling. This also helps prevent the food from sticking to the grill.

Seasoning. Always season the vegetables with salt. This can be done while the vegetables cook, since any moisture drawn out by the salt will evaporate immediately.

Additional Flavor. Grilling imparts a smoky flavor to the vegetables, but you can also give grilled vegetables an additional flavor boost with fresh herbs, flavored oils or a vinaigrette after cooking.

Rules for grilling vegetables:

Be sure the grill is well pre-heated. The grill is hot when you can hold your hand near the surface of the grill for no more than 2 to 3 seconds before needing to pull it away.

Most quick cooking vegetables are good vegetables to grill. Vegetables that take longer to cook need to either be thinly sliced or partially cooked before grilling, so that the exterior of the vegetables doesn't burn before the interior is cooked through.

Oil the vegetables to prevent them from sticking on the grill, to help get the best grill marks and to add flavor.

Try to flip the vegetables as little as possible. One turn to get grill marks on both sides is all that is required. Turning the vegetables too often will mess up the grill marks you want to see on the vegetables, plus it can cause the vegetables to fall apart.

Skewering often makes turning vegetables easier. Be sure to soak wooden skewers in water for 20 minutes before using on an open grill.

Equipment needed:

An outdoor grill (charcoal or gas) OR an indoor grill pan

Tongs

Grilled Portobello Mushrooms
with Cilantro Pesto

If you're not a fan of cilantro, replace the cilantro with basil in this recipe and make a traditional pesto. Presto!

1½ cups packed fresh cilantro leaves

½ cup packed fresh parsley leaves

1 clove garlic

2 tablespoons toasted pine nuts, almonds or pistachios

¼ cup grated Parmesan cheese

2 tablespoons lemon juice

¼ to ½ cup extra virgin olive oil

½ teaspoon salt

freshly ground black pepper

4 Portobello mushrooms, stems removed

2 tablespoons olive oil

salt

freshly ground black pepper

1. Pre-heat the outdoor grill for at least 10 to 15 minutes, or pre-heat an indoor grill pan over medium-high heat for 5 minutes.

2. While the grill is pre-heating, make the pesto. Combine the cilantro, parsley and garlic in a food processor and process until finely chopped. Add the pine nuts, Parmesan cheese and lemon juice and process again. With the processor running, drizzle in the olive oil through the feed tube until the pesto comes together as a smooth paste. Season with the salt and pepper and set aside.

3. Brush the Portobello mushrooms on both sides with the olive oil and season well with salt and pepper.

4. Grill mushrooms on the hot grill for 6 minutes per side, or until the mushrooms are tender to the touch. Remove from the grill, slice on the bias and drizzle the pesto over the top.

TIP

Portobello mushrooms are very meaty and make a great vegetarian substitute for a hamburger. Just leave the mushroom whole, spread the pesto on a grilled Kaiser roll, add some butter lettuce and a slice of tomato for a delicious vegetarian main meal.

Grilled Romaine
with Caesar Dressing

Grilling romaine is quick and easy, and can change a normal Caesar salad into something special and unique. You could use a pre-made Caesar dressing for this, but this dressing is very simple and gives such a lovely lemony finish to the grilled romaine. With this recipe you'll have leftover dressing for your next salad as well.

SERVES

4

1 egg yolk

1 tablespoon lemon juice

¼ teaspoon salt

freshly ground black pepper

½ to 1 clove garlic, very finely minced or mashed into a paste

3 anchovy fillets, finely chopped

⅓ cup olive oil

⅓ cup vegetable oil

4 hearts of romaine lettuce

1 to 2 tablespoons olive oil

salt

freshly ground black pepper

1. Pre-heat the outdoor grill for at least 10 to 15 minutes, or pre-heat an indoor grill pan over medium-high heat for 5 minutes.

2. While the grill is pre-heating, make the Caesar dressing. Whisk the egg yolk, lemon juice, salt and pepper together in a bowl. Add the garlic and anchovy and beat to mix in and distribute the flavor. Slowly drizzle in the oils, whisking constantly. Add very slowly at first, so that the ingredients don't separate. Whisk patiently until all the oil has been incorporated.

3. Slice the hearts of romaine in half, lengthwise. Brush the cut surface with olive oil and season with salt and pepper. Grill the romaine halves on a hot grill for 3 minutes per side. Remove from the grill and serve with each half overlapping the other. Drizzle the dressing over the top.

TIP

To make this into a real Caesar preparation, add some croutons and shavings of Parmesan cheese.

Grilled Corn on the Cob
with Chipotle Butter

Corn really must be grilled on an outdoor grill, rather than on an indoor grill pan. Seasoning the kernels before grilling is key to getting the best tasting result.

4 corn on the cob, husks intact

1 tablespoon olive oil

salt

4 tablespoons butter, room temperature

1 Chipotle pepper in adobo, chopped

½ teaspoon salt

1. Pre-heat the outdoor grill for at least 10 to 15 minutes.

2. Remove some of the husks of the corn, but leave a few layers on the cob. Pull those remaining layers back from the kernels and rub the silk off the kernels. Brush the kernels with olive oil, and season with salt. Pull the husks back over the kernels and wrap up tightly.

3. Using a food processor, or just a fork, combine the butter and the Chipotle in adobo. Mix well to distribute the Chipotle throughout the butter. Add the salt and mix again.

4. Grill the corn in the husks for 15 to 20 minutes, rotating occasionally. The husks will become charred. Remove the corn and let it sit for a minute or two. Using a hand towel to protect yourself from the heat, peel back the husks and tear them off the cobs. If desired, place the corn back on the grill for a minute or two, just to get grill marks. Serve with a dollop of Chipotle butter.

TIP

A Chipotle pepper is a dried smoked Jalapeño pepper. Chipotle peppers in adobo sauce can be found in the Mexican section of your grocery store. You can make the Chipotle butter ahead of time and keep it in your fridge or freezer. The best method is to roll the finished butter into a log in a piece of plastic wrap, and then freeze it. Pull the butter out of the freezer and let it defrost a little before serving. Slice off a piece and serve it on grilled vegetables, chicken or fish.

Grilled Eggplant
with Romesco Sauce

Romesco sauce is a delicious mixture of almonds, bread, red pepper and tomato that originated in Catalonia, Spain. This recipe will make about two cups of sauce. That's perfect because you will love having this sauce on hand. It brightens up and adds flavor to vegetables – grilled, steamed or roasted – as well as to fish, meats and seafood. It's also a great spread for sandwiches.

SERVES

4

1 large or 2 medium eggplant, sliced
(½- to 1-inch thick slices)

kosher salt, for the eggplant

1 large red bell pepper
(or ½ cup canned roasted red pepper)

1 thick slice of Italian bread

olive oil, for the bread

½ Jalapeño pepper, seeded

1 tablespoon fresh parsley leaves

2 cloves garlic

1 cup almonds, toasted

2 Roma tomatoes, peeled and seeded
(or ⅓ cup canned crushed tomatoes)

1 tablespoon red wine vinegar

¼ teaspoon smoked paprika

½ teaspoon salt

½ to ¾ cup olive oil

2 tablespoons olive oil

1. Pre-heat the outdoor grill for at least 10 to 15 minutes, or pre-heat an indoor grill pan over medium-high heat for 5 minutes.

2. While the grill is pre-heating, prepare the eggplant by generously sprinkling kosher salt on both sides of the eggplant slices and laying them flat between sheets of paper towel. Set aside.

3. Roast the red pepper on the hot grill until the skin turns black all over. Remove the pepper from the grill, place in a closed up paper bag and close the bag. This will allow the pepper to cool and also help to steam off the skin. When it is cool enough to handle, peel the pepper and remove the seeds.

4. Brush the bread with olive oil and toast on the hot grill. When nicely browned on both sides, remove from the grill and when cool enough to handle, tear the bread into pieces.

5. Place the bread, roasted red pepper, Jalapeño pepper, parsley, garlic, toasted almonds, tomatoes, vinegar, smoked paprika and salt in a food processor. Process until smooth. With the processor running, add ½ to ¾ cup of olive oil through the feed tube, using just enough oil for the sauce to come together in a smooth paste that is still pourable.

6. Brush off any excess salt from the eggplant slices and brush both sides with the olive oil. Grill the eggplant until nicely marked on both sides and soft to the touch – about 6 minutes per side. Remove to a serving plate and serve with the Romesco sauce.

Spaghetti Squash
with Marinara and Parmesan

Spaghetti squash is a unique winter squash, with fibrous flesh that shreds into strands that look like spaghetti or vermicelli when cooked. It is often used as a substitute for pasta, potatoes or rice. Once cooked, spaghetti squash has a mild flavor, but with a marinara on top, it is a great and healthful substitute for a big bowl of pasta.

SERVES

4

1 spaghetti squash (about 4 to 5 pounds)

1 to 2 tablespoons olive oil

salt

freshly ground black pepper

Basic Marinara Sauce (from page 72) or a store-bought marinara sauce

Parmesan cheese, grated or a block

1. Pre-heat the oven to 400° F.

2. Cut the squash in half and scrape out the seeds from the center of the squash. Brush the cut sides of the squash with olive oil and season well with salt and freshly ground black pepper. Place the squash in a roasting pan, cut side down and bake in the oven for 35 to 45 minutes, or until the squash is tender to a knifepoint.

3. While the squash is roasting, heat the marinara sauce in a saucepan on the stovetop.

4. Remove the squash from the oven, turn it over in the roasting pan and let it cool for just a minute or two. When it is cool enough to handle, scrape the squash with a fork, pulling the strands of squash away from the skin. Transfer the strands of squash to a serving dish or individual plates and top with the marinara sauce. Grate or peel shards of Parmesan cheese over the top and enjoy.

 You can also cook spaghetti squash in the microwave. Prepare the squash the same way as above and place one half of a squash in a baking dish, cut side down, and cover the squash with plastic wrap. Cook in the microwave for 7 to 10 minutes, turning it every few minutes if your microwave doesn't have a turntable.

Breakfast

I'm not sure breakfast is THE most important meal of the day, but it is important and it can be a lot of fun to prepare if you have the time. Starting the day right with a frittata, pancakes, French toast or the perfect plate of scrambled eggs seems like a luxury to many these days, but it doesn't have to. A little preparation the night before can make breakfast a quick fix in the morning.

Basic Cheese Frittata

A frittata is a perfect way to start a lazy weekend, but it's also nice as a dinner on some occasions. It is, after all, much like a quiche but without the crust. For breakfast, serve a frittata with a nice slice of rustic Italian bread and some pan-fried potatoes. For dinner, serve with a side salad and a glass of nice red wine.

SERVES

2

6 eggs

½ cup grated cheese, any type (Cheddar, goat cheese, Swiss, etc.)

1 tablespoon chopped fresh parsley (or other fresh herb)

2 teaspoons butter

¼ to ½ teaspoon salt

freshly ground black pepper

1. Pre-heat the oven to 450° F while you prepare your other ingredients. Crack the eggs into a bowl. Grate or crumble the cheese. Chop the parsley or other fresh herb.

2. Pre-heat an 8-inch oven-safe non-stick skillet over medium-high heat for 2 to 3 minutes.

3. When the skillet is hot, add the butter and swirl it around the skillet while it melts. You should hear the butter sizzling. Once it stops sizzling, lightly beat the eggs with a fork, add them to the skillet and stir them around with a fork or a spatula. Stir the eggs so that the uncooked egg has a chance to contact the hot skillet.

4. Cook like this for just 1 minute while the eggs start to set up. Remove the skillet from the heat and immediately add the cheese and almost all the chopped parsley, reserving some for a garnish. Season with salt and pepper and stir once more to evenly distribute the ingredients.

5. Transfer the skillet to the 450° F oven for 8 to 10 minutes, or until the frittata has puffed up and is lightly browned. Remove from the oven and turn the frittata out onto a plate. Cut the frittata in half and serve immediately, garnishing with the reserved parsley.

Recipe Explained!

● A frittata is an open-faced Italian omelette, which is slightly different from a traditional French omelette. A French omelette is cooked entirely on the stovetop and then folded over the filling ingredients. A frittata is much easier to make. The filling ingredients and egg are combined on the stovetop, and then the whole dish is baked in the oven. When it is finished, just slide it out of the skillet and serve it face-up on a plate or cut into wedges.

● I like a frittata that is airy and tender, has lots of colorful ingredients and is lightly browned on the bottom as well as the top.

● In order to end up with a light frittata, you need to incorporate air into the eggs and use a high heat in the oven so the eggs can rise like a soufflé. Lightly beat the eggs with a fork right before adding them to the skillet. You

don't want to over-beat the eggs, but whisking with a fork right beforehand is helpful.

● Pre-heating the skillet and having a very hot oven is also essential to making a fluffy and tender frittata. The skillet should be hot enough that the butter melts as soon as it hits the skillet. When the butter stops sizzling, it is a sign that all the water in the butter has evaporated and it is time to add the eggs to the skillet. I stir the eggs for just 1 minute on the stovetop to get the whole cooking process started and to distribute the filling ingredients evenly. Then transfer the skillet to a very hot oven.

● The oven needs to be hot so that the frittata cooks quickly, and doesn't dry out or become tough. These recipes have the oven at 450° F, but you could also just pop the skillet under the broiler to finish the frittata,

as long as you're paying attention and watch that you don't burn the top of the eggs.

● Because eggs cook so quickly, it is important to make sure your filling ingredients are cooked before you add them to the egg. Otherwise, they won't have enough time to cook before the frittata is finished.

● To make a frittata for more than two, just increase the ingredients, the size of the skillet you use, and the time in the oven.

● Frittatas can be served hot, at room temperature or cold, although the frittata won't be puffy if you let it cool. A frittata makes a perfect brunch item since you can serve it at room temperature. Serving it that way allows you to do your brunch preparation well in advance in a relaxed manner, whereas traditional French omelettes must be made one at a time and served immediately.

Asparagus, Goat Cheese and Herb Frittata

The goat cheese gives a nice bright flavor to this frittata. When asparagus comes into season in the spring, this makes a delicious breakfast.

6 eggs

½ cup goat cheese, crumbled

1 tablespoon chopped fresh chives
(or other fresh herb)

6 stalks of asparagus, sliced on the bias
(1-inch slices)

2 teaspoons butter

½ teaspoon salt

freshly ground black pepper

1. Pre-heat the oven to 450° F while you prepare your other ingredients. Crack the eggs into a bowl. Crumble the goat cheese. Chop the chives or other fresh herb.

2. Bring a small amount of water to a boil in an 8-inch oven-safe non-stick skillet. Once the water is boiling, season the water with salt and blanch the asparagus until tender – about 2 to 4 minutes depending on the thickness of the stalks. Drain and reserve the asparagus. Wipe out the skillet and place it back on the stovetop.

3. Pre-heat the skillet again over medium-high heat for 2 to 3 minutes.

4. When the skillet is hot, add the butter and swirl it around the skillet while it melts. You should hear the butter sizzling. Once it stops sizzling, lightly beat the eggs with a fork, add them to the skillet and stir around with a fork or a spatula. Stir the eggs so that the uncooked egg has a chance to contact the skillet.

5. Cook like this for just 1 minute while the eggs start to set up. Remove the skillet from the heat and immediately add the asparagus, cheese and almost all the chopped fresh chives, reserving some for a garnish. Season with salt and pepper and stir once more to evenly distribute the ingredients.

6. Transfer the skillet to the 450° F oven for 8 to 10 minutes, or until the frittata has puffed up and is lightly browned. Remove from the oven and turn the frittata out onto a plate. Cut the frittata in half and serve immediately, garnishing with the reserved chives.

TIP

Choose asparagus that is bright green, has firm stalks and tightly closed heads with no discoloration. To store asparagus, wrap the stalks in a wet paper towel and store in a loose plastic bag in the refrigerator. Alternately, trim the stalks, place the asparagus cut side down in a jar or glass with an inch of water in the bottom, cover the top of the stalks with a plastic bag and place in the refrigerator. Use within 2 to 3 days for best results.

Smoked Salmon, Cream Cheese and Chive Frittata

SERVES

2

Not just for bagels! Smoked salmon and cream cheese make this frittata smooth and silky.

6 eggs

2 ounces cream cheese, cut into little pieces (about ¼ cup)

3 ounces smoked salmon

1 tablespoon chopped fresh chives

2 teaspoons butter

¼ to ½ tsp salt

freshly ground black pepper

1. Pre-heat the oven to 450° F while you prepare your other ingredients. Crack the eggs into a bowl. Cut up the cream cheese. Cut the smoked salmon into 1-inch pieces and chop the fresh chives.

2. Pre-heat an 8-inch oven-safe non-stick skillet over medium high heat for 2 to 3 minutes.

3. When the skillet is hot, add the butter and swirl it around the skillet while it melts. You should hear the butter sizzling. Once it stops sizzling, lightly beat the eggs with a fork, add them to the skillet and stir them around with a fork or a spatula. Stir the eggs so that the uncooked egg has a chance to contact the skillet.

4. Cook like this for just 1 minute while the eggs start to set up. Remove the skillet from the heat and immediately add the cream cheese, smoked salmon and almost all the chopped chives, reserving some for a garnish. Season with salt and pepper and stir once more to evenly distribute the ingredients.

5. Transfer the skillet in the 450° F oven for 8 to 10 minutes, or until puffed up and lightly browned. Remove from the oven and turn the frittata out onto a plate. Cut the frittata in half and serve immediately, garnishing with the reserved chives.

Bacon, Cheddar and Tomato Frittata

Why serve bacon WITH a frittata when you can serve it IN a frittata?

6 eggs

½ cup grated Cheddar cheese

½ cup chopped tomato

1 tablespoon chopped fresh parsley
(or other fresh herb)

6 slices of bacon

2 teaspoons butter

½ teaspoon salt

freshly ground black pepper

1. Pre-heat the oven to 450° F while you prepare your other ingredients. Crack the eggs into a bowl. Grate the Cheddar cheese. Chop the tomato and parsley, or other fresh herb.

2. Chop the slices of bacon into 1-inch pieces. Place the bacon in an 8-inch oven-safe non-stick skillet and cook until the bacon is almost crispy. Drain the bacon on a plate lined with paper towel and set aside. Wipe out the skillet and place it back on the stovetop.

3. Pre-heat the skillet again over medium-high heat for 2 to 3 minutes.

4. When the skillet is hot, add the butter and swirl it around the skillet while it melts. You should hear the butter sizzling. Once it stops sizzling, lightly beat the eggs with a fork, add them to the skillet and stir them around with a fork or a spatula. Stir the eggs so that the uncooked egg has a chance to contact the skillet.

5. Cook like this for just 1 minute while the eggs start to set up. Remove the skillet from the heat and immediately add the bacon pieces, Cheddar cheese, chopped tomato and almost all the chopped parsley, reserving some for a garnish. Season with salt and pepper and stir once more to evenly distribute the ingredients.

6. Transfer the skillet in the 450° F oven for 8 to 10 minutes, or until puffed up and lightly browned. Remove from the oven and turn the frittata out onto a plate. Cut the frittata in half and serve immediately, garnishing with the reserved parsley.

TIP

If you are watching your fat intake, try substituting lean smoked ham, prosciutto or turkey bacon for the bacon.

Spicy Sausage and Broccoli Frittata

This frittata makes a hearty meal. Though there's no cheese in this recipe,
it's always a welcome addition.

SERVES

2

6 eggs

1 cup small broccoli florets

4 ounces hot Italian sausage, removed from casing and coarsely crumbled (1-inch chunks)

¼ cup chopped roasted red pepper (store-bought is fine)

1 teaspoon olive oil

½ teaspoon salt

freshly ground black pepper

1. Pre-heat the oven to 450° F while you prepare your other ingredients. Crack the eggs into a bowl. Cut the broccoli into bite-sized florets. Crumble the sausage. Roast and/or chop the red pepper.

2. Bring a small amount of water to a boil in an 8-inch oven-safe non-stick skillet. Once the water is boiling, season the water with salt and blanch the broccoli until tender – about 2 minutes. Drain and reserve the broccoli. Wipe out the skillet and place it back on the stovetop.

3. Add the oil and sausage to the pan, and cook the sausage completely over medium heat. Once cooked, remove the sausage to a side plate, leaving just a little of the fat in the pan. Lightly beat the eggs with a fork, add them to the skillet and stir them around with a fork or a spatula. Stir the eggs so that the uncooked egg has a chance to contact the skillet.

4. Cook like this for just 1 minute while the eggs start to set up. Remove the skillet from the heat and immediately add the sausage, broccoli and roasted red pepper. Season with salt and pepper and stir once more to evenly distribute the ingredients.

5. Transfer the skillet in the 450° F oven for 8 to 10 minutes, or until puffed up and lightly browned. Remove from the oven and turn the frittata out onto a plate. Cut the frittata in half and serve immediately.

TIP

Though you are only using the florets in this recipe, don't throw away the broccoli stems. These can be used in soups or sautéed on their own as a vegetable side dish. Peel the tough stems, blanch in boiling water for two minutes and then freeze them for a future use.

Scrambled Eggs
with Mushrooms and Herbs

You might wonder why I would include a recipe for something so seemingly simple. It's because most people make scrambled eggs the wrong way and made properly they are one of my favorite foods, any time of the day or night. No high heat is used here, except to sauté the mushrooms. Low heat and slow cooking makes the creamiest eggs you've ever had.

SERVES

2

2 tablespoons butter, divided

4 ounces fresh mushrooms (any variety), tough stems removed and sliced

2 teaspoons chopped fresh parsley

2 teaspoons chopped fresh chives

salt

freshly ground black pepper

4 eggs

1. Heat a non-stick skillet over medium-high heat. Add 1 tablespoon of the butter and cook the mushrooms until they are nicely browned and tender. Add the parsley and chives and season with salt and pepper. Transfer to a small bowl and set aside.

2. Wipe out the skillet and let it cool completely. Beat the eggs lightly in a small bowl with a fork. Add the eggs and the remaining butter to the skillet on low heat. Stir constantly to allow the eggs to set up evenly. A rubber spatula is perfect for this. Keep the heat on low or medium-low, but no higher. (A higher heat will cause the curds to harden and dry.) It should take at least 5 minutes for the eggs to cook properly. If they start to set up too quickly, remove the skillet from the heat for a few seconds and continue to stir. If they are taking too long to set up, add just a little more heat to the skillet, but be patient and resist the temptation to cook over too high a heat.

3. Once the eggs have set up, but are still moist, stir in the mushrooms and herbs and season with more salt and pepper to taste.

4. Serve over a thick slice of toasted rustic bread. Heaven!

Basic **Pancakes**

Growing up in Canada, I always had maple syrup on my pancakes and accepted no substitutes. My brother, however, sprinkled sugar and squeezed lemon juice on his pancakes. To each his, or her, own. Another nice serving option is to top the pancakes with a fruit compote, store-bought or homemade. This is another dish that can serve as breakfast or as a fun once-in-a-while dinner!

SERVES

3 – 4

1 cup flour

1 tablespoon sugar

1 teaspoon baking powder

¼ teaspoon salt

1 egg, yolk and white separated

1 cup milk

1 teaspoon lemon juice

2 tablespoons vegetable oil or melted butter

butter or oil for greasing the pan

1. Mix all the dry ingredients together in a large bowl. Whisk together the egg yolk, milk, lemon juice and oil or butter in a separate bowl or large glass measuring cup. In a third bowl, beat the egg white with a whisk until the egg white is fluffy and soft peaks form.

2. Add the liquid ingredients to the dry ingredients and mix until the two are just combined. Fold in the egg white until you can't see streaks of white anymore, but be careful not to over-mix the batter.

3. Pre-heat a non-stick griddle or skillet over medium heat. Add a little oil or butter and lightly coat the surface of the griddle. When the butter no longer sizzles, but a droplet of water splashed onto the griddle does sizzle, the griddle is ready to make the pancakes.

4. Pour batter onto the griddle, making pancakes of whatever size you wish. Do not disturb the pancakes until you see many little bubbles on the uncooked surface of the batter – about 2 to 3 minutes. Flip the pancake and cook the other side until brown. Remove the pancakes from the griddle and repeat for the next batch, adding butter or oil between batches if desired.

Recipe Explained!

● There are two tricks to making beautiful fluffy pancakes. The first is to separate the egg yolk and the egg white. By beating the egg white to soft peak stage (when the egg whites can almost stand up on their own when you lift the whisk out of the bowl) and then folding the beaten egg white into the batter, you incorporate air into the pancake, making it light and fluffy.

● The second trick is to have the griddle at just the right temperature. Using an electric griddle (or skillet) for this is ideal, because once you've found that right temperature, the griddle will keep the temperature even and you won't have to adjust the heat. (Set an electric griddle or skillet to 375° F.) The right temperature griddle will make the pancakes puff slightly as they cook, and won't let the surface burn before the inside has cooked.

● Many recipes for pancakes include buttermilk. This recipe uses milk and lemon juice instead. While it's not exactly the same as buttermilk, it's a good substitute, and you won't be saddled with three leftover cups of buttermilk, which you'll throw away in a couple of months when you find it in the back of your fridge on the top shelf chatting with the open can of tomato paste!

● Letting the pancake batter rest for at least 15 minutes is a good idea if you have the time. This will let the proteins in the batter relax and result in a tender pancake. You can even make the batter the night before and let it rest in the fridge.

● Finally, I like to add just a little butter or oil to the griddle before adding each new batch of pancakes. The butter gives the pancake a lacey browned pattern on the top and crisp edges. You may prefer a solid browned pancake, in which case you may not need to butter the pan in between batches of pancakes. Regardless of whether or not you grease the griddle in between batches, using a non-stick griddle is a good idea when making pancakes.

Maple Bacon Pancakes

Oh, how I love the combination of bacon and maple syrup, which is why bacon is a regular accompaniment to pancakes at my house. When a friend of mine told me she always puts chopped up cooked bacon in her waffle batter, I was sold and decided to add not only the bacon to my pancake batter, but the maple syrup too! Please don't think this means that you won't want more syrup at the table, however.

1 cup flour

1 tablespoon sugar

1 teaspoon baking powder

¼ teaspoon salt

4 slices of bacon, cooked and chopped

1 egg, yolk and white separated

1 cup milk

1 teaspoon lemon juice

3 tablespoons maple syrup

2 tablespoons vegetable oil or melted butter

butter or oil for greasing the pan

1. Mix all the dry ingredients with the cooked bacon pieces together in a large bowl. Whisk together the egg yolk, milk, lemon juice, maple syrup and oil or butter in a separate bowl or large glass measuring cup. In a third bowl, beat the egg white until the egg white is fluffy and soft peaks form.

2. Add the liquid ingredients to the dry ingredients and mix until the two are just combined. Fold in the egg white until you can't see streaks of white anymore, but be careful not to over-mix the batter.

3. Pre-heat a non-stick griddle or skillet over medium heat. Add a little oil or butter and lightly coat the surface of the griddle. When the butter no longer sizzles, but a droplet of water splashed into the griddle does sizzle, the griddle is ready to make the pancakes.

4. Pour batter onto the griddle, making pancakes of whatever size you wish. Do not disturb the pancakes until you see many little bubbles on the uncooked surface of the batter – about 2 to 3 minutes. Flip the pancake and cook the other side until brown. Remove the pancakes from the griddle and repeat for the next batch, adding butter or oil as desired between batches.

TIP

About ¼ cup of batter makes a perfect sized pancake.

Lemon Blueberry Cornmeal Pancakes

The cornmeal in these pancakes gives them a little crunch and a lovely yellow color. Add the lemon and blueberries and they are delightful little pancakes.

1 cup flour

¾ cup cornmeal

2 tablespoons sugar

1½ teaspoons baking powder

¼ teaspoon salt

2 teaspoons lemon zest

3 eggs, yolks and whites separated

1½ cups milk

1 tablespoon lemon juice

3 tablespoons vegetable oil or melted butter

1 cup fresh blueberries

butter or oil for greasing the pan

1. Mix all the dry ingredients with the lemon zest together in a large bowl. Whisk together the egg yolks, milk, lemon juice and oil or butter in a separate bowl or large glass measuring cup. In a third bowl, beat the egg whites until the egg white is fluffy and soft peaks form.

2. Add the liquid ingredients to the dry ingredients and mix until the two are just combined. Stir in the blueberries and then fold in the egg whites until you can't see streaks of white anymore, but be careful not to over-mix the batter.

3. Pre-heat a non-stick griddle or skillet over medium heat. Add a little oil or butter and lightly coat the surface of the griddle. When the butter no longer sizzles, but a droplet of water splashed into the griddle does sizzle, the griddle is ready to make the pancakes.

4. Pour batter onto the griddle, making pancakes of whatever size you wish. Do not disturb the pancakes until you see many little bubbles on the uncooked surface of the batter – about 2 to 3 minutes. Flip the pancake and cook the other side until brown. Remove the pancakes from the griddle and repeat for the next batch, adding butter or oil as desired between batches.

Chocolate Chip Walnut Pancakes

One of my basic rules of cooking is that a finished dish can only be as good as its ingredients. For this recipe, use high quality chocolate chips or chunks and you won't regret it.

1 cup flour

1 tablespoon sugar

1 teaspoon baking powder

¼ teaspoon salt

¼ cup walnuts, toasted and chopped into small pieces

⅓ cup good quality chocolate chips or chunks

1 egg, yolk and white separated

1 cup milk

1 teaspoon lemon juice

2 tablespoons vegetable oil or melted butter

butter or oil for greasing the pan

1. Mix all the dry ingredients including the chopped toasted walnuts and chocolate chips together in a large bowl. Whisk together the egg yolk, milk, lemon juice and oil or butter in a separate bowl or large glass measuring cup. In a third bowl, beat the egg white until the egg white is fluffy and soft peaks form.

2. Add the liquid ingredients to the dry ingredients and mix until the two are just combined. Fold in the egg white until you can't see streaks of white anymore, but be careful not to over-mix the batter.

3. Pre-heat a non-stick griddle or skillet over medium heat. Add a little oil or butter and lightly coat the surface of the griddle. When the butter no longer sizzles, but a droplet of water splashed into the griddle does sizzle, the griddle is ready to make the pancakes.

4. Pour batter onto the griddle, making pancakes of whatever size you wish. Do not disturb the pancakes until you see many little bubbles on the uncooked surface of the batter – about 2 to 3 minutes. Flip the pancake and cook the other side until brown. Remove the pancakes from the griddle and repeat for the next batch, adding butter or oil as desired between batches.

TIP Walnuts can turn rancid quickly because of their high polyunsaturated fat content. Store them in an airtight container in a cool, dark and dry place, or keep them in the refrigerator for a longer shelf life. You can also freeze walnuts (and other nuts).

Peach and Toasted Almond Pancakes

Peaches and almonds are both members of the rose family. While they are more like distant cousins than siblings, I think they work very nicely together.

SERVES

3 – 4

1 cup flour

1 tablespoon sugar

1 teaspoon baking powder

¼ teaspoon salt

¼ cup almonds, toasted and chopped into small pieces

1 egg, yolk and white separated

1 cup milk

1 teaspoon lemon juice

2 tablespoons vegetable oil or melted butter

1 medium peach, peeled and chopped (¼-inch pieces; about ½ cup)

butter or oil for greasing the pan

1. Mix all the dry ingredients including the chopped toasted almonds together in a large bowl. Whisk together the egg yolk, milk, lemon juice and oil or butter in a separate bowl or large glass measuring cup. In a third bowl, beat the egg white until the egg white is fluffy and soft peaks form.

2. Add the liquid ingredients to the dry ingredients and mix until the two are just combined. Stir in the peaches and then fold in the egg white until you can't see streaks of white anymore, but be careful not to over-mix the batter.

3. Pre-heat a non-stick griddle or skillet over medium heat. Add a little oil or butter and lightly coat the surface of the griddle. When the butter no longer sizzles, but a droplet of water splashed into the griddle does sizzle, the griddle is ready to make the pancakes.

4. Pour batter in the griddle, making pancakes of whatever size you wish. Do not disturb the pancakes until you see many little bubbles on the uncooked surface of the batter – about 2 to 3 minutes. Flip the pancake and cook the other side until brown. Remove the pancakes from the griddle and repeat for the next batch, adding butter or oil as desired between batches.

TIP

If you don't like its fuzzy skin, peel the peach by blanching and shocking it first. Cut a shallow cross mark through the skin on the end of the peach opposite the stem. Place the peach into boiling water for a minute and then submerge it in ice water immediately. The skin should then be easier to peel. If it is still resistant, repeat the blanching and shocking process and try again.

Basic French Toast
Pain Perdu

French toast was originally a way of using stale bread instead of throwing it away – by moistening it and frying it in butter. In France, French toast is called "Pain perdu", which translates as "lost bread". If you've lost your bread, but made it into French toast, I'd say that's a find!

SERVES

4

2 eggs

1½ cups milk

½ teaspoon salt

3 tablespoons sugar

1 tablespoon pure vanilla extract

8 to 10 thick slices French or Italian bread (¾-inch thick slices)

butter, to grease the pan

powdered sugar, maple syrup or a fruit compote (for serving)

1. In a wide and shallow bowl, lightly beat the eggs. Add the milk, salt, sugar and vanilla extract to the eggs and beat together until well combined.

2. Pre-heat a non-stick skillet or griddle over medium heat. While the skillet is heating up, soak the first batch of bread slices in the egg custard. The slices should soak in the egg custard for about 20 to 30 seconds per side.

3. Add about 2 teaspoons of butter to the skillet and let it melt. Transfer the bread slices from the egg custard to the skillet and cook each side until it is golden brown – about 1 to 2 minutes per side. While each batch of bread is finishing, soak the next batch of bread in the egg custard and repeat this step until all the bread has been cooked.

4. You can keep the finished French toast warm in a 200° F oven, but it is better to serve it immediately, drizzled with powdered sugar, maple syrup or a fruit compote.

Recipe Explained!

● French toast should be crispy on the outside, and silky smooth and soft on the inside. The key components are very simple.

● The bread is the most important ingredient. Although it is called French toast, the bread doesn't have to be French. Try using Challah, sourdough, brioche, Texas toast, cinnamon raisin bread, Panettone, or even croissants and quick breads. Store-bought pre-sliced bread will not make the best French toast. Instead, use bread that you can slice to at least ¾-inch thick. Thick slices of bread can hold up to the egg custard better

than thin slices, and won't fall apart when you try to dip and fry them.

● It is ideal if the bread is actually a little stale. Stale bread will soak up more of the egg custard and therefore be more custard-like in the center. If you don't have stale bread on hand, leave slices of bread out in the open for several hours or overnight.

● This basic recipe does not use a heavy egg custard. More egg would make the finished French toast denser and taste like fried egg. If you prefer dense French toast, use 3 eggs instead of 2 in the recipe.

● Try to get your skillet (or griddle) at just the right temperature. The goal is to get a crispy exterior without burning the French toast before the inside is cooked through. Butter should melt rapidly on the surface of the skillet, but not burn. An electric skillet or griddle is perfect for French toast because it will hold the heat steady. Set it at 375° F.

● While you can pile the slices of French toast on top of each other, it is also nice to slice each slice of bread diagonally and then shingle the slices on a plate. Either way, drizzle with powdered sugar and some maple syrup or a fruit compote.

Carrot Cake French Toast
with Maple Cream Cheese

Carrot cake slices make dense French toast, but it's such a nice way to use up any leftovers – if you ever have leftover carrot cake. If you make carrot cake for this recipe, bake it in a loaf pan so that it is easy to slice. This recipe is also great with banana bread in place of the carrot cake.

SERVES

4

2 eggs

1½ cups half and half

½ teaspoon salt

3 tablespoons sugar

½ teaspoon pure vanilla extract

8 to 10 thick slices carrot cake, store-bought, or homemade (¾-inch thick slices)

butter, to grease the pan

Topping:

4 ounces cream cheese

1 tablespoon maple syrup

¼ cup powdered sugar

1. In a wide and shallow bowl, lightly beat the eggs. Add the half and half, salt, sugar, and vanilla extract to the eggs and beat together until well combined.

2. Pre-heat a non-stick skillet or griddle over medium heat. While the skillet is heating up, soak the first batch of carrot cake slices in the egg custard. The slices should soak in the egg custard for about 30 to 60 seconds per side.

3. Add about 2 teaspoons of butter to the skillet and let it melt. Transfer the carrot cake slices from the egg custard to the skillet and cook each side until it is golden brown – about 1 to 2 minutes per side. While each batch of carrot cake slices is finishing, soak the next batch of carrot cake slices in the egg custard and repeat this step until all the carrot cake has been cooked.

4. While the French toast is cooking, whip the cream cheese with the maple syrup and powdered sugar until it is well combined and spoon-able. Place in a serving bowl.

5. You can hold the finished French toast warm in a 200° F oven, but it is better to serve it immediately. Serve the maple cream cheese in a bowl alongside the French toast so people can put a dollop on their plate –along with some extra maple syrup if they like.

Orange Stuffed French Toast

As a kid, a creamsicle was one of my favorite popsicles (after chocolate of course). This version of French toast reminds me of a creamsicle – a delicious combination of orange and cream. Garnish with fresh orange segments and enjoy.

2 eggs

1½ cups milk

½ teaspoon salt

3 tablespoons sugar

2 tablespoons orange zest, divided

1 tablespoon frozen orange juice concentrate, defrosted

6 ounces whipped cream cheese, at room temperature

8 thick slices Texas toast bread (¾-inch thick slices)

butter, to grease the pan

1. In a wide and shallow bowl, lightly beat the eggs. Add the milk, salt, sugar, 1 tablespoon of orange zest and orange juice concentrate to the eggs and beat together until well combined.

2. Pre-heat a non-stick skillet or griddle over medium heat. While the skillet is heating up, prepare the stuffed breads. Combine the remaining tablespoon of orange zest with the cream cheese. Mix well. Spread the orange cream cheese mixture on one side of four bread slices, spreading evenly all the way to the edges of the bread, and top with the other half of the bread, making cream cheese sandwiches. Then, soak the first batch of sandwiches in the egg custard. The sandwiches should soak in the egg custard for about 30 seconds per side.

3. Add about 2 teaspoons of butter to the skillet and let it melt. Transfer the sandwiches from the egg custard to the skillet and cook each side until it is golden brown – about 1 to 2 minutes per side. While each batch of sandwiches is finishing, soak the next batch of sandwiches in the egg custard and repeat this step until all the sandwiches have been cooked.

4. You can keep the finished French toast warm in a 200° F oven, but it is better to serve it immediately.

Pumpkin Pie Spiced French Toast
with Maple Whipped Cream

This is a great breakfast to enjoy in the fall, as you anticipate the pumpkin pie of Thanksgiving in November.

1 cup heavy cream

2 teaspoons maple syrup

1 teaspoon powdered sugar

2 eggs

1½ cups milk

½ teaspoon salt

3 tablespoons sugar

2 teaspoons pumpkin pie spice

8 to 10 thick slices French or Italian bread (¾-inch thick slices)

butter, to grease the pan

1. Whip the cream until soft peaks form. Add the maple syrup and powdered sugar and beat again to combine. Set aside in the refrigerator until you are ready to serve.

2. In a wide and shallow bowl, lightly beat the eggs. Add the milk, salt, sugar, and pumpkin pie spice to the eggs and beat together until well combined.

3. Pre-heat a non-stick skillet or griddle over medium heat. While the skillet is heating up, soak the first batch of bread slices in the egg custard. The slices should soak in the egg custard for about 20 to 30 seconds per side.

4. Add about 2 teaspoons of butter to the skillet and let it melt. Transfer the bread slices from the egg custard to the skillet and cook each side until it is golden brown – about 1 to 2 minutes per side. While each batch of bread is finishing, soak the next batch of bread in the egg custard and repeat this step until all the bread has been cooked.

5. You can keep the finished French toast warm in a 200° F oven, but it is better to serve it immediately with the maple whipped cream.

TIP

You can make your own pumpkin pie spice by combining 2 teaspoons of ground cinnamon with 1 teaspoon of ground ginger, ½ teaspoon of ground allspice and ½ teaspoon of ground nutmeg.

Baked Apple Cinnamon French Toast

If you're short on time in the morning, this is a great way to make French toast ahead of time. The preparation of this recipe happens the night before, making it a perfect dish to feed a crowd during the holidays when mornings can be hectic.

3 tablespoons butter, divided

2 tablespoons brown sugar

1 teaspoon ground cinnamon

¼ teaspoon ground nutmeg

2 Granny Smith, Macintosh or other good cooking-apples, peeled, cored and sliced (¼-inch slices)

8 thick slices French or Italian bread (¾-inch thick slices)

2 eggs

1½ cups milk

½ teaspoon salt

3 tablespoons sugar

1 tablespoon pure vanilla extract

powdered sugar and maple syrup for serving

1. Heat a 10-inch oven-safe non-stick skillet or casserole pan over medium high heat. Add 2 tablespoons of butter to the pan and let it melt. Add the brown sugar, cinnamon and nutmeg and mix well to dissolve the sugar.

2. Remove the skillet from the heat and toss the apples into the skillet, coating them evenly in the brown sugar and butter mixture. Slice the bread slices in half diagonally and fan the bread around the skillet on top of the apples, over-lapping the slices like shingles.

3. In a bowl, lightly beat the eggs. Add the milk, salt, sugar, and vanilla extract to the eggs and beat until well combined. Pour this mixture over the bread and press down slightly so the bread absorbs the liquid. Allow the mixture to rest for 1 hour to as long as overnight in the fridge.

4. When ready to bake, pre-heat the oven to 350° F and dot the top of the French toast with the remaining tablespoon of butter. Bake the French toast in the oven for 55 minutes. When ready to serve, you can invert the casserole onto a platter so that the apples are on top or simply leave the French toast in the skillet. Dust with powdered sugar and serve with maple syrup.

Cinnamon Apple Fritters

When you make these fritters with apple rings they look a lot like doughnuts, but inside is a soft warm bite of apple. Substitute any other fruit for the apples for something completely different. Banana, peach, pear, pineapple and mango all work nicely.

2 cups flour

1 tablespoon baking powder

½ cup sugar

1 tablespoon salt

1 tablespoon ground cinnamon

2 eggs, lightly beaten

1⅔ cups milk

2 tablespoons butter, melted

1 to 3 quarts vegetable or peanut oil for deep-frying

5 Granny Smith apples, peeled, cored and cut into rings or wedges

powdered sugar and maple syrup for serving

1. Combine the flour, baking powder, sugar, salt, cinnamon, eggs, milk and melted butter in a medium sized bowl. Mix well. Let the batter rest for at least 15 minutes. This will allow the protein in the flour to relax and help prevent a rubbery batter.

2. Fill a deep sauté pan or deep fryer with enough oil to cover the fritters. How much oil will depend on the size of pan you are using and whether you are making rings or wedges. If you are using an electric deep fryer, heat the oil to 375° F. If you are using a sauté pan on the stovetop, either measure the temperature of the oil with a deep fat thermometer or heat the oil until bubbles form around the handle of a wooden spoon when submerged in the oil. You can also just test a little of the batter in the oil to see if it is hot enough – the batter should sizzle and start to bubble immediately.

3. Dip the apple rings or wedges into the batter and gently drop the battered apples into the hot oil. Fry until the fritters are golden brown and crispy, turning once.

4. Drain the fritters on a paper towel and dust with powdered sugar. Serve immediately with maple syrup.

Desserts

I always try to save room for a little treat at the end of the day. It can be a small bite like a piece of chocolate or a special treat like a butter tart, but I like to have something sweet at the end of a meal. These recipes range from bake sale candidates to dinner party desserts, so there's something here for everyone. End the day on a sweet note!

Basic Dessert Soufflé

The first time I ever made a soufflé was when I was at university. My best friend, Tanya, and I took turns beating the egg whites by hand, not really knowing what it was we were looking for. The soufflé turned out fine, but had we a little more information, we would not have felt so blind along the way. Here is the information you need to pass Soufflé 101.

¼ cup + 1 tablespoon sugar, plus more for sugaring the soufflé ramekins

3 tablespoons flour

3 egg yolks

1 cup whole milk

2 teaspoons pure vanilla extract
(or a whole vanilla bean if available)

1 cup fruit purée

3 egg whites, room temperature

pinch salt

powdered sugar, for dusting finished soufflés

1. Pre-heat the oven to 400° F. Butter four 6-ounce ramekins, dust the insides with sugar and set aside.

2. Combine the ¼ cup of sugar and flour and whisk together. Add the egg yolks and beat until light in color – about 4 to 6 minutes. In a medium saucepan, bring the milk and vanilla extract to a simmer. (If you are using a whole vanilla bean, slit the bean lengthwise and let it steep in the milk for at least 10 minutes. Scrape the seeds from the bean into the milk and then discard the vanilla pod.) Pour the milk into the egg yolk mixture, whisking constantly.

3. Add the fruit purée to this mixture and allow it to cool slightly.

4. In a separate mixing bowl, whisk the egg whites to soft peak stage (the point at which the whites can almost stand up on the end of your whisk), adding 1 tablespoon of sugar and a pinch of salt near the end. Using a plastic spatula, fold the whipped egg whites into the egg yolk mixture in three stages, folding gently after each addition - start with a third of the whipped egg whites, continue with the second third of egg whites, and finally fold in the remaining egg whites.

5. Transfer the batter carefully to the prepared soufflé ramekins, piling the batter to the rim of each ramekin.

6. Bake for 20 to 25 minutes. When the soufflés have risen, are golden brown on top and jiggle only slightly when tapped, remove them from the oven, dust with powdered sugar and serve immediately.

The Science Behind a Dessert Soufflé

The science behind a soufflé is quite simple. Air is beaten into egg whites, which are then folded into a savory or sweet base and heated in the oven. By beating the egg whites to soft peak stage, air pockets are trapped in the soufflé. When these air pockets get hot in the oven, the air expands and causes the soufflé to rise. As the air pockets cool, they contract again and the soufflé will fall. That is why you always have your guests seated before you take a soufflé out of the oven — everyone waits for a soufflé because the soufflé waits for no-one!

The three parts to a soufflé are a base, egg whites and air. The base can be any flavor you choose, but it must be smooth without any chunks of food. Chunks, like whole berries for instance, are too heavy to rise and will just remain on the bottom of the soufflé dish.

Whipping the egg whites is the most important step in making a soufflé. There are a few rules to follow. First of all, if egg whites come into contact with ANY fat (even a drop of egg yolk), they will not whip and you will have to start over with new egg whites. Taking some simple precautions is helpful. Thoroughly wash and dry the bowls and beaters you will use to whip the egg whites. Separate the egg whites from the yolks carefully, using three bowls. Start with one small bowl to catch the egg white. Separate the first egg, putting the yolk in a second medium-sized bowl. Make sure there is no fat in the egg white and then transfer it to a third larger bowl (the mixing bowl you will use for beating the whites). Repeat this step with each egg, keeping the yolks together and transferring the whites into the large bowl one at a time. This way, should you break a yolk into the egg white, you can discard just that one white and will not have to start again.

It is easier to separate the egg white from the yolk when eggs are cold. However, it is easier to whip egg whites when they are at room temperature. So, separate the eggs at the beginning of the cooking process and let them sit at room temperature while you prepare the rest of the soufflé.

You can use an electric hand mixer or stand mixer to whip the egg whites, but it is also possible to beat them by hand. Often, a copper bowl is used to beat egg whites, but it is not essential. Copper reacts with the egg whites, creating whites that rise higher in the oven. If you think you might make several soufflés, a copper bowl would be a nice investment and it looks beautiful hanging in your kitchen. If you don't have a copper bowl, you can add ⅛ teaspoon of cream of tartar to the egg whites and get a similar effect.

Once the egg whites have been whipped, folding them gently into the flavorful base is the next critical step. Folding is different from stirring or mixing. It is a gentle way of incor-porating two sets of ingredients. Use a flat rubber spatula and turn the ingredients over onto each other. Folding the egg whites and the base together will make the base lighter, but will deflate the egg whites. To reduce the amount of air loss, fold the egg whites into the base in three stages. Fold a third of the egg whites into the base to initially lighten it. Then repeat with a second third of the egg whites and finally the remainder of the egg whites. As the base becomes lighter, you will deflate the egg whites less.

Soufflé dishes of all sizes always have straight sides, which make it easier for the soufflé to rise. It is the shape of the dish, rather than the size, that is important. If you are making individual soufflés, use small ramekins. Buttering and sprinkling sugar on the sides of the dish will give a sweet soufflé a chewy exterior.

Sometimes, a soufflé recipe will call for a collar on the dish. This is a way of extending the sides of the soufflé dish upwards. Butter a piece of parchment paper, and wrap it around the outside of the soufflé dish (butter side in) so that the paper extends beyond the top of the dish. Secure the paper around the dish with some kitchen twine. When the soufflé is finished, remove the collar carefully and show off your spectacular dessert. Again, a collar is not necessary, but it does help the soufflé rise as high as it can.

Chocolate Soufflé
with Molten Center

This soufflé does not rise as high as the other recipes, but the molten chocolate center will soon make you forget about that.

¼ cup unsalted butter, plus more for buttering the soufflé ramekins

4 tablespoons flour

1 cup whole milk

1½ ounces high quality semi-sweet or bittersweet chocolate

2 tablespoons + 1½ teaspoons cocoa powder

1 teaspoon pure vanilla extract

4 egg yolks

5 egg whites, room temperature

6 tablespoons sugar

pinch salt

6 (1-inch) chunks of high quality semi-sweet or bittersweet chocolate

heavy cream (for serving)

1. Pre-heat the oven to 400° F. Butter six 6-ounce ramekins.

2. Pre-heat a medium saucepan over medium-high heat. Add the butter and melt until frothy. Stir in the flour and cook over medium heat, stirring for 2 minutes. Add the milk, whisking vigorously and bring the mixture to a boil to thicken. Remove from the heat.

3. Meanwhile, melt 1½ ounces of chocolate in a double boiler or in the microwave. Add the melted chocolate to the saucepan and stir in the cocoa powder, vanilla extract and egg yolks. Mix well and let cool slightly.

4. In a separate mixing bowl, whisk the egg whites to soft peak stage (the point at which the whites can almost stand up on the end of your whisk), adding the sugar and a pinch of salt near the end. Fold the whipped egg whites into the chocolate base in three stages, folding gently after each addition - start with a third of the whipped egg whites, continue with the second third of egg whites, and finally fold in the remaining egg whites.

5. Transfer the batter carefully to the soufflé ramekins, placing a 1-inch chunk of chocolate in the center of each ramekin when it is half full. Spoon more batter on top of the chocolate chunks, filling the ramekins almost to the top.

6. Place the ramekins on a baking sheet and bake for 15 to 18 minutes. When the soufflés have risen slightly, are lightly browned on top and jiggle only slightly when tapped, remove them from the oven. Break the soufflé open gently with a spoon and pour heavy cream inside. Serve immediately.

TIP To melt chocolate in a microwave, first chop it into uniformly sized pieces so that it melts evenly. Place the chopped chocolate in a microwave-safe bowl and microwave on 50% power for 1 minute. Stir and repeat the process until the chocolate has melted.

Pumpkin Pie Spiced Soufflé

Use canned pumpkin for this soufflé. This is a great dessert for the fall and winter months when you need a little 'rise' in your spirits.

3 tablespoons butter,
plus more for buttering the soufflé ramekins

3 tablespoons flour

1 cup whole milk

½ cup canned pure pumpkin
(not pumpkin pie filling)

¾ teaspoon pumpkin pie spice

½ teaspoon orange zest, finely chopped

2 egg yolks

¼ cup + 1 tablespoon sugar,
plus more for sugaring the soufflé ramekins

pinch salt

6 egg whites, room temperature

1 tablespoon sugar

1. Pre-heat the oven to 400° F. Butter six 6-ounce ramekins and dust the insides with granulated sugar, tipping out any excess sugar.

2. Pre-heat a medium saucepan over medium-high heat. Add 3 tablespoons of butter and melt until frothy. Stir in the flour and cook over medium heat, stirring regularly for 2 minutes. Add the milk, whisking vigorously and bring the mixture to a boil to thicken. Remove from the heat.

3. Transfer to a large bowl and add the pumpkin, pumpkin pie spice and orange zest.

4. In a separate bowl, beat the egg yolks with ¼ cup sugar until thick – about 4 minutes. Stir the egg yolk mixture into the pumpkin mixture.

5. In a third mixing bowl, whisk the egg whites to soft peak stage (the point at which the whites can almost stand up on the end of your whisk), adding 1 tablespoon of sugar and a pinch of salt near the end. Fold the whipped egg whites into the egg yolk base in three stages, folding gently after each addition - start with a third of the whipped egg whites, continue with the second third of egg whites, and finally fold in the remaining egg whites.

6. Transfer the batter carefully to the soufflé ramekins, piling the mixture to the rim of the dishes.

7. Bake for 20 to 25 minutes. When the soufflés have risen, are lightly browned on top and jiggle only slightly when tapped, remove them from the oven and serve immediately with heavy cream, vanilla ice cream, or Crème Anglaise.

 Crème Anglaise is a pouring custard made from eggs, milk, sugar and vanilla.

Light and Airy Raspberry Soufflé

This is the easiest of all the soufflé recipes in this book and it is also fat-free! If you choose to use sugar-free jam, then this truly can be a diet dessert… but no-one needs to know.

Butter, for the soufflé ramekins

5 egg whites, room temperature

6 oz seedless raspberry jam
(sugar-free jam, if desired)

pinch salt

powdered sugar, for dusting the finished soufflés

1. Pre-heat the oven to 400° F. Lightly butter six 6-ounce ramekins.

2. Place the raspberry jam into a large mixing bowl and stir to loosen with a fork or spoon.

3. Whisk the egg whites to soft peak stage (the point at which the whites can almost stand up on the end of your whisk), adding the pinch of salt near the end. Fold the whipped egg whites into the jam in three stages, folding gently after each addition – start with a third of the whipped egg whites, continue with the second third of egg whites, and finally fold in the remaining egg whites.

4. Transfer the batter carefully to the soufflé ramekins, piling the mixture to the rim of the dishes.

5. Place the ramekins on a baking sheet and bake for 8 to 10 minutes. When the soufflés have risen, are lightly browned on top and jiggle only slightly when tapped, remove them from the oven, dust with powdered sugar and serve immediately.

TIP
You can make soufflés ahead of time. Store filled unbaked ramekins in the refrigerator for up to 4 hours. Then bake as directed and serve immediately

Grand Marnier® Soufflé

Grand Marnier® Soufflé is a classic and one I'm sure you will enjoy. When I taught my father to make a soufflé, this is the one he chose to perfect.

SERVES

6 – 8

3 tablespoons butter,
plus more for buttering the soufflé dish

3 tablespoons flour

1 cup whole milk

4 egg yolks

¼ cup + 1 tablespoon sugar,
plus more for sugaring the soufflé dish

pinch salt

¼ cup Grand Marnier® liqueur

6 egg whites, room temperature

1. Pre-heat the oven to 400° F. Butter a 2-quart soufflé dish and dust the inside with granulated sugar, tipping out any excess sugar.

2. Pre-heat a medium saucepan over medium-high heat. Add 3 tablespoons of butter and melt until frothy. Stir in the flour and cook over medium heat, stirring regularly for 2 minutes. Add the milk, whisking vigorously and bring the mixture to a boil to thicken. Remove from the heat. Transfer to a large bowl and cool slightly.

3. In a separate bowl, beat the egg yolks with ¼ cup of sugar and salt. Beat in the Grand Marnier®. Stir the egg yolk mixture into the milk mixture.

4. In a third mixing bowl, whisk the egg whites to soft peak stage (the point at which the whites can almost stand up on the end of your whisk), adding the remaining 1 tablespoon of sugar and a pinch of salt near the end. Fold the whipped egg whites into the egg yolk base in three stages, folding gently after each addition – start with a third of the whipped egg whites, continue with the second third of egg whites, and finally fold in the remaining egg whites.

5. Transfer the batter carefully to the soufflé dish, piling the mixture to the rim of the dish.

6. Bake at 400° F for 30 to 35 minutes. When the soufflé is puffed, golden brown on top and jiggles only slightly when tapped, remove it from the oven and serve immediately with heavy cream, vanilla ice cream, or Crème Anglaise.

Basic Chocolate Almond Bark

A chocolate bark is very easy to make and wrapped up in cellophane, it makes a great gift during the holidays. With only two ingredients in this recipe, they really must be of the best quality. The chocolate should be at least 60% cocoa and toasted, lightly salted almonds are best for this bark.

12 ounces high quality semi-sweet chocolate (at least 60% cocoa), chopped

1 cup almonds, toasted and lightly salted

1. Melt roughly three quarters of the chopped semi-sweet chocolate in a double boiler or the microwave, stirring until smooth. When the chocolate has melted completely, remove the chocolate from the heat, add the remaining chopped chocolate and stir again until melted and smooth.

2. Pour the chocolate onto a baking sheet lined with parchment paper, or better yet, use a silicone baking sheet. Tip the baking sheet to spread the chocolate out evenly, creating a smooth surface.

3. Scatter the toasted almonds across the surface of the chocolate and press them lightly into the bark.

4. Transfer the baking sheet to the refrigerator and let the bark set. When firm, break the bark into pieces and store in an airtight container. Serve within a day or two.

Ahhh....Chocolate!

Ahh ... chocolate! Few foods compare to chocolate in my world. If I had to live on a desert island and could only take one food with me… you know where I'm going. The keys to melting chocolate are simple: don't heat it too much and keep it dry. Chocolate, not surprisingly, melts at a very low temperature – just below human body temperature (think of this the next time you put a chocolate bar in your pocket!). If you heat chocolate at too high a temperature, it will burn and once burnt, it is good for nothing. Burning chocolate is very easy to avoid, however, by melting chocolate in one of two ways.

The most traditional method of melting chocolate is in a double boiler. A double boiler consists of a vessel suspended over a pot of simmering water. You can purchase double boilers, which are easy to handle, or you can assemble your own double boiler by holding a heat-safe bowl over a saucepan of water. The bowl should rest above the water, but not touch the water. The disadvantage of a homemade version is that the bowl often gets too hot to handle. If you are melting a small amount of chocolate, bring the water in the pan to a boil and then remove it from the heat and place the bowl of chocolate on top. If you are melting a substantial amount of chocolate, chop the chocolate into uniform pieces, keep the heat underneath the water at the lowest possible setting and stir the melting chocolate often.

You can also melt chocolate in a microwave. First chop the chocolate into uniformly sized pieces to help it melt evenly. Then, place the chopped chocolate in a microwave-safe bowl and microwave on 50% power for 1 minute. Stir and repeat the process until the chocolate has melted.

In a perfect world (or a chocolate factory), chocolate is tempered before being made into chocolate bark. Tempering is a process that keeps the chocolate shiny and retains its snap. It requires heating the chocolate to a certain temperature (115˚ F for dark chocolate; 110˚ F for milk and white chocolate), cooling it to below 82˚ F, heating it again (but only to 88˚ to 91˚ F) and holding it there. That's a lot to pay attention to and makes chocolate bark more challenging than it needs to be. These recipes cheat a little and make the process much easier. Reserving a quarter of the chocolate and adding it to the rest of the chocolate already in a melted state brings the temperature down to roughly the right degree. The result is a bark that breaks neatly and has some shine to it. Occasionally, chocolate can bloom, or look like it has a white dust all over it. This can happen when chocolate has not been properly tempered, or if the chocolate goes through temperature changes (into the refrigerator, out of the refrigerator, etc.) This does not affect the taste of the bark, but does affect the appearance. For this reason, make chocolate bark at most a day or two before you want to serve it.

The other key rule to melting chocolate is to keep it dry. If any amount of water gets into the chocolate, the chocolate will seize or clump up. For this reason, some people prefer to microwave chocolate to melt it, rather than having chocolate near to water and steam from a double boiler. If the chocolate does seize up, the only remedy is to add more water or cream. It will loosen up again, but it can no longer be used for bark. Instead, you can use the chocolate cream mixture to make a chocolate ganache or glaze (but that's a whole other story!).

Make sure you pour the melted chocolate onto a surface that will allow the chocolate to be removed again easily when solid. Silicone baking sheets are ideal for this purpose. They are flexible and can peel away from the solidified chocolate. If you don't have a silicone baking sheet, line a regular baking sheet with some parchment paper, which can also be peeled away from the bark. Just make sure there are no folds or creases in the parchment paper when you pour the chocolate. Creases get caught in the chocolate when it cools and little bits of parchment paper will be stuck in your bark.

Store the bark in the refrigerator in an airtight container until you are ready to serve.

White Chocolate Peppermint Bark

When Christmas comes along, this is the bark that you'll most likely see at parties and gatherings. Its white and red colors, along with the chocolate and mint flavors, fit the holiday theme perfectly.

6 ounces high quality semi-sweet chocolate (at least 60% cocoa), chopped

6 ounces high quality white chocolate, chopped

¼ teaspoon pure peppermint extract

20 to 30 red and white peppermint swirl hard candies or candy canes

1. Melt roughly three quarters of the chopped semi-sweet chocolate in a double boiler or the microwave, stirring until smooth. When the chocolate has melted completely, remove the chocolate from the heat, add the remaining chopped semi-sweet chocolate and stir again until melted and smooth.

2. Pour the chocolate onto a baking sheet lined with parchment paper, or better yet, use a silicone baking sheet. Tip the baking sheet to spread the chocolate out evenly, creating a smooth surface. Transfer the baking sheet to the refrigerator and let the bark set.

3. Melt three quarters of the chopped white chocolate in a clean double boiler or the microwave, stirring until smooth. When the white chocolate has melted completely, remove it from the heat, add the remaining chopped white chocolate and stir again until melted and smooth. Add the peppermint extract and stir to combine well.

4. Place the candies in a zipper sealable plastic bag and crack them into small pieces by banging them with a rolling pin or meat tenderizer. Stir the candy pieces into the white chocolate.

5. Pour the melted white chocolate on top of the dark chocolate on the baking sheet and spread it out to create a smooth surface.

6. Transfer the baking sheet to the refrigerator and let the bark set up. When firm, break the bark into pieces and store in an airtight container. Serve within a day or two.

TIP All white chocolates are not made equal! Many inferior confections called "white chocolate" are actually made with a vegetable fat instead of cocoa butter. These imposters are the "white chocolates" that real chocolate lovers can't stand. When you're buying white chocolate, look at the ingredient list to make sure cocoa butter is listed there. Real white chocolate should have 20% cocoa butter.

Dark Chocolate Caramel Bark
with Fleur de Sel

Here's an adult version of chocolate bark that combines sweet and salty flavors. This recipe makes a truly elegant chocolate bark.

1 cup sugar

12 ounces high quality semi-sweet chocolate (at least 60% cocoa), chopped

1 to 2 teaspoons fleur de sel (or coarse sea salt)

1. Place the sugar in a saucepan and heat over medium heat. Watch the sugar as it begins to melt. Do not stir the sugar, but tilt the pan to help the sugar dissolve evenly. Watching constantly, bring the sugar to a boil. As soon as it has turned a mahogany brown color remove it from the heat. You should start to see just a little smoke rising from the pan when it is ready. Immediately pour the caramel onto a baking sheet lined with parchment paper, or better yet, use a silicone baking sheet. Working quickly, tip the baking sheet to spread the caramel out evenly, creating a smooth surface. Set the caramel aside to solidify.

2. Melt roughly three quarters of the chopped semi-sweet chocolate in a double boiler or the microwave, stirring until smooth. When the chocolate has melted completely, remove the chocolate from the heat, add the remaining chopped semi-sweet chocolate and stir again until melted and smooth.

3. Pour the chocolate onto the layer of caramel and spread it out to create a smooth surface. Set the bark aside and let it set up at room temperature or in the refrigerator, but before it has completely set up, sprinkle the fleur de sel over the top.

4. When firm, break into pieces and store in an airtight container.

TIP Fleur de sel is the hand-harvested top layer of the sea salt from the salt marshes of France. The most renowned fleur de sel comes from Guèrande, in Brittany. Fleur de sel has moist, flaky crystals and a more delicate taste and a higher mineral content than regular table salt. Because it is relatively scarce, it is not inexpensive, but you will only use it sparingly to finish foods. It is well worth the price.

Marbled Dark Chocolate and Peanut Butter Bark

The classic combination of chocolate and peanut butter will never go out of style.

6 ounces high quality semi-sweet chocolate (at least 60% cocoa), chopped

2 ounces high quality milk chocolate, chopped

3 ounces peanut butter chips

½ cup salted roasted peanuts

1. Melt roughly three quarters of the chopped semi-sweet chocolate in a double boiler or the microwave, stirring until smooth. When the chocolate has melted completely, remove the chocolate from the heat, add the remaining chopped semi-sweet chocolate and stir again until melted and smooth. Pour the chocolate onto a baking sheet lined with parchment paper, or better yet, use a silicone baking sheet. Tip the baking sheet to spread the chocolate out evenly, creating a smooth surface. Set aside.

2. Melt the milk chocolate and peanut butter chips together in a separate clean double boiler or in a bowl in the microwave. Pour the melted milk chocolate and peanut butter chip mixture on top of the dark chocolate in a zigzag pattern. Run a knife blade through the two chocolate mixtures, creating a swirl or marble effect.

3. Scatter the peanuts over the top and press lightly into the bark.

4. Transfer the baking sheet to the refrigerator and let the bark set. When firm, break the bark into pieces and store in an airtight container. Serve within a day or two.

Chocolate Bark
with Dried Fruit, Nuts and Seeds

This is a bark where every bite is different from the last. If you want a bark packed full of ingredients, increase the quantities below to ¾ cup of dried fruit, ¾ cup of nuts and seeds and ½ cup of candied ginger.

1 pound high quality semi-sweet chocolate (at least 60% cocoa), chopped

¼ cup dried sweetened cranberries

¼ cup dried apricots, chopped

¼ cup hazelnuts, toasted and chopped

¼ cup pecans, toasted and chopped

¼ cup pumpkin seeds

¼ cup candied ginger pieces, chopped

1. Melt roughly three quarters of the chopped semi-sweet chocolate in a double boiler or the microwave, stirring until smooth. When the chocolate has melted completely, remove the chocolate from the heat, add the remaining chopped chocolate and stir again until melted and smooth.

2. Pour the chocolate onto a baking sheet lined with parchment paper, or better yet, use a silicone baking sheet. Tip the baking sheet to spread the chocolate out evenly, creating a smooth surface.

3. Combine all the remaining ingredients in a bowl and sprinkle this mixture over the surface of the chocolate, pressing in lightly.

4. Transfer the baking sheet to the refrigerator and let the bark set. When firm, break the bark into pieces and store in an airtight container. Serve within a day or two.

Basic Vanilla Fudge

I know few people who can resist a piece of fudge. This recipe makes fudge in the traditional way, using a candy thermometer and a fair amount of time. The other fudge recipes that follow are a little easier to make because they use marshmallow cream instead of cooking the sugar and beating the fudge. I think you'll find either style results in a tasty treat.

1½ cups (12 ounces) evaporated milk

¼ cup heavy cream

1 vanilla pod, split
(or 1 tablespoon pure vanilla extract)

2½ cups sugar

1 tablespoon light corn syrup

⅛ teaspoon salt

7 tablespoons butter

1. Combine the evaporated milk and heavy cream in a medium saucepan and heat gently. Split the vanilla pod open by slicing into it lengthwise, but not cutting it in half. Add the split vanilla pod to the saucepan, scraping the seeds out into the milk and cream. Let this mixture steep for 15 minutes on very low heat. Remove the vanilla pod and discard.

2. Add the sugar, corn syrup and salt to the milk and stir to dissolve the sugar. Bring the mixture to a boil. Reduce the heat to medium and boil until the temperature reaches between 236° and 240° F on a candy thermometer. While the sugar is boiling, use a pastry brush to brush the insides of the pot down with water to make sure no residual crystals of sugar are left on the sides.

3. Pour the boiling sugar mixture into a clean bowl. Cover with a clean kitchen towel to stop dust or anything else from falling in, and let it cool to 110° F. This will take 1 to 2 hours.

4. Add the butter and beat the fudge with an electric hand mixer until it no longer has any gloss to it and the path of ripples from the beater remain visible. This will take 10 to 20 minutes.

5. Pour the fudge into a 9-inch square pan (either buttered well, lined with parchment paper or coated with a non-stick surface), spread out the fudge until smooth and let it cool. When it has set, cut the fudge into squares and enjoy. Store the fudge in an airtight container in the refrigerator.

Recipe Explained!

● Traditional fudge is not difficult to make, but recipes have been made easier by using marshmallow cream in recent years. This basic recipe follows the traditional method. There are a few key stages, which if you have a candy thermometer and know what you're looking for, ensure success.

● Boiling the sugar is the first important step. The sugar needs to be brought to a temperature called the "soft ball" stage — between 236° and 240° F. During this step, the sugar will want to crystallize, and the goal is to prevent this from happening.

Having both corn syrup (glucose) and sugar (sucrose) in the recipe will help because the two types of sugar compete with each other and slow crystallization. Brushing down the sides of the pot with water to wash away any stray crystals of sugar will also help prevent crystallization.

● The second important step is the cooling stage. The fudge must cool to about 110° F before it can be beaten. You can check the temperature with an instant read thermometer. It can take as long as 2 hours to reach 110° F.

● Once the fudge has reached 110° F, it is time to beat the fudge. Beating breaks up the sugar crystals that form as the fudge cools, and is key to a smooth fudge that is not grainy. Beat the fudge for 10 to 20 minutes, until you can clearly see a path of ripples from the mixer remaining in the fudge. Beating will also make the fudge lose its glossy appearance. If the fudge starts to thicken, you're on the right track.

● Then, all that is left to do is wait for the fudge to cool and set. Patience is a virtue and it does have its rewards!

Chocolate Pecan Fudge

Marshmallow cream makes this recipe much easier than traditional fudge recipes. There's no need for a candy thermometer or for the arm strength required to beat the fudge. The results are still delicious.

1½ cups sugar

⅔ cup evaporated milk

¼ cup butter

7 ounces marshmallow cream

¼ teaspoon salt

1 cup milk chocolate chips

2 cups semi-sweet chocolate chips

1 teaspoon pure vanilla extract

1 cup pecans, toasted and chopped

1. Combine the sugar, evaporated milk, butter, marshmallow cream and salt in a medium saucepan and bring to a boil. Reduce the heat to medium and cook for 5 minutes, stirring regularly.

2. Remove the pan from the heat and stir in the two different chocolates. Stir until the chocolates have melted and are well combined.

3. Add the vanilla extract and pecans and stir.

4. Pour the fudge into a 9-inch square pan (either buttered well, lined with parchment paper or coated with a non-stick surface), spread out the fudge until smooth and let it cool. When it has set, cut the fudge into squares and enjoy. Store the fudge in an airtight container in the refrigerator.

Dark Chocolate Orange Fudge

Another great holiday gift! Purchase tins at your local craft store and fill them with this fudge. Wrap a ribbon around the tin, attach a gift card and you're ready to make someone very happy.

1½ cups sugar

⅔ cup evaporated milk

¼ cup butter

7 ounces marshmallow cream

¼ teaspoon salt

2 cups bittersweet chocolate chips or chunks

1 cup semi-sweet chocolate chips or chunks

1 teaspoon pure vanilla extract

1 teaspoon pure orange extract

2 tablespoons orange zest, coarsely chopped

1. Combine the sugar, evaporated milk, butter, marshmallow cream and salt in a medium saucepan and bring to a boil. Reduce the heat to medium and cook for 5 minutes, stirring regularly.

2. Remove the pan from the heat and stir in the two different chocolates. Stir until the chocolates have melted and are well combined.

3. Add the vanilla and orange extracts and orange zest and stir.

4. Pour the fudge into a 9-inch square pan (either buttered well, lined with parchment paper or coated with a non-stick surface), spread out the fudge until smooth and let it cool. When it has set, cut the fudge into squares and enjoy. Store the fudge in an airtight container in the refrigerator.

TIP You can make your own vanilla extract by combining 1 cup of vodka with two split vanilla beans. Store in a cool dark place for two months, gently shaking the jar from time to time.

Marbled Fudge

Dragging a knife through the two different colored fudges makes a beautiful marbled effect that is enhanced when the finished fudge is cut into squares.

1½ cups sugar

⅔ cup evaporated milk

¼ cup butter

7 ounces marshmallow cream

¼ teaspoon salt

½ cup white chocolate chips or chunks

1 teaspoon pure vanilla extract, divided

2 cups semi-sweet chocolate chips or chunks

1. Combine the sugar, evaporated milk, butter, marshmallow cream and salt in a medium saucepan and bring to a boil. Reduce the heat to medium and cook for 5 minutes, stirring regularly. Remove the pan from the heat.

2. Pour a quarter of this mixture into a bowl. Add the white chocolate and ½ teaspoon of vanilla extract and stir to melt the chocolate and to combine.

3. Add the semi-sweet chocolate to the saucepan with the remaining marshmallow mixture. Stir until the chocolate has melted and is smooth. Stir in the remaining ½ teaspoon of vanilla extract.

4. Pour the dark chocolate mixture into a 9-inch square pan (either well-buttered, lined with parchment paper or coated with a non-stick surface). Drizzle the white chocolate mixture into the dark mixture in a zigzag pattern.

5. Drag a knife through the fudge, in a zigzag motion perpendicular to the rows of white chocolate. Let the fudge cool. When it has set, cut the fudge into squares and enjoy. Store the fudge in an airtight container in the refrigerator.

White Chocolate Fudge
with Macadamia Nuts and Dark Chocolate Chunks

Look for true white chocolate, with at least 20% cocoa butter for this recipe. It will be smoother and much tastier than the less expensive imposters.

1½ cups sugar

⅔ cup evaporated milk

¼ cup butter

7 ounces marshmallow cream

¼ teaspoon salt

3 cups high-quality white chocolate chips

1 teaspoon pure vanilla extract

1 cup Macadamia nuts, roughly chopped

1 cup high-quality semi-sweet chocolate chunks

1. Combine the sugar, evaporated milk, butter, marshmallow cream and salt in a medium saucepan and bring to a boil. Reduce the heat to medium and cook for 5 minutes, stirring regularly.

2. Remove the pan from the heat and stir in the white chocolate. Stir until the chocolate has melted and is smooth.

3. Add the vanilla extract and macadamia nuts and stir.

4. Pour the mixture into a non-stick 9-inch square pan (either well-buttered, lined with parchment paper or coated with a non-stick surface). Sprinkle the semi-sweet chocolate chunks over the top and press into the fudge. Let the fudge cool. When it has set, cut the fudge into squares and enjoy. Store the fudge in an airtight container in the refrigerator.

TIP
Macadamia nuts have more beneficial monounsaturated fats than any other nut. Macademias are very nutritious for humans, but can be toxic to dogs. With their high fat content, macadamia nuts can turn rancid quickly. Store in the refrigerator and use within two months.

Basic Cheesecake

I like a cheesecake that is dense and rich, rather than light and airy. I've kept the number of ingredients in this basic recipe to a minimum to make it simple and to allow you to add your own flavors later on. Remember that you never make cheesecake for dinner tonight... you make it for dinner tomorrow. It needs several hours to chill.

MAKES 1

9-inch

10 to 12 graham crackers, crushed (about 2 cups)

¼ cup butter, melted

2 pounds cream cheese, room temperature

1⅓ cups sugar

1½ teaspoons pure vanilla extract

4 eggs

1. Pre-heat the oven to 325° F. Wrap the outside of a 9-inch spring-form pan with aluminum foil to create a completely waterproof seal.

2. Crush the graham crackers into crumbs either using a rolling pin or with a food processor and combine with the melted butter. Press the crumb mixture into the base of the springform pan. Refrigerate the crust while you prepare the cheesecake batter.

3. Using the paddle on a stand mixer on low speed, or the regular beaters on a hand mixer on low speed, blend the cream cheese until it is completely smooth with no lumps.

4. When all the lumps in the cream cheese have disappeared, add the sugar and vanilla extract. Blend to just incorporate the ingredients and then add the eggs one at a time, beating just a little after each addition. Continue to mix until the eggs have been mixed in, but do not over-beat.

5. Pour the batter into the springform pan on top of the graham cracker crust. Place the springform pan in a larger baking pan. Fill the larger baking pan with water until it is halfway up the sides of the springform pan, creating a water bath.

6. Bake at 325° F for one hour. After one hour, the center of the cheesecake should still jiggle when you tap the pan gently. Turn off the oven and leave the cheesecake in the closed oven for another hour. Then remove the cake from the oven and let it cool to room temperature on your kitchen counter before refrigerating. Refrigerate for at least 8 hours before serving.

Keys to a Successful Cheesecake

There are more varieties of cheesecake in the world than I can mention here. They range from airy to dense, rich to light, cookie crust to pie crust. No one style is better than another. It's all a matter of personal preference. My preference is for the rich, dense variety.

The most important quality of a good cheesecake is texture. It should be smooth and melt in your mouth. There are three tricks to attaining this goal.

First of all, start with room temperature cream cheese. It makes sense that a smooth cheesecake should start with smooth ingredients. Save yourself the agony of working with cold cream cheese. The cream cheese absolutely must be room temperature. If you don't have time to let the cream cheese come to room temperature, cut it into small chunks and place in a microwavable bowl.

Microwave for 20 seconds. Then beat the cream cheese until it is completely smooth using low speed on an electric mixer.

The second key to cheesecake success is to avoid incorporating air into your batter. Low speed on an electric mixer is important to limit the amount of air that gets beaten into the batter. Once the eggs are in the batter, low speed and not over-beating is even more important, because eggs tend to hold air when they are whipped. Air in the batter will expand in the oven and escape through the top of the cake, causing a crack in the cake's surface and compromising the cake's texture.

Finally, the third consideration in making a cheesecake is to always gradually transfer the cake from one temperature to another temperature. A sudden change in temperature will cause the cake to sink or crack.

Baking the cheesecake in a water bath slows the rate at which the cheesecake heats. Leaving the cheesecake in the oven for an hour after the oven has been turned off allows the cheesecake to cool over a longer period of time. Another hour on the kitchen counter before you refrigerate the cheesecake also allows it to cool more gently.

With these three rules in hand, the only other thing you need to know is how to tell when the cheesecake has finished baking. Check the cheesecake after an hour in the oven by tapping the pan with a wooden spoon. There should be a circle about 3 to 4 inches in the center of the cake that still jiggles. This is normal and will set after the cheesecake cools.

Chocolate Swirl Cheesecake

The cream filling of the cookies in this recipe works as the "glue" to hold the cookie crumb crust together.

30 chocolate cream-filled cookies, crushed (with the filling)

2 pounds cream cheese, room temperature

1⅓ cups sugar

1½ teaspoons pure vanilla extract

4 eggs

2 ounces semi-sweet chocolate, melted

1. Pre-heat the oven to 325° F. Wrap the outside of a 9-inch spring-form pan in aluminum foil to create a completely waterproof seal.

2. Crush the cookies, including the filling, with a food processor. Press the crumb mixture into the base of the springform pan. Refrigerate the crust while you prepare the cheesecake batter.

3. Using the paddle on a stand mixer on low speed, or the regular beaters on a hand mixer on low speed, blend the cream cheese until it is completely smooth with no lumps.

4. When all the lumps in the cream cheese have disappeared, add the sugar and vanilla extract. Blend just to incorporate the ingredients and then add the eggs one at a time, beating just a little after each addition. Continue to mix until the eggs have been mixed in, but do not over-beat.

5. Transfer 1 cup of the batter to a small bowl. Stir the melted chocolate into this batter and set aside.

6. Pour the plain batter into the springform pan on top of the crumb crust. Drizzle the chocolate batter into the plain batter in a zigzag motion. Then, drag the blunt edge of a butter knife through the two batters to create a marbled effect. Place the springform pan in a larger baking pan. Fill the larger baking pan with water until it comes halfway up the sides of the springform pan, creating a water bath.

7. Bake at 325° F for one hour. After one hour, the center of the cheesecake should still jiggle when you tap the pan gently. Turn off the oven and leave the cheesecake in the closed oven for another hour. Then remove the cake from the oven and let it cool to room temperature on your kitchen counter before refrigerating. Refrigerate for at least 8 hours before serving.

 Cheesecakes taste better served at room temperature. Take the cheesecake out of the refrigerator 30 minutes before serving.

Raspberry Cheesecake

Light and fruity, but still luxurious and rich, this raspberry cheesecake is a delight in the summer months with fresh raspberries, but can still be made all winter long with frozen fruit.

12 graham crackers

¼ cup butter, melted

2 pounds cream cheese, room temperature

1⅓ cups sugar

1½ teaspoons pure vanilla extract

4 eggs

1½ cups fresh raspberries or
1 (10 ounce) package frozen raspberries

1 cup fresh raspberries

powdered sugar

1. Pre-heat the oven to 325° F. Wrap the outside of a 9-inch spring-form pan in aluminum foil to create a completely waterproof seal.

2. Crush the graham crackers into crumbs either by hand or with a food processor and combine with the melted butter. Press the crumb mixture into the base of the springform pan. Refrigerate the crust while you prepare the cheesecake batter.

3. Using the paddle on a stand mixer on low speed, or the regular beaters on a hand mixer on low speed, blend the cream cheese until it is completely smooth with no lumps.

4. When all the lumps in the cream cheese have disappeared, add the sugar and vanilla extract. Blend just to incorporate the ingredients and then add the eggs one at a time, beating just a little after each addition. Continue to mix until the eggs have been mixed in, but do not over-beat.

5. Puree the 1½ cups fresh or frozen raspberries in a food processor and strain to remove the seeds if desired. Stir the raspberry purée into the batter and mix well.

6. Pour the batter into the springform pan. Place the springform pan in a larger baking pan and pour water in the larger baking pan until it comes halfway up the sides of the springform pan.

7. Bake at 325° F for one hour. After one hour, the center of the cheesecake should still jiggle when you tap the pan gently. Turn off the oven and leave the cheesecake in the closed oven for another hour. Then remove the cake from the oven and let it cool to room temperature on your kitchen counter before refrigerating. Refrigerate for at least 8 hours before serving.

8. Serve with fresh raspberries on top and dust with powdered sugar.

Milk Chocolate Polka Dot Cheesecake

Creating the polka dots in this cheesecake can be a little tricky, but never fear. If you don't like the dots you've created, simply swirl a knife through the batters and create a marbled cheesecake instead.

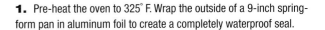

MAKES 1

9-inch

30 chocolate cream-filled cookies, crushed (with the filling)

2 pounds cream cheese, room temperature

1⅓ cups sugar

1½ teaspoons pure vanilla extract

4 eggs

2 ounces milk chocolate, melted

1. Pre-heat the oven to 325° F. Wrap the outside of a 9-inch spring-form pan in aluminum foil to create a completely waterproof seal.

2. Crush the cookies, including the filling, with a food processor. Press the crumb mixture into the base of the springform pan. Refrigerate the crust while you prepare the cheesecake batter.

3. Using the paddle on a stand mixer on low speed, or the regular beaters on a hand mixer on low speed, blend the cream cheese until it is completely smooth with no lumps.

4. When all the lumps in the cream cheese have disappeared, add the sugar and vanilla extract. Blend to just incorporate the ingredients and then add the eggs one at a time, beating just a little after each addition. Continue to mix until the eggs have been mixed in, but do not over-beat.

5. Transfer 1 cup of the batter to a small bowl. Stir the melted chocolate into this batter and set aside.

6. Pour the plain batter into the springform pan on top of the crumb crust. Place the chocolate batter into a piping bag, fitted with a plain tip. Insert the tip of the piping bag into the plain batter, pushing it all the way to the crust. Pipe out some of the chocolate batter while simultaneously drawing out the piping bag until you reach the top of the cake. The goal is to create tubes of chocolate batter throughout the plain batter, making it look like there are chocolate polka dots on the surface of the cake.

7. Place the springform pan in a larger baking pan. Fill the larger baking pan with water until it comes halfway up the sides of the springform pan, creating a water bath.

8. Bake at 325° F for one hour. After one hour, the center of the cheesecake should still jiggle when you tap the pan gently. Turn off the oven and leave the cheesecake in the closed oven for another hour. Then remove the cake from the oven and let it cool to room temperature on your kitchen counter before refrigerating. Refrigerate for at least 8 hours before serving.

Pumpkin Cheesecake

Here's another substitute for pumpkin pie at the holidays. The ginger crust really adds to the pumpkin pie flavor.

30 ginger snaps, crushed (about 2 cups)

¼ cup butter, melted

2 pounds cream cheese, room temperature

1⅓ cups sugar

1½ teaspoons pure vanilla extract

4 eggs

1 (15 ounce) can pure pumpkin puree (not pumpkin pie filling)

½ teaspoon pumpkin pie spice

heavy cream, whipped (for serving)

1. Pre-heat the oven to 325° F. Wrap the outside of a 9-inch spring-form pan in aluminum foil to create a completely waterproof seal.

2. Crush the ginger snaps into crumbs either by hand or with a food processor and combine with the melted butter. Press the crumb mixture into the base of the springform pan. Refrigerate the crust while you prepare the cheesecake batter.

3. Using the paddle on a stand mixer on low speed, or the regular beaters on a hand mixer on low speed, blend the cream cheese until it is completely smooth with no lumps.

4. When all the lumps in the cream cheese have disappeared, add the sugar and vanilla extract. Blend to just incorporate the ingredients and then add the eggs one at a time, beating just a little after each addition. Continue to mix until the eggs have been mixed in, but do not over-beat.

5. Stir in the pumpkin puree and the pumpkin pie spice. Mix well.

6. Pour the batter into the springform pan on top of the ginger snap crumb crust. Place the springform pan in a larger baking pan and pour water in the larger baking pan until it comes halfway up the sides of the springform pan.

7. Bake at 325° F for one hour. After one hour, the center of the cheesecake should still jiggle when you tap the pan gently. Turn off the oven and leave the cheesecake in the closed oven for another hour. Then remove the cake from the oven and let it cool to room temperature on your kitchen counter before refrigerating. Refrigerate for at least 8 hours before serving with a dollop of whipped cream.

Basic Pie Dough

Everyone should make pastry at least once in their life. Making it by hand is satisfying, but using a food processor is a huge time saver. This pastry is crisp and tasty and freezes well.

2 cups all purpose flour,
plus more for dusting the work surface

½ teaspoon salt

8 ounces unsalted butter,
cut into cubes and well chilled

½ teaspoon lemon juice

⅓ to ½ cup ice-cold water

1a. By hand: Mix the flour and salt together in a bowl. Use a pastry cutter to cut the cold butter into the flour, or pinch the butter in the flour with your fingers until it has the consistency of coarse meal.

2a. Add ⅓ cup of water and lemon juice, drizzling it as evenly over the flour as possible. Fold the dough together with your hands until you are able to collect it into a dough ball. You may need to add more water in order to get to this stage, but avoid adding too much which will toughen the dough.

3a. Shape the dough into two disks of even size. Wrap with plastic wrap and refrigerate for at least 30 minutes before proceeding to step 4.

1b. Using a food processor: Freeze the butter cubes for 15 minutes before starting. Blend the flour and salt together in the food processor bowl. Add the semi-frozen butter cubes and pulse together with the flour until the butter chunks in the flour are about the size of peas.

2b. Add ⅓ cup of water and lemon juice, drizzling over the flour as evenly as you can and pulse the mixture again to get the dough to come together. You may need to add more water in order to get to this stage.

3b. Transfer the dough to a counter lined with plastic wrap and shape the dough into two disks of even size. You may need to knead the dough a little or add a little more water to get the dough to come together as a ball. Refrigerate the dough for at least thirty minutes before proceeding to step 4.

4. To blind bake (bake without a filling): Roll the dough out on a floured surface until it is a circle about ¼-inch thick. Place the dough into the pie dish and gently press the dough into the edges of the dish. Trim the edges of the pastry and refrigerate the pie shell for 30 minutes.

5. Meanwhile, pre-heat the oven to 375° F. Line the pastry shell with parchment paper and fill the interior of the pastry shell with pie weights, dried uncooked beans, or uncooked rice. You can also use copper pennies to line the dough.

6. Bake in the oven for 20 to 30 minutes or until the edges of the pastry start to turn brown. Remove the pie weights, rice, beans or pennies and prick the pastry with a fork all over. Return it to the oven for 15 more minutes. Cool the pastry shell in the pan on a cooling rack for 10 minutes. Then fill with desired filling.

The Basics of Pie Dough

The rule to making pastry is simple — keep everything cold, including your hands. The goal is to work butter into the dough without completely blending it into the flour. In a finished pastry, you should still be able to see patches of butter. Those patches of butter will separate the proteins in the flour when baked, resulting in a flaky pastry. By keeping the butter cold, you run less risk of blending it into the flour. By using ice-cold water, you also increase your chances of keeping the butter in small chunks.

It is important not to over-work or over-mix your pastry dough. Not only will too much kneading blend the butter into the dough, reducing the flakiness, it will also develop the protein in the flour, making the pastry more elastic and inclined to shrink. When making bread dough, the opposite is true. Bread dough is kneaded for a long time because you are trying to develop those elastic proteins. Try to bring the pastry together without handling it too much. As soon as the water allows you to gather the butter and flour together, flatten the pastry dough into a disk and refrigerate.

Finally, let the pastry rest. Resting is important because it allows the proteins to relax. If you've ever baked a pastry shell that shrank in the pie dish, it is because the pastry did not have enough time to rest before baking. Rest the pastry after making it and again after rolling it out.

Baking blind (which means baking a pie shell without a filling) is done when you intend to add a filling to the pie that doesn't require any cooking - a fresh fruit tart or a chocolate mousse pie, for example. When blind baking, you need to weigh down the dough in the pie plate to stop it from rising up and doming in the center. You can use a variety of objects to weigh down the pastry. Ceramic pie weights can be found in gourmet stores. Ceramic distributes the heat evenly, helping to conduct heat to the pastry underneath. Dried beans or uncooked rice can also be used, but be sure to discard them afterwards. Copper pennies work effectively as well, but remember they will be super hot when they come out of the oven, so handle them carefully.

Once the pastry shell has set in the oven, you can remove the weights and then prick the bottom crust with a fork. This creates little steam vents for the pastry, again helping to keep it flat in the bottom of the pie dish. Return the pastry shell to the oven to finish cooking.

Tarte Tatin

Legend has it that Tarte Tatin was a mistake that turned out to be a good thing. Two young French sisters with the last name 'Tatin' were baking apple tarts when one realized she'd forgotten to put the pastry in the bottom. Her sister told her to just put the pastry on top and that they'd turn the pie over afterwards. The rest is history...

SERVES

6

1 cup sugar

2 tablespoons water

8 Granny Smith apples, peeled, cored and quartered

2 tablespoons sugar

4 tablespoons butter

Basic Pie Dough (see page 281) for 1 (9-inch) circle

1. Pre-heat the oven to 375° F.

2. Combine the sugar and water in a saucepan and heat over medium high heat until the sugar has melted and starts to brown. Don't walk away at this point, since sugar browns very quickly once it begins to color. As soon as the sugar is light brown in color, quickly pour the sugar into the bottom of a 9-inch cake pan or oven-safe skillet and rotate the pan so that the sugar coats the entire bottom surface.

3. Combine the apples and 2 tablespoons of sugar in a bowl and toss well. Transfer the apples to the pan on top of the sugar. Dot the apples with butter.

4. Roll the pastry out to fit the 9-inch pan and drape it over the apples, tucking the edges into the sides of the pan as though tucking the apples into bed. Bake in the oven for 45 to 60 minutes, or until pastry is nicely browned. Carefully drain off some of the excess juice from the apples (the juice will be extremely hot). Let the tart cool slightly and then invert onto a plate, still being careful not to spill any extra hot juice onto your hands.

Mile High Apple Pie

Apples shrink when baked in an apple pie, so to make this pie a "mile" high, you'll need more apples than you think. Straining the juice from the apples and simmering it before returning it to the apples produces a thicker pie filling without losing any of the great apple flavor.

Basic Pie Dough (see page 281)
for 2 (9-inch) circles

9 cups peeled, cored and sliced apples
(about 3 pounds; ½-inch slices)

⅓ cup brown sugar

⅓ cup sugar, plus more for sprinkling on top

1 teaspoon ground cinnamon

¼ teaspoon ground nutmeg
(or preferably freshly grated nutmeg)

¼ teaspoon allspice

¼ teaspoon salt

4 teaspoon cornstarch

1 to 2 tablespoons butter, cut into cubes

1 egg, lightly beaten

1. Pre-heat the oven to 425° F.

2. Roll out the pastry circles on a floured surface until they are about ¼-inch thick. Place one circle of rolled out dough into the pie dish and gently press the dough into the edges of the dish. Trim the edges of the pastry and refrigerate the pastry shell for 30 minutes. Place the other circle of dough in the refrigerator, either rolling it up in parchment paper or a silicone baking sheet.

3. Combine the apples, sugars and spices together in a large bowl. Stir and then let sit for at least 30 minutes. Strain the apples through a colander into a bowl, reserving the liquid. Bring this liquid to a simmer in a small saucepan on the stove and reduce it almost by half.

4. Toss the apples with the cornstarch and then return the reduced liquid to the apple mix. Transfer the apples to the pie dish with the rolled out pastry. Pile the apples high in the dish and dot the apples with the butter. Drape the remaining rolled out pastry circle over the top.

5. Brush the lower edge of the pastry with water and seal the top edge of the pastry down onto the bottom edge. Once sealed together, trim the pastry around the dish. Make 5 or more slits or cut outs in the pastry to allow steam to escape during cooking. Brush the surface of the pie with the lightly beaten egg, and sprinkle the surface with sugar.

6. Bake in the oven for 30 minutes. Reduce the heat to 350° F and continue to bake for another 20 to 25 minutes. If at any point the edges of the crust are getting too dark, cover the edges with aluminum foil. The pie is finished when nicely browned on top and the apples inside are tender and soft when pierced with a paring knife through one of the vent slits.

 Good apple varieties for apple pie are: Cortland, Jonathan, Baldwin, Golden Delicious, Pink Lady, Pippin or Granny Smith.

5 lbs Apples
brown sugar
butter
cinnamon
Vanilla Ice Cream

Mixed Berry Pie with Crumble Topping

I love this pie. The berries are not sweetened too much, which allows their flavor to be the center of attention. The crumble topping is delicious too – a nice alternative to a double-crusted pie.

Basic Pie Dough (see page 281)
for 1 (9-inch) circle

Topping:

1 cup flour

1 cup rolled oats

¾ cup brown sugar

pinch salt

1½ sticks (6 ounces) butter, cut into cubes

Filling:

½ cup sugar

2 tablespoons cornstarch

4 cups mixed berries (strawberries, raspberries, blueberries, blackberries)

1 tablespoon lemon zest

¼ teaspoon nutmeg
(freshly grated if possible, otherwise, ground)

1. Pre-heat the oven to 425° F.

2. Roll the pastry out to fit a 9-inch pie plate. Press the pastry into the corners of the dish, and cut the pastry around the pie plate, leaving about 1 inch hanging over the side. Fold the extra inch of pastry up to make a thick rim around the perimeter of the pie dish. Place the pastry shell in the refrigerator for at least 30 minutes while you prepare the rest of the pie.

3. Make the crumble topping. Combine the flour, oats, brown sugar and salt in a bowl. Mix well. Add the cubed butter and pinch the mixture together to form lumps about the size of peas. Set aside in the refrigerator.

4. In another mixing bowl whisk the sugar and cornstarch together. Add the berries, lemon zest and nutmeg. Toss well and transfer the berries to the pie shell. Bake the pie for 30 minutes, checking the edges of the pie after 15 minutes. If the edges are getting too brown, make a ring of aluminum foil to rest over the edge of the pie to protect it. After 30 minutes of baking, reduce the heat to 400° F, sprinkle the crumble topping over the berries and return the pie to the oven for another 15 to 20 minutes. The berries should bubble, the pastry should be brown and the topping should be browned and crisp.

Butter Tarts

I didn't know Butter Tarts were Canadian until I left Canada and never saw them again! I've always wondered why they haven't made it big south of the border and after you try one or three, you'll wonder too!

MAKES

12 - 14
tarts

2 eggs

1½ cups brown sugar

½ cup corn syrup

3 tablespoons butter, melted

1 cup raisins

2 teaspoons white vinegar

½ teaspoon pure vanilla extract

pinch of salt

Basic Pie Dough (see page 281) for 2 (9-inch) circles

1. Pre-heat the oven to 350° F.

2. Beat the eggs well with a stand mixer, hand mixer or vigorously by hand with a whisk until smooth and light in color.

3. Add the sugar, corn syrup and melted butter to the eggs, and beat again. Add the raisins, vinegar, vanilla extract and salt and mix well.

4. Roll the pastry out to ¼-inch thick. Using a circle cutter, cut the pastry into circles about 2 inches wider in diameter than the muffin pan cups you plan to use. Place circles of pastry into the cups of a muffin pan. Fill the shells two thirds full with the batter and bake until the pastry is light brown – about 25 to 30 minutes.

5. Let the tarts cool in the pan. Then un-mold and serve.

TIP There are three varieties of Butter Tarts: plain, with raisins or with walnuts. I prefer Butter Tarts made with raisins.

Basic Rice Pudding

Rice puddings have been around for ages. In ancient times, rice pudding was prescribed as a medical cure, recommended for the old, the very young or anyone with stomach trouble. These days, I recommend it for anyone wanting the quintessential comfort food dessert.

3 cups whole milk
(or a combination of milk and heavy cream)

1 tablespoon butter

¼ cup sugar

⅛ teaspoon salt

½ vanilla bean, split open
(or 2 teaspoons pure vanilla extract)

¾ cup long grain rice, uncooked

½ cup currants (or raisins)

1. Combine the milk, butter, sugar and salt in a large saucepan. Slit the vanilla bean lengthwise and scrape the seeds out of the bean into the milk with a paring knife. Drop the vanilla pod into the milk as well. Stir well to ensure that the vanilla seeds are dispersed throughout the mixture.

2. Bring the mixture to a boil, remove the vanilla pod and add the rice. Reduce the heat to a simmer. Cover and simmer for at least 20 minutes. Remove the cover and continue to cook the rice, stirring regularly until the desired consistency is reached – as much as 25 more minutes.

3. Add the currants and stir well.

Recipe Explained!

● Rice pudding is another dish whose qualities can lead to much debate amongst devotees. Some like it thick, some like it thin, some like it super soft, others like it a little chewy. I think it should fall somewhere in the middle. Rice pudding should be creamy with a little texture left in the rice. It should not be gluey or chewy or mushy or soupy. If you understand how the different qualities develop, you'll be able to adjust the rice pudding to suit your own taste.

● First you must decide which type of rice to use. Long grain rice makes a pudding with more bite to the rice. Short grain rice results in a softer pudding.

● The choice of dairy products also affects the final product. This recipe calls for whole milk, but if you want to make the pudding a little richer and more decadent, you can substitute heavy cream for part, or all of the milk. I often just use half and half and some people use evaporated milk, which is delicious. Reduced or nonfat milk is not really an option. Regardless of what dairy product you choose, you'll notice that rice pudding uses a lot more liquid than if you were making regular rice. The ratio of liquid to rice is roughly 2:1 for regular rice, but 4:1 for rice pudding. The rice absorbs the liquid as it cooks and the starch released by the rice will thicken the remaining liquid in the rice pudding.

● If you like your rice pudding loose and wet, cook the pudding for a shorter time. If you prefer a thicker rice pudding, keep cooking it until the consistency you like has been reached. Remember to stir the pudding more regularly as it thickens to prevent it from burning on the bottom.

● This is just one method of making rice pudding – simmering it on the stovetop. The other method is to bake it in the oven in a dish. When it is baked, a skin forms on the top of the pudding. Some love the skin; others hate it. I have not found that baking the rice pudding produces any significant benefit over simmering it, so have used the stovetop method here.

● You may also see recipes that incorporate eggs into the pudding at the end of cooking to enrich and thicken the pudding. This is certainly an option, but I find that the rice pudding is rich enough as it is, especially if you choose to use some cream.

Coconut Rice Pudding

Rice pudding takes a Caribbean vacation in this recipe.

1 cup coconut milk

1 cup heavy cream

1 cup water

1 tablespoon butter

¼ cup sugar

1 cinnamon stick

⅛ teaspoon ground nutmeg

⅛ teaspoon salt

½ vanilla bean, split open
(or 2 teaspoons pure vanilla extract)

¾ cup long grain rice

½ cup shredded coconut, toasted

½ cup pineapple chunks

1. Combine the coconut milk, heavy cream, water, butter, sugar, cinnamon stick, nutmeg and salt in a large saucepan. Slit the vanilla bean lengthwise and scrape the seeds out of the bean into the milk with a paring knife. Drop the vanilla pod into the milk as well. Stir well to ensure that the vanilla seeds are dispersed throughout the mixture.

2. Bring the mixture to a boil, remove the vanilla pod and add the rice. Reduce the heat to a simmer. Cover and simmer for at least 20 minutes. Remove the cover and continue to cook the rice, stirring regularly until the desired consistency is reached – as much as 25 minutes more.

3. Serve warm with toasted shredded coconut and pineapple chunks on top.

TIP

Coconut milk often separates in the can, leaving a thick layer of coconut cream on top of the thin coconut milk. Shake the can before opening it to recombine the coconut cream and milk. If you are trying to separate the coconut cream from the milk, refrigerate the can before opening. I don't recommend light coconut milk because it has very little flavor. If calories are a concern, thin regular coconut milk with water or another liquid.

White Chocolate Hazelnut Rice Pudding

Delicious white chocolate hides in this white rice pudding. It can be the flavor that keeps your guests guessing.

3 cups milk

1 tablespoon butter

¼ cup sugar

1 cinnamon stick

⅛ teaspoon ground nutmeg

⅛ teaspoon salt

½ vanilla bean, split open
(or 2 teaspoons pure vanilla extract)

¾ cup long grain rice, uncooked

4 ounces high quality white chocolate, chopped

4½ teaspoons hazelnut liqueur

½ cup hazelnuts, toasted and chopped

1. Combine the milk, butter, sugar, cinnamon stick, nutmeg and salt in a large saucepan. Slit the vanilla bean lengthwise and scrape the seeds out of the bean into the milk with a paring knife. Drop the vanilla pod into the milk as well. Stir well to ensure that the vanilla seeds are dispersed throughout the mixture.

2. Bring the mixture to a boil, remove the vanilla pod and add the rice. Reduce the heat to a simmer. Cover and simmer for at least 20 minutes. Remove the cover and continue to cook the rice, stirring regularly until the desired consistency is reached – as much as 25 minutes more.

3. Remove the pan from the heat and add the white chocolate and hazelnut liqueur. Stir until the chocolate has melted.

4. Serve warm with toasted hazelnuts on top.

 TIP White rice will keep almost indefinitely in a tightly sealed container to keep out moisture, dust and insects. Brown rice, on the other hand, should be kept in the refrigerator or freezer. The oil in the bran of brown rice gives it a shelf life of only 6 months if kept at room temperature.

Lemon Rice Pudding
with Blueberry Anise Compote

This rice pudding is topped with a fruit compote, which is also wonderful with pancakes or French toast.

SERVES

4

3 cups milk

1 tablespoon butter

¼ cup sugar

⅛ teaspoon salt

zest of 2 lemons, chopped
(reserving 1 tablespoon for garnish)

½ vanilla bean, split open
(or 2 teaspoons pure vanilla extract)

¾ cup long grain rice, uncooked

Compote:

1½ cups blueberries, fresh or frozen

⅓ cup sugar

⅓ cup water

1 teaspoon lemon juice

1 star anise pod

1 cinnamon stick

⅛ teaspoon salt

pinch freshly ground black pepper

1. Combine the milk, butter, sugar, salt and all but 1 tablespoon of lemon zest in a large saucepan. Slit the vanilla bean lengthwise and scrape the seeds out of the bean into the milk with a paring knife. Drop the vanilla pod into the milk as well. Stir well to ensure that the vanilla seeds are dispersed throughout the mixture.

2. Bring the mixture to a boil, remove the vanilla pod and add the rice. Reduce the heat to a simmer. Cover and simmer for at least 20 minutes. Remove the cover and continue to cook the rice, stirring regularly until the desired consistency is reached – as much as 25 minutes more.

3. While the rice pudding is cooking, make the compote. Combine all the ingredients for the compote in a medium saucepan and stir well. Bring the mixture to a boil and reduce the heat to a simmer for 30 minutes. You can make this compote well in advance if desired. Just keep it refrigerated and warm it for serving.

4. When the rice pudding has reached the desired consistency, spoon portions into bowls and top with the compote and the remaining lemon zest.

TIP You will find star anise in the spice section of your grocery store, but star anise is actually the star-shaped fruit of a small oriental tree. The fruit is picked and dried before it ripens. Each pointed arm of the star is a seedpod, containing one seed. Usually the whole star is used in recipes, although sometimes it is ground. It has a licorice-like flavor.

Dark Chocolate and Cherry Rice Pudding

Two of my favorite foods – chocolate and cherries!

SERVES

4

1½ cups milk

1½ cups heavy cream, plus more for serving

1 tablespoon butter

¼ cup sugar

⅛ teaspoon salt

½ vanilla bean, split open
(or 2 teaspoons pure vanilla extract)

¾ cup long grain rice, uncooked

3 ounces high quality semi-sweet chocolate, chopped

⅛ teaspoon pure almond extract

1 cup pitted cherries, roughly chopped

block of white chocolate, shaved for garnish (optional)

1. Combine the milk, cream, butter, sugar and salt in a large sauce-pan. Slit the vanilla bean lengthwise and scrape the seeds out of the bean into the milk with a paring knife. Drop the vanilla pod into the milk as well. Stir well to ensure that the vanilla seeds are dispersed throughout the mixture.

2. Bring the mixture to a boil, remove the vanilla pod and add the rice. Reduce the heat to a simmer. Cover and simmer for at least 20 minutes. Remove the cover and continue to cook the rice, stirring regularly until the desired consistency is reached – as much as 25 minutes more.

3. Add the chocolate, almond extract and cherries and stir well until the chocolate has melted.

4. Serve with a drizzle of heavy cream or sprinkle white chocolate shavings on top.

TIP

Pitting cherries is most easily done with a cherry pitter. If you don't have a cherry pitter, you can use a paper clip! Bend the paper clip open so that it looks like an "S". Stick one end of the clip into the stem end of the cherry. Run the paper clip under the pit and pull it out.

Cornmeal Layer Cake
with Lemon Cream

This cake is light and tasty, and the cornmeal gives it a nice little crunch. My dear friend Mary claims it is her favorite birthday cake. Happy Birthday Mary!

SERVES

8 - 10

Cake Batter:

8 ounces unsalted butter, room temperature plus more for buttering the pans

3 cups granulated sugar

4 teaspoons pure vanilla extract

4 eggs

4 cups flour

⅔ cup cornmeal

2 teaspoons baking soda

½ teaspoon baking powder

½ teaspoon salt

2 cups buttermilk

1 (8 ounce) jar raspberry jam

Lemon Cream Frosting:

2 cups heavy whipping cream

1/2 cup powdered sugar

1 teaspoon lemon zest

1/4 teaspoon lemon extract

1. Pre-heat the oven to 350° F and lightly butter two 9-inch round cake pans.

2. Using a stand mixer or hand mixer, cream the butter and sugar together until light and fluffy – at least 5 minutes. Add the vanilla extract and the eggs, one at a time. Beat after each addition until the eggs are well incorporated into the batter.

3. Combine the dry ingredients in a separate bowl. Add the dry ingredients and the buttermilk alternately to the creamed butter mixture. Mix until the ingredients are just combined, but do not over-mix. Divide the batter between the two buttered cake pans.

4. Bake the cake pans in the oven for 35 to 45 minutes. When a skewer inserted into the center of the cake comes out clean, remove the cake pans and allow them to cool completely. Remove the layers from the cake pans and slice the domed top off one or both of the cake layers so that they can sit on each other evenly. Spread the raspberry jam between the cake layers. (Make sure the top surface of the cake (the surface that you intend to frost) is not a cut surface. If you slice the domed top off both layers, invert the top cake layer so that the cut surface is in the center of the cake. This will make it easier when you come to frost the cake.)

5. For the lemon cream, whip the heavy cream with a stand mixer or hand mixer until it forms soft peaks. Sift in the powdered sugar and add the lemon zest and extract. Frost the cake just before serving. Garnish with long strands of lemon zest, or with twisted lemon slices.

TIP
It is best to frost this cake close to serving time, so that the frosting doesn't have time to weep. Alternately, you can stabilize the cream with store-bought cream stabilizer.

Chocolate Espresso Mousse

I have always loved chocolate mousse. How could I not? It's a perfect way to end a meal... or a book.

SERVES

4

4 ounces bittersweet chocolate, chopped

2 tablespoons butter

2 egg yolks

½ teaspoon pure vanilla extract

1 teaspoon instant espresso powder

2 egg whites

4 teaspoons sugar

½ cup heavy cream, plus more for garnish

espresso beans, for garnish

1. Melt the chocolate and butter together in a double boiler or in a bowl in the microwave. Let the chocolate cool slightly. Add the egg yolks to the chocolate one at a time, beating well between each addition. Add the vanilla extract and the instant espresso powder and mix well.

2. Whip the egg whites to soft peak stage (when the egg whites will almost stand up on their own at the end of the whisk – looking like a chocolate kiss). Add the sugar and beat again until glossy.

3. In a separate bowl, whip the heavy cream until it reaches soft peaks.

4. Fold the egg whites into the chocolate mixture carefully, trying not to deflate the egg whites too much. Then, fold in the whipped cream and combine gently until no more streaks of white appear.

5. Transfer to individual serving bowls or glasses. Refrigerate for 30 minutes and then serve garnished with a dollop of whipped cream and an espresso bean or two. If you make the mousse ahead of time and store it in the refrigerator, let it sit on the kitchen counter for 20 to 30 minutes before serving.

Index

Index

Index

Index

Index

Index

Index

Tip Index